The Green Crow

SEAN O'CASEY

New York
GEORGE BRAZILLER, INC.
1956

Copyright © 1956 by Sean O'Casey

Manufactured in the United States of America

ACKNOWLEDGMENTS

The following copyrighted items are reprinted in this volume with the permission of their original publishers:

"The Arts Among the Multitude" reprinted from *7 Arts #2*, edited by Fernando Puma, published by Falcon's Wing Press, Indian Hills, Colorado.

"St. Pathrick's Day in the Morning," "Always the Plough and the Stars" and "Bernard Shaw: Appreciation of a Fighting Idealist" reprinted from *The New York Times*.

"A Flutter of Flags," "The Power of Laughter" and "Come to the Fair" reprinted from *Saturday Night*.

"No Flowers for Films" reprinted from *Leader Magazine*.

Preface

This is a nest of Ids and Trends, made up of a few short stories and articles, written on divers occasions; added to a laughing look-over of things said about the Theater, here and elsewhere; besides some merry and amusing comments thereon; including a squint and a few quips at Irish notice-writers (popularly called critics); accompanied with a skirl of shrewd remarks made by the Author on the tendencies of the theater of today.

This collection of literary jorum-gems is respectfully dedicated to the Readers of Past Works by the Author, who freely acknowledges, and with a zealous thankfulness, that for years he had but faintly subsisted if he had not often tasted of their bounty. As you, dear Readers, have been so kind to his works in the past, the Author hopes you may read this book, when time and serious occasions may give leave, and find something in it worthy of your approbation.

Truly devoted to your Service,

Sean O'Casey

Contents

[v]

Foreword

The crow is a common bird, flying almost in every sky and known to all who have a sky over them and a cliff or a tree to spare. He is a laddo that can't afford any gorgeousness in his feathers; all black, except for a better-off brother who decorates his plumage of brilliant black with snow-white bands—the magpie, the cleric of the Corvidae, a dignified chap, fond of chattering as a cleric is fond of preaching. The crow has a bad one in the family—the Jackdaw, a cunning chap who is fond of gathering glittering gewgaws to himself that rightfully belong to others. We've all heard of the Jackdaw of Rheims, the little bastard who stole the Bishop's ring and, in the end, had to confess and do penance for his sin. A common bird, the crow, as I am a common man, as we all are, in a wide sense, of the common family of man, brother to every other man, with every woman a sister, whatever their race, their color, their creed. We all caw together and live the same way; we all respond to Shylock's passionate outburst (like it or not) making Gentile and Jew one: Man most miserable, man most glorious; man most mean, man most generous. The great Thought, for from the first man came Cnossos, Egypt, Greece, Rome, Great Britain, America, the Soviet Union, and Ireland.

The crow, however, isn't all that common but, in ways, a remarkable bird, clever and cute. Indeed, many naturalists lift him into the highest rank of bird-life: a bird of extreme intelligence, and extreme intelligence isn't so common that it is to be picked up in every strand of mind like pebbles on a beach; but it is common to the crow. Let us all learn from the bird.

The crow can fly through a bitter wind over the sea with the waves tossing up white spray from the top of the tumbling ridges; he can fly bravely even with the deep tinge of famine touching his bones, with the peak of a breast bone cutting his skin. Firm on the wing, high in the sky, when the east wind blows, when the frost blenches the grass and the gorse-buds faint with the cold. Lean and pinched with hunger as he may be, he can fly bravely and confidently through the dusk of the evening to the shelter of a fir-tree grove. As he himself has often done—flown through the dusk of uncertainty, flown bravely, his breast bone nearly as sharply outlined as that of the many-wintered crow, flying before the red bitterness of the east wind.

A cute one, the old crow ponders over things. He asks questions, wants to know. Why does a bee have a sword to his fiddle—buzzzzzz buzzzzzzzz? As well as a cunning mind, the crow has a rakish eye and looks, or seems to look, on the world with a careless and, at times, a reckless air, as if it had the lord of creation, Man, well taped; a roving eye, too, watching left, right, down, almost within the same fraction of a second, maintaining a keen regard over his sense of danger.

Once, opposite where I lived, a big old crow haunted a fir tree, tall and intensely bushy. The crow was fond of eggs and was hated by all who had hens. One fine morning as I roved out, I saw Sergeant Roche halting me with a gesture as he pointed a finger cautiously up to the higher branches of the spreading fir tree. His other hand stretched out slowly to take a gun handed to him slowly and cautiously by a comrade constable who was himself looking heavenwards. Their two wives stood motionless a little distance away, both solemnly gazing, too, up to the top of the tree. Slowly the gun was taken by the Sergeant, who was a dead shot; taken by touch, for he kept his head high, his eyes fixed in their stare towards the top of the tree, his thought tying the crow to where he perched alone and unaware of an exploding doom.

"He'll do it to she," whispered an old jobbing-gardener who had been a vedette in the long-lost Boer War. "He'll do it to she, right proper."

Slowly the gun came across the Sergeant's chest; slower it mounted, gradually, silently creeping up with the butt coming nearer and nearer to the shoulder.

"He'll do it to she," again whispered the old gardener. "Divide she into splinters, proper o."

But the Sergeant didn't do it to she, for when the butt of the gun had reached his shoulder, the gun came down again, though the Sergeant still stared up to the top of the tree.

"The blighter's gone!" he said. "Given us the slip."

No one saw it go; no one heard a flutter of a wing; nothing. No sound had crept into or startled the silence, but the bird was no longer there, nothing left of she but what sounded like, and seemed to be, a derisive caw-caw in a distant and alien sky.

"Outa range," said the Sergeant. "Gone, with her belly full of our eggs."

Think, too, of the common crow's bigger brother, Corvie Corax. Look close, watch the raven well and you'll see more than a suit of solemn black, for with the raven the black is shot with green, ay, and with purple too. Not showy, but there all the same. Yessir, there, all right. Corvie is a gay chap for all his inky cloak. Not, of course, the petted and paunched stooges strutting about on London's Tower Hill. They are there for show and have gone from life. No, not them, but the bohemian boys flying away over the Devon moors and valleys, at times getting so furious with joy that they tumble over and over as they fly, croak shrilly, and go over head and heels again and again with a skill no airman could imitate. Tumblers in the sky, tumbling as if they were full of Devon's rough cider; gallant lads, linking the heavens up with careless jollity. Well, we can do a little of this tumbling ourselves on the green; we can let our hearts now and again resent and resist the duties of life, the threat of death, and relax in loud hilarity as if the sun himself were a dancer, sorrow and pain merely mists on a mirror.

The crow or his brother, the raven, may appear in heraldry, but no national flag carries a crow on its field. It used to flaunt itself on the flag of the Vikings, but the Scandinavians have long abandoned the crow for the cross. The Lusk Irish Pipers' Band alone carries a huge crow on its big white field, commemorating the fact that the people of this part of North Dublin are descendants of the valiant old Vikings. Nor is the sound of the crow's song blended into any C-sharp or D-flat piece of music; it never sounds from a symphony, a sonata, or a serenade, though the voices of other birds may, here and there, be heard rippling through a bar of music. But the crow's caw is part of heaven's choir, like it or not. Let the lark soar past, its song in full flower of sound; the crow's caw cuts through it, tinting the lark's romantic light with the duskiness of a more earthly day. Let him have and let him enjoy his tenor notes, says the crow, but I'm always here to sing the bass for the birds.

The caw of the green crow has been heard in Irish skies and English skies this long time, as the dark one flew along side by side with Picasso's white dove, the one cooing, the other cawing, for peace when most of the other birds—the thrush, the wren, the warblers, the lark—were silent; when even the eagle seemed to have forgotten his whistle. Now the skies everywhere are full of the piping of all the birds, piping for peace: a merry throng chanting in unison and in harmony for that peace which the world alone can give. The Parliament of Foules denounces war.

When I think—as I do at times—of the frequently expressed belief that the sojourn in the English skies of the Green Crow has weakened the crow's caw, the belief seems, for various reasons, comical, illogical. It was W. B. Yeats who began the impression at the time of his rejection of *The Silver Tassie*. Since then, the titwillows have echoed and made shriller the old eagle's whistle. But in thinking of me for his own good or bad reasons, Yeats forgot about himself. Yeats got his first schooling in Hammersmith, London; he lived for over twenty years in Bloomsbury, London; and, if we add the time he spent afterwards in England (he had a house in Oxford), the South of France, in Italy and in the United States, it will easily be found that the eagle was far longer and far further away from Ireland than ever the Green Crow was; and, as far as I know, the titwillows of the time never bothered to chirrup the eagle back to his home. James Stephens, the Irish poet and story-teller, was never gagged and nagged at to come back to Eirinn, however far away he went into England or the

United States. Neither was there any of this fuss over the clever dramatist, Denis Johnston; nor was any ruaille buaille made to bring back George Moore, who did return once and went back to England quicker than he had left it. No one, of course, would or could bother about Joyce's going. Then there were the hundreds of actors and actresses who left hot-foot for London, for New York, and for Hollywood to spend the rest of their years there if God would favor them. Yet, no one ever did, or ever does, nag at them to return or warn them that their acting-art is in danger of decay if they remain in Hollywood. Indeed, if they do come back for a quick look round, they are hailed as representatives of Irish culture and Irish achievement; the playwrights, actors, and actresses left behind watch them enviously and wait for the first chance of a favoring wind to carry them off and leave them gently down in London's West End or New York's Broadway.

Another thing never noticed, never questioned, is why the many dramatists still under Irish skies, still breathing Irish air, don't do better than it is said they do. The plays that are done, both in English and Irish, seem to sink to the same mediocre level, to be fitted with little life and varnished by but a few sparkles of music or song. The Irish sky is over their heads, the Irish sod clings to their feet, Ireland plays her part all around them, yet home-stuck Irish playwrights pluck from experience neither nettle nor rose. God knows, I wish they did. In my opinion, they would have a better sight of drama if they ventured to spend a few years in London, for however poor the theater here may be, it is livelier, firmer, more venturesome than its timid and tired sister of Dublin. Hot and handsome prizes are given now for plays in English and in Gaelic, but so far there hasn't been even one flash in a pen. Nothing yet

in the Irish mirror held up to nature but shadowy silhou-
ettes. Of three Gaelic plays done yesterday, two of which
won prizes, O Glaisne says in his Gaelic article, "The three
dramas gave us a pleasant evening, but that was all." However, O Glaisne scented promise in one of the playwrights,
a Richard Power, and hoped he "would have another day."
May God hasten it on!

The Irish drama critics are indeed a dull bunch. It is
very doubtful if there be any like them in any other clime.
A correspondent, writing to the Irish papers to warn the
world about them, says: "The Irish drama critic is very
often 'the fella who got the job' because other working
journalists were too busy or too valuable to be spared. It is
unfair to call them critics; they are notice-writers." Young
or old, it is the writer who remains to live on in Ireland
that has the tough time face to face with bullies and bend-
the-knee bastards; those who try to create something in the
shape of article, story, or poem in the press or in magazines
like *The Bell* or *Irish Writing*. The poet Austin Clarke has
a couple of significant pieces in the current quarterly number of *Irish Writing*. Clarke is no friend of mine, but he is
a poet of no mean stature and a man of no mean mind. He
has had a hard time making a living for his family and
for himself. In one piece he tells of his flight from England
back to Ireland, bringing his family back "wave after wave
from exile," and ends with the remark

> *Could I have known*
> *That I would sleep in England*
> *Still, lie awake at home?*

Lie awake at home! Ireland has murdered sleep. In another
poem, he tells us how he was startled from sleep by a clang:
realization that "The Holy Ghost Fathers had bought a
bigger bell" followed by a question of "Why should our

blessed truth be measured by the mile?" Looks like the
blinds are down for the poet in Dublin, and only through
a slit or two can he ever see the sun.

So, let those who are growing care-worn over the Green
Crow's absence from Irish woods interest themselves rather
in the birds that haunt the trees, the hedges, and the shrubbery of Ireland's four beautiful fields. And should a one of
them grow a colored feather or two in chest or on back,
let not the rest pounce on him to pluck them out so that
he may not escape from the common color of the common
flock.

Some Latin writer once said, "If a crow could feed in
quiet, it would have more meat." A thing this Green Crow
could never do: it had always, and has still, to speak and
speak while it seeks and finds its food, and so has had less
meat than it might have had if only it had kept its big
beak shut. Never mind: many have listened to its caw, some
listen still, and this book is another caw-caw for those who
may wish to hear more, the Green Crow hoping that the
hoarse voice may sound mellower if it is remembered that
the crow

> *Renders good servant as your man-at-arms,*
> *Crushing the beetle in his coat of mail,*
> *And crying havoc on the snail and slug.*

Some don't like the caw of the crow when it has in it
any hint of the lark's song. Most of the Irish critics, using
any stick by which to beat a god, object to the lyrical
quality in O'Casey's later plays. One said, "After *The Plough
and the Stars* O'Casey's playwriting took a curious twist that
disturbs and grieves his true admirers." True admirers—
aha, ahem! Another, in an impassioned appeal, begged

O'Casey, almost on his knees, "to return to first principles." Yet the same chaps complain when plays on the stage or that come over the radio have any signs of O'Casey's influence in them, though they go on urging O'Casey to go on, go on imitating himself. If these critics were honest, they would know that O'Casey's later plays belong to his first purr-ins-a-pulls. His first play ever to appear in print was in his later manner. The play *Roisin's Robe* was printed in *The Plain People* years before the appearance of *The Shadow of a Gunman*. This paper was then edited, I think, by Erskine Childers who was afterwards executed by the Free State Government during the dreadful and foolish civil war. Again, in the same year that saw *The Shadow of a Gunman* on the Abbey stage, *Cathleen Listens In,* a satirical fantasy, was done on the same stage; and the very same critic who bleats about the return to first principles acted the part of a fantastic character in the fantastic play. Oddly enough, when I think of it, the play speaks still, for the politics in Ireland today—minus a civil war—are as they were then and the question of the merits or demerits of Compulsory Irish is still a theme of battledore and shuttlecock.

So, my friends, among the gay and gentle sounds of lark, thrush, robin, and nightingale, I beseech you silence for a few moments that you may hear the caw of a Green Crow. Here is the gathering together of a variorum making a strange nest from twigs, gay-colored feathers, and a few sprigs of thyme. Here are some short stories long out of print, articles on the British theater, taken from a book that has been out of print, too, for a long, long time; other articles asked for, from time to time, by editors of various journals, to all of whom I am beholden for permission to reprint them here.

What is all this for? Why have these things been written? Does one write for posterity? For a living? For a living, undoubtedly. One of the Irish critics, warning me of calamity for writing as I have done now for over twenty years, says, "The long view of posterity may turn out to be a poor one." So it may, indeed, but I won't be there to hear it. My conscience lies within myself and not within the soul of posterity. T. S. Eliot writes somewhere: "We write to keep something alive, and not because we believe in success or expect a triumph." To keep something alive: there it is, and it is good enough. So, to posterity I say

Fare thee well! and if forever,
Still forever fare thee well.

Caw! caw! caw!

The Flying Wasp

Overture

THERE ARE A LOT OF CRITICS IN THE WORLD, just as there are a lot of authors, too. High-born ladies and high-born gentlemen, like other courting couples, they have their differences; differences that cause a coolness between them, sometimes lasting a lifetime. It is but fair to say, though, that, when it lasts so long, the fault is usually with the author; the critic is usually the readier to forgive. I fear we writers of novel, play, biography, imagine the critic to be gifted, not only with ordinary sight, but with foresight, back-sight, and the sight of seeing things which aren't there. They differ among themselves, as all human minds do and must; and they differ in different countries. The American critics, for instance, are very different from those who hover over the banks of the Thames. The Americans, though they have the beaks and talons of a hawk, can coo like a sucking dove; they can be friendly, they can be damn good companions. They are as happy, possibly even happier, among others as they are among themselves. The English critics seem to be uncomfortable outside of their particular stalls or when absent from their own Critics' Circle. They aren't good mixers.

[3]

They seem to be forever afraid that they may be asked any questions. Especially by playwrights. They act as if they were captains in the theater, and the playwrights not members of the crew, but only sad stowaways. They seem to be unaware that the critic and the playwright are fifty-fifties, of equal importance, both assigned to the hard, but enjoyable, task of keeping the theater alive; of bringing before the view the drama-blossoms of the past that have proved themselves to be everlasting in color and perfume, and to select from the newer crowd of daisy and dandelion a blossom that has suddenly taken on the beauty of a lily or a rose. The drama critic, of surety, and the playwright, having the same quality, are one: the playwright presents the blossom he has grown to the theater, and the critic takes it, and puts it in a vase that he has made for all to view and admire; so we have a fine flower in a fine vase, living together, and lasting forever.

The critic who is afraid of a challenger is really afraid of himself; he hasn't got the gift of criticism, which is to shove the bad aside, make room for the good, lead it forth, and show it to the world. There will always be a difference between author and critic, living in the same house, eating the same bread, and drinking the same wine. The author can never be satisfied with all a critic says about him, if he be living to read what the critic has written. The critic-rose, however he may open his petals to waft perfume over an author, one day or another, the fondling author will feel the prick of a thorn, and shy away, pained, surprised, and a little angry. There is no use of kicking against the pricks, for guard himself as he may, the author will, one day or another, when he is least suspecting, suddenly feel a stab of pain in the hand, and see a finger trickling blood. Humility isn't a common virtue, and the critic mustn't be put out either if a few hot curses singe his hair. Let the author remember, should the

work he creates be good, that there will be always some critics of understanding, wide-breasted and brave enough to
take on their shields venomous thrusts made at an original
author, and blunt the points that seek to slay. Let the author
vaguely remember that his work may not always be good,
the time he feverishly realizes that the critic is sometimes
wrong; that though some critics don't know how to read,
there are also some authors who don't know how to write.
Scholar as he must be, experienced as he should be, the critic
lays aside his scholarship, forgets his experience, when he
sits down to analyze and enjoy a work that sings a new song,
or an old one in a new way; and his criticism becomes a cry
from the heart as much as the work that flames beneath him
with agony or laughter on his table or on his desk. Criticism
is the guide, the defender of every lovely thing written in a
book, picturing itself on a canvas, thrusting itself from stone
or bronze, or strutting on a stage in finery of jewelled laughter or weeping in black over the grave of a lost woman or a
lost cause. The effective critic should, as George Jean Nathan
says, ally the "mind of a gentleman with the emotions of
a bum."

The American critics, however mistaken they are, however
bitter they may be, however exasperating they may become,
are invariably friendly. Meeting them, they will come to you
with hands outstretched, will sit you down, make you take it
easy, and trate you dacent. So long as you aren't a bore, and
so long as you don't want to be forever talking about yourself
and your work; for these critics take an interest in many
things away from colored lights and make-believe, where
silken curtains neither go up nor come down to reveal or hide
away a fantasy; they talk Republican or Democratic; most
of them choose Jefferson rather than McCarthy; the pipe,
cigar, or cigarette is usually in a hand or near an elbow; they

would look at a flower in the field, an animal in the zoo, as
as well as a play on the stage. I know one eminent American
drama critic who was as interested in the making of a grand
table for a room in his little country home as he would be in
any play, even in one whose words and actions rang a
hundred melodious bells about strong and striving man,
pealing out life's coronation, or tolling miserably over a grave
marking where life had failed, had faded, and had died without one defying sigh. The making of the table linked him
down to ardent and arduous life, giving him a keener insight
into pictures he might see on a wall, or living pictures glow-
ing fantastic on a stage, uniting life he saw and felt with the
colored and speculative strutting and posing on the stage.

The English drama critics don't seem to be so simple; they
don't divide themselves, unless with their particular cronies.
They try to keep themselves unspotted from the world outside the theater. They rarely doff their drama-miters, and
usually carry their pastoral-comical, historical-pastoral croziers in their hands. They have an Athanasian creed of their
own. To make things cozy for themselves, they have built up
a nice little code of law which says that no one criticized
by them should have the vulgarity or indecency to answer
back (the Irish critics go one better by declaring that no
indignant playwright should answer back or forward). The
late James Agate once said in the *Manchester Guardian*
that he "willingly accepted the principle that the criticized
should reply to a criticism only for two reasons, namely: one,
if a misstatement of fact occurred; and, secondly, if the critic
refutes himself."

A cozy little code of honor for the English critics. The
critic is to have a mile of paper-space a year to go for the
playwright, while the playwright isn't to have an inch of
spare space in which to say a word about the critic. A nice

little self-arrangement of theatrical logic on the part of the English critics. The natural and revealed religion of the Theater is that a playwright must never attempt to answer a critic back. No back answers! When was this law handed down from the theatrical heaven, and who was the first critic to grab hold of it, I wonder? Sainte-Beuve? In a letter to the press, Ernst Toller once complained that an English critic had suggested a play by the dramatist contained lines of doubtful taste (in spite of Shakespeare, the English critics remain the unflinchible and invincible chumpions of good taste in the drama). Toller said in his letter of complaint: "It is an unwritten law that the author has to present his play to the public and the critics, be they the worst, and then remain silent." Dumb. Poor dumb wounds, we cannot bid them speak for us. But why not, if we have hope for the play that we have put before them? It's bad enough that the English critics should create a law to suit themselves, but it is worse when playwrights themselves decide to mount and trim a golden frame around it. If the critic has hope for the criticism he puts before the playwright, he won't fear anything that may be said against it; for he is not an enemy, but a comrade of the playwright.

Why do so many English critics cling so lovingly to this law? Is it because of their love for the greatness and dignity of the English Theater, and their fear that a cross word flung at a critic might mean the death of the drama? In my opinion they hang on to this dainty law because they are so unsure of themselves that they must guard their opinions, at all costs, against intelligent challengers who take a living interest in the Theater.

This law wins a lot of its power from the fact that so many playwrights seem to be intensely afraid of calling critics to question for the silly, pretentious, and unfair things some of them sometimes say; because, on the whole, playwrights are as poor in spirit as they are in thought and imagination, and their mouths are always watering for what is termed a "good notice," however bad their play may be; because they have little confidence in themselves as writers, and trust to the critics to swell them out bigger than they are, or ever will be—as, indeed, the critics sometimes do; and because they are more interested in what they can commercially get out of what they do than in any quality that ought to be in their work.

Some time ago, one well known in the journalistic world, who is also a playwright, coined a play which was deservedly received by a silent boo from the critics. He rang me up, and complained bitterly that the critics had done him wrong, insisting that the play had what the critics said it had not. I suggested that he should answer the critics back, and fearlessly point out where he thought them to be astray. He couldn't do that; oh no, he wouldn't do that; such a thing wasn't done, and there was the end of it. I had a big suspicion that he thought I might do it for him. "They decided to slate the play," he moaned, "and I'll have to take my gruel without complaining," and he complaining all the time—to me. A timid play followed by a timid complaint. Critics, on the whole, respond to a very bad play with all their gongs sounding the same note; a fine play is bound to react in different ways on different critics, just as it does, in varying ways, on members of an audience who see and hear it. But, whatever the impact, there will always be critics who will mingle their minds with the imagination of a good play, and courageously use their powers to add new oil to the new lamp in the Theater, turn up its light more firmly, and hold the lamp high for farther souls to see.

It matters little or less when different persons feel parts of a play in a different way. It is said that no eye sees the same thing in exactly the same way; that no ear hears the same sound exactly the same way; and it isn't surprising that the same part of a play excites differing emotions in differing breasts. For instance, I remember that the late Mr. Agate called the frolic drunkenness of Joxer and Captain Boyle, in the ending of *The Plough and the Stars,* a master touch, though a fine Shakespearean scholar and critic, a Mr. Lawrence, referred to it as a disaster. It was that to this, and this to that, without doing any harm to the critics or to the play. Both responses were genuine, though one condemned and the other applauded. Very different from this impulsive rejection, and equally impulsive acceptance, was the feeling for Rosie Redmond, the prostitute, in the second act of the same play, by the Irish drama critics of that time. With one accord, they shoved the character aside as unnecessary and utterly irrelevant; she smirched the play with a redundant character. There was neither impulsiveness nor honesty in this response. Why do I say that, now? Why? I'll tell you: Not a saint or sinner of them took the slightest notice of A Woman, a character in the same play, in a following act, who had neither rhyme nor reason for being there; a character that was in every way a false introduction; one who could have no conceivable connection with any of the others from the play's beginning to the play's end. Rosie Redmond was as natural in the pub as a wallflower would be sprouting from the crevices of a crumbling wall; the Woman as unnatural where she was as a bishop would be were he found as a lodger in a Dublin tenement. But the Irish critics pushed and pulled Rosie towards the door, while they looked upon the Woman with nonchalant eyes, and heard her few stuttering remarks with nonchalant ears. Why? I'll tell you: There was no honesty in the reviews; none then as there is none now. The criticisms that left the Woman alone and harried Rosie showed that when the critics aimed, they aimed sideways, so that they would hit, not the play alone, but through the play, the playwright. As these Dublin critics were then—hooting down any that contradicted them—so are they now, hooting now from the dusty, musty hide-hole James Agate left behind them. Today, the thirtieth of May, nineteen hundred and fifty-five, a commentator, Niall Carroll, says in the *Irish Press*: "As far as I can recall, none but the minor and unimportant authors in this country have ever rushed into print to attack the critics when their work was not well received. The worst mud-slinger would hardly class Mr. O'Casey as minor or unimportant, but it looks as if he is resorting to the habits of the lesser dramatic breeds."

The lesser breeds within the critics' own sweet law. May it not be, on the other hand, that it is the less important and lesser breeds of the critics who writhe and cry fie when their opinion is challenged? No gifted criticism is so brittle as to shake at a cry of scorn, or break at a shout of anger. As with the playwright, there is no critic who, one time or another, will not be challenged, if not by a playwright, then by a comrade-critic who cannot see as he has seen, or hear as he has heard; and the critic who shrivels up before the searchlight of another mind is dead before the same searchlight has reached him. As for O'Casey and the Irish critics, he doesn't attack them: he merely laughs at them, and the laughter is enough to change the elegant, waddling swan into common, comical, conceited goose.

The critic and the playwright are in the same boat—if both be good, they will both live, and each will have a stimulating effect upon the other: each makes room for the other. *Nil desperandum* is the motto of good dramatist and good critic alike, even when assailed and surrounded by snakes and bladdhers.

None but the minor and unimportant authors in this country have ever rushed into print to attack the critics when their work wasn't well received. None? Never? Even were this so—though it isn't—there is no warrant for a literary status quo to become immortal. "This country," Mr. Niall Carroll, may have known no authors over unimportance; and, of course, you have read little, or your memory may be bad when you shout "never." As I write, June begins, and purple lilac, yellow laburnum, and red hawthorn are nodding to each other in gardens and over walls, using all that is in the ground beneath and in the air around to express themselves in different colors, and their own fancied forms, within a rare and curious unity of truth and loveliness. If only the Irish drama critics could move halfway to this colorful achievement: could use all that has been, all that is, to make themselves wiser, more colorful, within a unity of knowledge and adventurous suggestion. This lad, then, would know that artists are as fond of challenging the critics as the critics are of challenging the artists. We know what Yeats thought of the snakes and the bladdhers that hissed and slobbered venom over his *Countess Cathleen*; of what he thought of them who hissed and spat at Synge's *Playboy of the Western World*. He not only criticized the Irish critics, but the English ones, too, advancing from this redoubt to make an onslaught on the whole aspect and tinselled tatters of the theater shown there, as it gasped out the mean and meager view it took of life, and the miserable knowledge it had of the theater's art. As in the days of Yeats and Synge, more than fifty years ago, so are the Irish critics, ninety-nine per cent of them, today. Fleas hanging on to bigger backs, for that is the one way in which they can achieve a part-time immortality.

> *Half-wits are fleas; so little and so light,*
> *We scarce could know they live, but that they bite.*

Irish critics, was it Yeats said this of you? Who, then? Guess, lads.

It is a very sad thing that our little Republic, so rich a day or two ago with such souls as Synge, Gregory, Moore, Joyce, and Yeats; so poverty-stricken today with few but flea-minds with us, unable to chirrup even as the cricket on the hearth. These fleas, inflated as they are from what they get out of the bites they give each other, are all of the same common measure: to give advice; to do nought but laugh, would be to give cordial to the dead. It is sad to think that applause or condemnation of fools is to be received no longer from the common audience, but from the critics; for the critics now stand on their toes to garland triviality with all the pomp the parish pump can give, and hasten to hunt the serious and the fanciful out of sight and out of sound. Most of these critics have a staling custom of saying, as they say a rosary, that I attack them because I cannot bear the various ways they find fault in, and with, my work. I don't think there's any reason to furnish themselves with this flattery; for I don't imagine, as they do, that their reporting from Liffey or Shannon becomes the dramatic law of half the world. I join my thought with what the poet thought of his parochial teasers:

> *Let those find fault whose wit's so very small,*
> *They've need to show that they can think at all.*

What they may say is of no consequence to me—spiritually or materially. They can do me no harm in the world outside, and not much on the banks of the Bann, the Shannon, or even the Liffey herself. What I fear is that they stand in the way of better and of braver minds; of some younger thought eager to thrust a braver tone and a sturdier spirit into Irish drama criticism. The present-day ones are but a foolish blend of arsenic and old lace. To give one instance, I remember one of the first of Liffey-bank critics running round the city like Solomon Eagle, in *Old Saint Paul's*, crying loud, Come all ye, come all ye! A good play, a grand play, a great play for Ireland and the world! The heart-cry and the head-cry lasted a month of Sundays, and then departed from the sounds of earth; for the good play, the grand play, the great play, has never been mentioned by name again by the Dublin critic. Yet the same critic howls down plays, better and wiser, more musical, than the good one, the grand one, the great one, that he tried to thunder into the notice of Ireland and the world. Ireland has forgotten it, and the world knows it not.

These critics do not injure O'Casey, but they disgrace Ireland. That offense is far worse, for in the gallant and competing world, we have no navy to shove out into the seven seas, no army to shake another land with its marching, no huge industrial activity to furnish a continent with amazing machinery, or the wherewithal to clothe a continent's millions. We have but our imagination and mind in poem and in play, in the form and use of home and church and public building, in a fiddle-tune woven out into a fine symphony, in the painting that will move half a world into staring, in the play that will honor any stage in any country good enough to put it on. We should not allow the grand shove to the world's front, given to Ireland by Yeats, Joyce, Shaw, Synge, Gregory, and a few others, to weaken for want of another hand or two to keep the shove going; and we might well begin with a young critic of the drama conscious of the people, but careless of Church and State, who, casting off the thin finery of fear, will stand up to speak out what he thinks, how he feels, about all he sees surging or crawling around him, careless of conduct and careless of comment by the fearful, the little-minded, and the cadging souls that prey on the courage they lack, and try to destroy any vision beyond their job, or the miserable prayers they mutter to slyly save their miserable souls.

It will be hard going for the young stag of criticism, maybe hard going for a long time, till he grows sturdy antlers to fence the yapping dogs away; but, in the end, the little ones, having saved their souls, shall lose them; and he, having had the courage to suffer loss, shall save his; for, as Ernest Newman, the music critic, once said: "If there is something in a man's music that appeals for its own sake to a fair number of people, he will become a classic in spite of all that critics can urge against him." What Ernest Newman said of music, can be said of drama, and can be said of criticism too. If there be anything in a drama, there will always be some critics who will stand by it, fight for it, and make it known; cap it with laurel. And as George Jean Nathan tells us, "There will always be intelligent laymen who can easily distinguish the values between the Brothers Minsky and the Brothers Karamazov." I myself have been called pretentious, dull, feeble, pagan, immoral, indecent, vile, vulgar, and blasphemous; so the young Irish critic needn't be afraid or ashamed, seeing that he has such a bad example to give him courage and give him faith.

The two—critic and dramatist—are two tassels hanging on the same wonderful curtain; attached to colored, silken cords pulling gorgeous curtains aside and then pulling them together again: between them they bind and loose all that is good, great, and glorious in the Theater. It isn't all solemn and serious: the clowns are here by the high altar of drama, too. The one place in the world where hero and clown go hand in hand together. Says Brooks Atkinson in his *Once Around the Sun*, "The clowns can run and sing, turn handsprings, tumble and bellow, and distort the ordinary materials of life into something rich and merry. . . . They are the royal minstrels—the antic comics, the skipping fools, the masters of the revels. For an hour or two in the evening they push back the walls of the universe." They are, they are; they do, they do, indeed.

What chance have we of survival—dramatist, critic, and actor—now that we are but a step away from the deluge and avalanche of radio, television, and film? Has the drama at last to hand in her gun and surrender her sword? The bodiless voice is forever sounding in our ears; the wolf of the film and the fox of television are running in and out of the house; now is the time of the Big Shows, blessed by the Big Business Man, when audiences come to the theater, not to see what dramatist and actor can do, not to hear what a critic can say; but just to see what money can buy. Have the rotten dramatists, the rotten critics, and all the bastard blazonry of big business shows put drama in a leaden coffin at last? No, for to destroy the living theater, these would have to destroy life itself. Few can come out over the wireless, though the audience number millions; as few can show themselves on the films, or on television, though the audience number millions; but we can all act; in the theater, on a platform, in a club, at home beside the fire; and no power or person can interfere with us acting a way through life. The little girl hugging a doll and believing herself a mother, the lad drawing a tin sword, believing himself a hero, are the beginning of all the world's a stage; and this inborn motive

will always urge life to go to see within the living theater how
life lives; how she sings her song or does her dance, dance of
joy or dance of death; how she behaves in magnificence or
in misery; what she looks like when bells ring for a wedding,
or how she looks when a bell tolls for the dead.

The Public Death of Shakespeare

The article above, and the one titled England,
Say When, *were written around the time of the
eminent desire for a National Theater. Shakespeare was slumbering heedlessly in his grave,
unbothered by a soul. The Memorial Theater
was a mausoleum, with a chantry where a few
actor-priests and actor-priestesses now and again
held off-record performances of hurried prayers,
under the light of the moon and stars; then flew
off again to London for the better and more
radiant rally of moon-ray and star-ray in the colored lights of Shaftesbury Avenue and Piccadilly
Circus. The Chairman of the Foreign Commission Union of Soviet Writers has sent me a request for an article giving an account of the
many performances of the plays of Shakespeare,
all over England, to mark an anniversary of a
birthday. There wasn't one; not a one anywhere.
The Stratford Memorial Theater was closed, and
the key taken out of the door. A famous Jewish
Soviet actor came to England on an invited visit.
"Where would you like to go, what would you
like to do?" he was asked.*

——*We weel go to see all de Shakespeare plays
being done in London, first of all.*
——*You can't do that; you can't do that—there's
none being done.*
——*What a peety! Vel we weel go to Stratford-
on-Avon to see dem doing dem der.*
——*You can't do that; you can't do that—the
Theater's shut up, the Caretaker has the
door-key in his back pocket, and is away,
away at the Cinema.*
*Shakespeare had disappeared out of England. He
wasn't to be seen anywhere this time, not even
under a cloud.*

SHAKESPEARE'S DEAD. PRODUCERS, ACTORS,
audience, and dramatists have all had a hand in it. He has
been half kicked to death by bad productions of his plays,
and finished finally by having no production at all. There's a
sigh of relief heard now that all is over, for he always stood
in the way of bad drama, and we are so used to this now,
that it is all we want and as much as we need. Actors can go
on serenely lisping their nancy numbers, mincing the English
language into shrivelled murmurs; managers can safely take
a chance with any damned thing that comes their way;
dramatists can go on brocading the English Theater with
one triviality after another; and the critics can go on writing
their golden scriptures of criticism about bum plays without
a single prod of pain assailing their artistic consciences. The
public death of Shakespeare is the symbol of the public death
of the Theater, though we have today what we never had
before, namely, six famous plays written, produced, and
scheduled every year as regularly as the import and export
records from the Office of Statistics. So, apparently, we have
improved on Shakespeare and the other great Elizabethans.
Six famous plays in a year! Why, the English dramatists

haven't given us six famous plays in a century. There isn't a single great play among the lot of them, and few of them have even a second-hand glory. Famous bowlers, famous batters, famous film stars and starinas, famous tennis players, famous rascals, we have many and various and hearty and strong, but famous plays we have none, even though many of them be tabarded with a golden-jacketed gospel of praise woven by a gusty gatherer-in of geniuses.

＊　　　＊　　　＊

We have the Memorial Theater (appropriate name that) on the Avon, housing Shakespeare's shade; we have the museum-like Old Vic presenting his plays as souvenirs; we have Sir Barry Jackson once a year burnishing Elizabethan swords and brushing a few Elizabethan velvets with elaborate ceremonial; and we have Mr. Sydney Carroll, when the humor takes him, doing a sun-spotlight Shakespearean dance in Regent's Park, with the critics solemnly attending and wishing that they were having a one-and-one with a crony in the peaceful glades of the Savage or the Garrick Clubs: these are about all, each of them pretty tired, and, in my opinion, none of them with a finger-strength power to even modify the recessional movement from Shakespeare and the drama on the one hand, or from the Theater on the other. But all this feverish activity shows how the English people love their William Shakespeare—Shakespeare and the *Sunday Express*. It has been said with extreme unction that he is the most popular English dramatist in England. England will have to travel a long way back or a good way forward before Shakespeare can become a popular dramatist. He isn't so easy to get on with as some people are pleased to think. He chooses his company carefully. He isn't "hail fellow well met" to everyone who stops to ask him who he was with last night.

You have to know a thing or two before Shakespeare will stop to have a chat with you. He makes quite a few demands on the intelligence, and you have almost to give as good as you get before he shakes your hand. Under the circumstances how could he be a popular dramatist? If you still think he is, have a look round, listen and see, and then judge for yourself. Go into the pleasant homes of England and listen to hear how often and often his name is mentioned. You will find that, so far from him being the most popular dramatist in England, he is unknown except as a well-known name. If Shakespeare were all that he is cracked up to be to the English people, their joy and their pride, their bright and morning star in dramatic literature, then all, or most, or, at least, some of the English dramatists would be influenced by his plays. How many have been influenced by him? Is there even one English dramatist of whom it can be said that he was influenced by Shakespeare? Even faintly influenced? Not even a vanishing sign of him in one of their works. The young, rising, risen dramatists of England have effectively bundled Shakespeare out of their minds, and, so signs on it, write as many famous plays in a year as Shakespeare wrote in his lifetime. Some time ago the young and graceful Beverley Nichols, the Prince Charming of the English Theater, wrote an article of advice to all who were ambitious to become playwrights, and he told these hopeful ones to follow, oh, not Shakespeare, but Lonsdale and Coward. Fall in and follow the band. Lonsdale and Coward will bring the young playwrights where the people want them to go, and where they want to go themselves. So off with the motley, and on with the blouse and the shorts and the sandals, and follow these two, leaving Shakespeare sitting like a wasted beggar on the wayside.

＊　　　＊　　　＊

Nietzsche has said that God is dead, and were he living here today, he would add to the name of God the name of Shakespeare, for Shakespeare, as far as the writing of drama, the speaking of drama, the acting of drama, the production of drama, are concerned, is as dead as Queen Anne. He is gone and almost forgotten, and with dead Shakespeare, English drama lies dead too. All the sirens, hooters, buzzers, and recording clocks of the theater will immediately cry out that this is nonsense. Let us see who have been the high lights and the limelights and the leading lights of the English Theater during the last ten years or so. Here they are, standing to attention with their chests out: Coward, Lonsdale, Phillpotts, Sherriff, with Beverley Nichols peeping round the corner. And their plays: *Bitter-Sweet* and *Cavalcade*; *Maid of the Mountains* and *Spring Cleaning*; *The Farmer's Wife* and *Yellow Sands*; *Evensong*. Here we have the highest mountain peak and the deepest sea of modern English drama. The sea isn't half a mile down and the mountain isn't capped with snow. A wheen of days ago the English Theater passed through a bonnie time of jubilation and glee when *Journey's End* swept the country, and its author, Mr. Sherriff, was hailed as the resurrection and the life of English drama. The plump brains among the critics sang and danced and lit bonfire-praises that flung a glare of glory over the whole of England, till their combined praise became a dramatic annunciation. And yet these brawny-brained fellows might have guessed something when they read that the author of this play had neither seen nor read a play by Shakespeare. They might have guessed more when they read that when this author was brought to see *Hamlet* for the first time, and was asked what emotions the play stirred in him, replied, frankly, neither pity nor admiration. His chief feeling, as he said, was that the Prince of Denmark wasn't a man with

whom he would like to spend a week-end. Hamlet talked far
too much and did too little. Imagine thinking that a man who
killed a courtier, drove his sweetheart mad, shook his mother
to the center of her soul, and slew his stepfather, had done
too little! This playwright went on to tell us that he wasn't
impressed by Shakespeare's technique, and thought that the
introduction of the ghost was a mistake, for the reason that
it made Mr. Sherriff dislike Hamlet's father. The ghost, said
he, was full of the spirit of revenge; such a little attitude
of mind for a man who had suffered physical death: *Hamlet*
would have been a better play if the ghost had not appeared;
it would have strengthened the play scene, in which, by the
way, he thought Claudius came out so well; a really practiced
villain might have sat unmoved. The king's ingenuous reaction showed what a human being he really was. As for
being moved by the tragedy, went on Mr. Sherriff, or being
interested in the stir of Hamlet's mind, it didn't move me
greatly. I was much more moved by Young Woodley, an
ordinary boy who only half understood what was happening
around him. Hamlet was perfectly aware of everything
(imagine any man being perfectly aware of anything), and
I could feel no pity for a man who could express his emotion
so lucidly. I had real pity for the young schoolboy in Mr.
van Druten's play, none for the Prince of Denmark. Hamlet
speaking his thoughts aloud is so unnatural on the stage (long
live naturalism!), and the glorious language got in the way
of the play.

* * *

Well, Mr. Sherriff and his fellow playwrights have seen to
it that glorious language gets into the way of a play no
longer. Here we see what a young playwright, accepted a
little wheen of days ago as the very head and front of Eng-

lish drama, thought of the greatest play yet written by an Englishman. We see how he had a pitiful admiration for comparatively trivial gnat-like pieces of naturalism when pitted against the majesty and grandeur of Shakespeare's *Hamlet*. What are we to think of a young dramatist who, having created an almighty hope in the breasts of the poor English critics for the future of the drama, confesses that he had never seen or read a play by Shakespeare, and who, when he sees *Hamlet*, cries out, "Not this man, but John van Druten!" It is only fair to say that Mr. Sherriff made it plain that it was his first impression of a Shakespeare play, and later on he would probably discover that he had been talking foolishly. Let us all hope that he has since discovered that he talked foolishly, though, as far as I know, nothing has yet been said by him that would lead anyone to think he had in any way altered his first impression. So from this example, and indeed from many others, it is fairly evident that the English dramatists have buoyantly sealed up their minds against any possibility of inspiration from the works of Shakespeare.

The English actors aren't much better. Look at George Robey, who recently squeezed himself into the massive part of Falstaff, and didn't seem to achieve, according to the critics, the glory that this great part ought to give a great comedian (and Robey is a great comedian). He told us, through an interview, that he had seen only one play by Shakespeare, and had read none. And the part of Macbeth wasn't the best-played part of the many parts played by Charles Laughton. The part of Caliban called out to be played by this actor, but he played the part of Prospero instead. Long ago I suggested that he should have a shot at Falstaff, but he told me Falstaff was a part he could never feel. In my young days there seemed to be few actors who hadn't had a shot at a part in a Shakespeare play; now there seem to be few who have filled a part in one of his plays. Mr. St. John Ervine sorrowfully told us a few days ago, in an article aglow with admiration for Miss Marie Tempest, that in all her long experience of many parts on the English stage she never had had the honor to play a part in a play written by Shakespeare. It must be a sad thought to an artist, however great and well-beloved he or she may be, to look back and, in the remembrance of things done, find among all not a single success or even a single failure in a part from a play by Shakespeare. But the chorus of "I never did" grows bigger and bigger year by year, and a decade or so hence there will be nobody left interested enough to ask the question. So it is becoming almost impossible for an actor great in many ways to give greatness to a great part written by Shakespeare. For it is certain that no great actor or actress can suddenly blossom greatly in a great part in a Shakespeare play. Indeed it is said that managers, when they are told by an artist looking for a job that the artist has had experience in Shakespeare plays, turn up their insignificant noses, and tell the artist to go, for what they want is experience in modern plays, and not experience in Shakespeare stuff. The plays that now troop on and off the stage are such poor and woebegone trivialities, and the actors have become so softened with what is called naturalism, that none of them has the mouth for speaking Shakespeare. This the critics call restraint, and one is sick of reading such things as he or she acted with suitable, or beautiful, or great, restraint. The actors now are satisfied with acting themselves. They talk as themselves, dress as themselves, move about as themselves, and feel to be themselves. They are one-finger composers of the music of life; they are do-me-so-do actors and nothing else and nothing more. So we'll leave poor Shakespeare's ghost flitting in and out of the Old Vic, while his body lies in state in Stratford, and pull down the flags to half-mast, waiting for a suitable interval when we can decently pull them down altogether, and then forget that Shakespeare ever existed.

*   *   *

But hold your horses for a second—something's happening that brings new hope to English drama. The foundation of a National Shakespeare Studio for young actors is announced by Alexandra Carlisle. Training in Shakespeare is, according to her, absolutely essential for any young actor, and at present it is a very difficult training to get. False alarm! This is taking place in New York.

But hold your horses again for a second. Something else's happening that brings new hope to England's drama. The Chronicle Plays of Shakespeare as a group are to be performed for the first time in the English-speaking world. Where, where, where? In California, U.S.A., under the nose of Hollywood!

It was a mistake. I thought I saw his eyelids fluttering. Shakespeare still lies stretched out in state in Stratford on the Avon.

National Theater Bunkum

The article below is from The Flying Wasp. *It was written in nineteen hundred and thirty-five, originally, for an English weekly journal called* Time and Tide. *At the time there was great disturbance of mind about the plan to give England a National Theater, a plan sponsored by Bernard Shaw, Granville-Barker, and many others, but laughed at, and vehemently opposed by, a lot of the English drama critics, headed by James Agate.*

Around this time, the event causing all the mockery went forward. A site had been bought in South Kensington from the money got together by many years of gathering, and this, through the Title Deeds, was presented to the Trustees, with bugles blowing amain, sennets sounding, and drums beating a tattdoo doodoodoodlelorum. The site is there to this day; fallow and lonely— not a mouse stirring. The article below was a twisted laurel leaf thrown in by me among the garlanded fuss of the time.

Later on, fifteen years or so later, another sennet was sounded during the holding of the National

*Festival of Britain (the greatest thing thought of
and done by any Labor Government, or by any
other). When spirits were high, pride manifest,
and dramatic patriotism afire, the English Parliament passed a resolution, acclamo passionata,
that One Million Pounds would be set aside for
the purpose of building a National Theater on
the South Bank of the Thames, near where the
Elizabethans used to revel round the Globe; the
Million to be given when economic conditions
permitted. Verboten. The site is there to this
day; fallow and lonely; not a mouse stirring;
nothing there but a mirage of the image of Hope.*

I

THERE IS A CURIOUS COMIC GROUP IN ENGLAND
who pine after what they are pleased to call a National
Theater. They will not be happy till they get one, and they
will be a damned sight unhappier when they do. A crude
and a rude fellow named Granville-Barker is at the head of
this irritating band of agitators who, among other things,
want Shakespeare's plays played often and Shakespeare's
plays played well. God knows we have had enough of this
boyo for the last decade or so, without having him bobbing
up before you every time you come in for a meal or go out for
a drink. It is really a sad and a shameful thing to have these
people gadding about saying we want a National Theater,
we ought to have a National Theater, we must have a National Theater. Surely we have had enough Shakespeare for
the rest of our unnatural lives. Who wants a National Theater,
anyway? It is all very well for Granville-Barker to flourish in
our faces a long and brightly colored string of names, with

his Sir John This and The Lord Bishop of That, as if we had not the power to do our own thinking, independently of interested persons, ready, as Mr. Agate says, to ram a National Theater down our throats. And there is not, for all its impudent and imposing display, a single solitary name of importance from one end of the list to the other. Not a single mention of a right- or a left-wing forward, a back, or goalie, of one well-known football club; not a mention of a famous tennis player, or a film star; no mention of a golfer with a handicap of less than two, or a beauty-queen of cotton, muslin, silk, georgette, or steel; or a bathing-belle who had won a prize in one of our great and grim dailies; a cricketer who has scored a thousand runs, a Derby winner, a pugilist with a suitable number of knockouts, a runner who has won the race from Brighton to London three times running; or even the name of one from the shoal of literary geniuses caught squirming on the hook of fame week in and week out by our far-seeing reviewers and publishers determined to make England a fit place for these geniuses to live in. So the claim that the English people want a National Theater is all cant *ad hoc* and *ad hominem,* as Mr. Agate might say, and is just cool air blown out broadcast to confuse people and cause them to make a hasty decision that they might regret for the rest of their days.

* * *

When is Shakespeare ever mentioned in the House of Commons debates, or at the quiet and orderly meetings of the Cabinet, or at the assemblies of the Trades Union Congress, or at the coming together of the Convocation of York or Canterbury, or at the yearly dinners given by the Critics' Circle? Never, if you ask me or Mr. Agate, and the same is, to any intelligent human being, proof positive that England does not want a National Theater. This indifference shows that the House of Commons, the Cabinet, the members of the Trades Union Congress, the Critics' Circle, the Rotarians, Y.M.C.A., Society for the Prevention of Cruelty to Children, and the King's Proctor, do not and never will want or submit to the *ad hoc* or *ad hominem* creation of a National Theater, and that the whole question is founded on cant and controversy. All this murmuring that a National Theater will make for better drama, that it will maintain the efficiency and dignity of acting, that it will keep the plays of Shakespeare on regularly, revive whatever is vital in English drama, prevent recent plays of merit from falling into oblivion, produce new plays, and further the development of modern drama, and produce translations of representative works of foreign drama, is nothing else but a venomous attempt on the part of highbrow coteries to fasten further burdens on the backs of the dramatic critics, and torment honest and simple-minded people, anxious to live out their lives in peaceful and imaginative recreation among old ladies, family affairs, and the old folks at home.

❊   ❊   ❊

It was most encouraging to the common sense of the country to read the exegetic and lordly comments called "Clearing Away Cant" on this subject, written recently by Mr. James Agate, and appearing in the *Sunday Times.* Here, without hesitation and in fine manner, he laid down the law on these matters raised by pompous and nerve-wracking people. He tells us, without putting cap or cloak on it, that if people wanted to see the best drama, past and present, the opportunity would be provided, even in the existing state of affairs; though in the phrase of "even in the existing state of affairs" there is an implication that in a different state of affairs there might be a better chance of seeing the best of drama, past and present. He does not tell us that when people want a thing like the best of drama, past and present, the providing of the opportunity takes trouble, time, energy, and many activities before the opportunity can be provided. And is not the lordly one right when he says that he does not see why a person living in Penzance should subscribe for a performance of *Volpone* which nobody in London thinks of going to see? Hear, hear—and another hear, hear—to that. Why the hell should he, indeed? I ask, alongside Mr. James Agate, looking confidently up in his face. But, unfortunately, there will always be fools with faith knocking around, living, maybe, in Penzance, who would fork out a subscription for a performance of *Volpone* in London, who are full of a foolish faith in the ultimate greatness of mankind, and thinking they touch the hand of God by loving and honoring the great plays of the past and the present. You know, Mr. Agate, and I know myself, that this is a fond delusion, a snare, and a dangerous deceit. What could be fairer than the profound philosophy of Mr. Agate when he says if an art has become so unattractive that it cannot keep up its own dignity, he sees no reason why its dignity should be kept up for it? Could anyone, by taking thought and pondering the livelong night through, give utterance to a deeper thought than this thought? And yet there are those who murmur against this, saying, this fellow mixes up the poverty and the wretchedness of the Theater with the great art of the drama; that the great art of the drama cannot lose its dignity; that the maintenance of the efficiency and the dignity of an art does not mean the restoration of a dignity that has been lost; and that the only efficiency and dignity that has been lost to the drama, and will have to be restored, is the dignity and efficiency of the critics themselves; that the unattractiveness and triviality of the present state of the English Theater is kept up by the dignity of the dramatic critics turning themselves almost inside-out to get kind phrases together with which to color over the bleak barrenness and stale triviality of the plays that go to make up the eunuch-minded English Theater of the present day. They keep the average so low that thousands are writing worthless plays in the certain hope that, if they be no better, they will be no worse than many that have brought a ding-dong dandy chorus of plaumas or praise from the critics.

As far as the playing of Shakespeare goes, have we not the Old Vic, as Mr. Agate succinctly points out in his comments. Of course we have, and what more does a satisfied and sensible people want? Here we have the finest productions that can be given of Shakespeare's old time and for all time plays, with the Old Vic, like an old satin-clad lady, mustering the loveliest lights, dresses, decors, sennets, alarums, advances, retreats, skirmishes, trumpet calls, drumbeats, kindling music, mixed with the ravishing declamation of Shakespeare's glorious poetry. Yet a little while ago the music critic of the *Sunday Times* had the audacity to turn up his nose and say that "he had not seen the performance of *Macbeth* at the Old Vic, and, by the grace of God, he never would. He heard a broadcast by the actors concerned in the production at the Old Vic; and if blank verse be spoken at the Old Vic as it was by the majority of the actors who spoke on the radio, he should continue to prefer his Shakespeare in his study. Most of the people gabbled verse as if it were a paragraph in a newspaper." So, regarding the Old Vic, there is a difference of opinion between Mr. Agate, the dramatic critic, on the one hand, and Mr. Ernest Newman, the music critic, on the other. Mr. Newman, probably, is a cousin of the fellow living in Penzance, and so I plump for Mr. Agate, for, as a dramatic critic, he ought to know more about dramatic values in the speaking of Shakespeare than Mr. Newman, who, when all is said and done, is only a music critic, and spends so much of his time listening to first-rate music and writing about it that he cannot, in the nature of things, see or understand the beauty and integrity hidden deep in the little critic-coddled plays that are now speckling the English Theater with the blue mold.

❖ ❖ ❖

Unfortunately Mr. Agate, while his feet are in the buskins, his french-quartered shield well in front of him, his long sword out, says *ad hoc* and *ad hominem* that "that which is vital does not need reviving; the need presupposes that the vitality is lost or impaired." In making this lunge Mr. Agate trips over his french-quartered shield and falls dead on his nose. That which is vital constantly needs reviving—surely any biologist would tell him that. The story of life is a story of revivals from the day Adam and Eve scuttled out of the Garden of Eden to the present hour in which the big party have rearranged their Cabinet in an effort to give new life and energy to their government. Living things are in constant need of revival; it is only the dead that need no recreation. Mr. Agate should know that it is the sense of living drama among the people that has to be revived, and not the living drama itself: that is as vital as ever. The biggest difficulty that those who strain and work for this revival will have to face is not the low dramatic vitality of the people in general, not even that of the dramatists, though this is pretty bad; not that of producers; but the revival of the devitalized critics themselves. They will probably die in the last ditch.

Recovering from his slip, Mr. Agate stands to attention and trumpets: "No good play ever fails to be produced. If it is really a good play, it may begin in a hole [begin in a hole—j'ever hear anything like that!], but it ends by reaching all the corners of the earth." The critics should assemble in a reverent circle and sing a threefold amen to that saying. Why, if it be a good play, should it have to be produced in a hole? Because of the fact of it being good it should be produced with banners and a trumpet call. Why is it that most bad plays are produced in a grand manner under the cocked-up noses of Mr. Agate and his brother critics? But we shall have more to say about this a little later on.

Strange, after all this, that Mr. Agate seems to expect that those who are trying to interest people in the creation of a National Theater should jump at the chance of getting him to go on a lecturing tour in support of a project which he seems to look upon with strongly seasoned scorn. *Le jeu n'en vaut pas la chandelle.*

II

IN AN ARTICLE WRITTEN RECENTLY BY MR. AGATE for the *Sunday Times*, this critic makes the point that a National Theater would have to be "the theater of a people, and not that very different thing, a people's theater, which means slum dramas performed by unfashionable actors and dowdy actresses before ill-dressed audiences." What can a sensible person make of a remark like this, when it is plain that the Theater today is, in its fashionable actors, fashionable actresses, and fashionable audiences, exactly, by implication, what Mr. Agate wants it to be, having but one fault, namely, that it is dead? Here we have the apostle of elegant, well-dressed Pinerovianism speaking. He wants fashionable actors

and actresses with all the loveliness of Worth and Rozane off
their backs but on their bottoms, parading their trivialities
before him. He wants a National Theater to be a theater of
the people in contradistinction to a people's theater. I smell a
rat there. Now a National Theater to be of any use must be,
not in fashionable actors and actresses, but in dignity and
integrity, a theater of the people; and it must be in dealing
with the whole life of those who live, a people's theater as
well. This man pines for Pinero with his expensive clothes,
his yachts, villas, grand cigars, liqueurs with golden names,
French *hors-d'œuvres,* added to plots that instead of painting
the lily or perfuming the violet, gild the louse. A theater of
the people, for the people, or by the people, will hardly
waste time in the revival of a dead thing like *Letty,* or of
Mrs. Tanqueray the Second or Mrs. Tanqueray the Third.

* * *

Strange, too, that there seems to be an echo knocking about
somewhere of Mr. Agate's voice saying that the one thing a
fashionable actor can't do is to act. If we carry the rejection
of ill-dressed audiences to its logical conclusion, then, we come
to the belief that the male and female well-dressed window
dummies are the noblest works of God. How can the actors
be anything else but unfashionable, the actresses anything
but dowdy, the audiences anything but ill-dressed, using
these terms without an implication of snobbery, if the play
they act in on the one hand, and go to see on the other, be
produced in the hole that Mr. Agate seems to think a sufficient
encouragement for the author of a good play? In a recent
article in the *New York Times* Mr. Brooks Atkinson, the
American dramatic critic of that paper, reviewing the past
theatrical season of New York, was compelled to say that the
one current vitality in the Theater he knew was pulsing

through the activities of those groups that Mr. Agate so virtuously despises. John Mason Brown, dramatic critic of the New York *Evening Post,* tells us that "it is both agreeable and timely to point out how in *Awake and Sing!* and in *Waiting for Lefty* the Group Theater has not only achieved the best ensemble production of its career, but also has discovered in Clifford Odets a vigorous young dramatist who is possessed of many uncommon and exciting potentialities." One must remember, too, the unfashionable actors, the dowdy actresses, and the ill-dressed audience that first played and first clapped eyes on the plays of Eugene O'Neill. And where is the dramatist here to compare with him? The fashionable actors wouldn't be able to play the parts in his plays; the elegant actresses would be as bad as the fashionable actors; and the well-dressed audiences would possibly rush away after the end of the first act.

There are other instances of dowdy actresses, unfashionable actors, and ill-dressed audiences doing something for the drama; and Mr. Agate himself reminds us that his interest in Shaw was aroused at a hole-and-corner performance of *Candida.* Anyway, ill-dressed audiences are to be found everywhere. Conventional women ill-dress themselves (if Mr. Agate used the word in that sense) as often as the arty groups, and will always do so till they use the brain more and the mannequin less.

*   *   *

It is ridiculous for Mr. Agate to think, and thinking, demand that a National Theater be above class. How often have we heard this before, and how little there is in it. It is to be above class, he says, because it appeals to all classes. This depends on the plays produced, and it would be hard indeed for any theater, much more a National Theater, to put on plays that would appeal to all classes, except that the policy of putting on different kinds of plays at different times, each in its own way, would appeal to a different class, and so, as time ran on, the theater would realize the ideal wished for by Mr. Agate by appealing to all classes in the heel of the hunt. But to expect a play to be written that would appeal to all classes (it wouldn't appeal even to all the critics) is to ask something more than any dramatist can do. What we want are worthly examples of drama, irrespective of whether they appeal to all, or only certain classes, or certain elements in all the classes that at present form the community.

Mr. Agate is, perhaps, afraid that in some play or another he may get a knock in the face with a bit of propaganda of the wrong sort. He wants, evidently, to sit composed, watching the coy movements and speech of fashionable actors, elegantly robed actresses, among a delightfully dressed audience, and a play that will bring back the nicely-pressed-out remembrances of earlier days as he strolled about with Letty on his arm and when his house was in order. Mr. Agate fails to see propaganda lepping about all around us. Most literature is livened with propaganda. Shakespeare has it. *The Trojan Women* is propaganda. So are the Bible and the Koran, the rulebook of the Y.M.C.A., the philosophy of Spinoza and Schopenhauer, and the hymn books of the Salvation Army. Mr. Agate's articles are propaganda, and this article is propaganda against the propaganda of Mr. Agate.

*   *   *

A man who has anything vital to say in the form of a play, says it with strength, and puts a comely shape on what he has to say, should be afforded the finest hearing the country can give him. This ideal will be hard to come by, for if a man has anything vital to say, and says it with strength and come-liness, a great part of his countrymen will be indifferent; a good many more (better than the others, anyway) will want him crucified; but we can and do expect that dramatic critics who are ever in a spate about the need for good plays, should warm their chilled hands with a little clapping when a fine play evolves in front of their eyes. And this is, of course, where a National Theater will come in: a National Theater will exist for the performance of such plays as are by com-mon consent or picked judgment the best of our time and of theater history, but of which the production would be un-remunerative. Surely Mr. Agate will agree that a government that is not deaf nor dumb nor blind should, at least mo-mentarily, relax its political agitations, to run up a few State Theaters throughout the country in every town and in every borough having in them a hundred thousand men, women, and children.

* * *

The question which Mr. Agate really raises is that of who cares a damn about fine drama? Well, at least, a National Theater would be a symbol of fine drama. At the present time England is without a symbol or sign of anything worthy of the name of fine drama. One might call the Old Vic a symbol of Shakespeare, for it is, at least, keeping the name of the great poet before his people. But it is a sad symbol for a greater, more vital performance of his plays. The Old Vic is only a hole-and-corner existence for England's greatest dramatist.

It is the English method of getting rid of him as quietly as possible. England, out of her generosity, her indomitable pride, in the power of her great nationhood, finds a cubby-hole for Shakespeare where he can get in nobody's way, and

where his name will not interfere with the nonchalant ease
and comfort of the critics who, perhaps, like plays that are
easy to write about, because there is nothing original or
strange in any of them.

* * *

In his book on *A National Theater*, Mr. Granville-Barker
tells us that English drama ranks high among the literature
of the world. Does it really? According to Mr. Agate it does
not rank very high in the opinion of the English people themselves, for he tells us that the English people are indifferent
to the creation of a National Theater that might serve to
make it rank a little higher than it does in the home of its
creation. English acting, goes on Mr. Granville-Barker, given
its chance, can compare with the best, but the English nation,
as a nation, cares nothing for the credit of either. The for-
eigner, the American, the visitor from the Dominions will
probably find the Theater Royal, Drury Lane, our National
Theater of the past, occupied by American musical comedy;
and for anything that can be called representative drama,
they may, as often as not, seek elsewhere in vain. This, says
Mr. Granville-Barker, is something of a reproach, surely, to
the capital city of an Empire. The English people, led by
some of the critics, can take such a reproach in their stride
as they march onward singing, "Keep right on to the end of
the road." The capital city of four hundred and forty-five
millions of people cannot afford the cost of a National
Theater. The Empire is too damned poor. In money or in
mind? Is England's mind so poverty-stricken that her people
cannot summon up enough thought to even desire a National
Theater? Mr. Agate seems to think so. Mr. Agate is an Englishman connected with the Theater during the longest part
of his life, and he ought to know. Does he really know? As an

Irishman I have no hesitation in saying that I think he does not know.

❋ ❋ ❋

That the English are not unanimous about the need for a National Theater there can be no manner of doubt, but then a people is never unanimous about the need for anything except war. Is there an important and intelligent minority in England of English people convinced that a National Theater would be a good and desirable thing for England to have? Mr. Agate notwithstanding, there undoubtedly is. Ought the desires and opinions of this intelligent and important minority to be held in honor? Is their opinion that England's contribution to the world's drama ranks high worthy of earnest consideration? Is England's rank in the dramatic literature of the world a high one? Is, then, this desire of an important minority, and the high rank of England's contribution to the world's drama, worthy of a National Theater? A great many have said yes to these questions. So far from nobody wanting a National Theater, it would seem, according to names appearing on the circular sent out by the British Drama League, and published in Mr. Granville-Barker's book, that almost everybody possessing in his soul more culture than would cover a sixpence is hot for the creation of what Mr. Agate thinks to be *non compos ad retardus* in the minds of the English people. The list has down on it the names of playwrights, critics, actors, actresses, politicians, professors, theater managers, clergymen, bishops, lords, ladies, publicists, poets, soldiers, sailors, scientists, authorities on children, painters, and composers. But it would seem, according to Mr. Agate, everybody down here is nobody, a miracle of conjuration of all into nothing that only a Mr. Agate could perform. Surely the number of intelligent people

who desire a National Theater is as great and as important
and as intelligent as the number who desire Mr. Agate to be a
dramatic critic. I think the ayes have it this time. What we
desire and what we honor in music, in literature, and in
drama is as much a mirror of England's mind as the huge
glass that gives the reflection in the *Daily Mail* or the *Sunday
Express*, with the difference that the one is a mass reflection
of dull and brittle British bounce, and the other is the mirror
of England's culture.

England, Say When

HOBBS, THE CRICKETER, HAS A BIGGER PLACE IN
the hearts of the English people than Shakespeare, the poet.
Millions have seen him batting on the field or on the screen,
or have read what he said about the majesty and mystery of
the game. Millions of English people have never yet seen a
play by Shakespeare. Millions more will soon be born who,
when they grow up and are asked what play by Shakespeare
they have seen, will shout in chorus, We have all seen *Peter
Pan*; but the old graybeards and grayheads will mutter that
Peter Pan was one of Shakespeare's worst works, and that his
greatest opus was really *The Private Life of Henry the
Eighth*. Hardly a state of things for England to be proud of,
or even to ignore.

Surely a National Theater is needed to bring about a
better state of things: a place where Shakespeare would be
played, and no longer falsely worshipped. A National Theater
is bound to be a good thing for dramatists, actors, and audience; good for all except, perhaps, the critics. It would be
certain to have an effect for good and evil on the dramatists
writing for the English Theater today: a good influence by

[41]

setting before them a standard that they could aim at, even
though they never reached it; an evil influence—as good
as the good—by showing that their work is something to
deplore, and to be finally got rid of as contributing nothing
but rubbish to the English drama. The actors and actresses
would develop a sense of shame to be seen acting in them,
the audience would develop a sense of shame for wasting
their time going to them, and the dramatists themselves
might develop a sense of shame in seeing their plays performed. Listen to what Mr. Granville-Barker has to say
about the acting that we see on the English stage: "The
history of the English Theater for the past thirty years has
been the history of a succession of actors who, having made
a reputation, have done little or nothing thereafter to fulfil it,
have in too many instances sagged back into mediocrity,
masking their impotence by an ever-increasing emphasis
upon their popular manner and their successful tricks . . .
so it comes about that we have an assortment of good actors
who never get any better; and really no great ones that we
know of." No great actors in England! So thinks Granville-
Barker, and the world thinks so too. A nice how-do-you-do
for the English Theater. And most of the few good ones
that remain have become the chained galley slaves of Hollywood. These good actors, who are galley slaves of Hollywood, think by displaying their handsome faces or ugly
mugs in close-ups on some well-and-yell-advertised film
that they are acting as they or any other actor never acted
before, and, from one point of view, they are quite right.
How many actors and actresses are there left in England
today—those in the sun and shade of Hollywood included
—who could play Hamlet, Macbeth, Falstaff, Lear, Antony
in the Caesar play and in the Cleopatra play, Pistol, Dog-
berry, Coriolanus, Doll Tearsheet, Volumnia, Desdemona,

Perdita, Cleopatra, Romeo, Juliet, Thersites, Bottom, Flute, or Snout, not to mention the characters abounding in the plays of Shakespeare's companions? Where are the English actors to play these characters as they ought to be played, and as they can be played? There ought to be hundreds able to play them and play them well; but those who are can be numbered only in twos and threes, and some of the characters in Shakespeare seem to be beyond the powers of the best of them. In fact, the greatest actor in England today, without the shadow of a doubt, is Mickey Mouse, *chargé d'affaires* in the theatrical art of England.

It isn't so very long ago when the whole of England was in arms against a *Kultur* that she thought would blacken the soul and redden the back of civilization. She conquered that power, and rolled that *Kultur* in a bloody dust under her feet in order to preserve—what? The culture of the Popular Press? That is the kind of culture she is honoring today. The Bardolphs, Nyms, Pistols, and Poins are busy leading England in politics, literature, and art. Only the other day, a kid called Maudie Mason wrote an essay in which she said that England was the loveliest land in the world, or something of that sort, and was told by an inspector that that sort of sentiment didn't lead England straight to Heaven, or something of that sort. Immediately Maudie Mason's essay became a *codex sinaiaticus Britannicorum*. A red-faced ballyhoo England came down on the inspector, and the Cabinet rent its garments and poured ashes over its head that such a rebuke should be given to such a saying. The standing orders of the House of Commons were postponed, and the House went into committee, and held an all-night sitting to prove that England was and is, and is to be, the loveliest and greatest land in all the world, with little Maudie Mason listening-in to it all and grinning her pleasurable approval, with others wondering if England was beginning to suffer from softening of the brain. What a different England we can imagine England would be if that debate had been held, not to magnify a child's essay, but to decide on ways and means by which a National Theater could be provided to the greater glory of England. Here they were blathering about the greatness of England through the wisdom of Maudie Mason, and all the time their greatest dramatist, Shakespeare, has to be content with an outhouse in which to have his plays performed. What a pity a Conservative member or a Liberal member or even a Labor member didn't introduce in the midst of the debate a motion asking the House to approve the creation of a National Theater so that England might be brought a little nearer to that state of greatness to which little Maudie Mason has been pleased to call her. But no word was spoken, and dramatic literature, one of England's greatest glories, remains one of England's greatest shames.

What is the State doing for the Theater? Damn all. The book about a National Theater, written by Granville-Barker, ought to be a White Book by now, putting before the English Parliament and the nation the need, the great need, for a National Theater. Granville-Barker's scheme as outlined in his book is an ideal one, and a modification of it might do well, and better than the ideal, for some if not many reasons. The details, many, careful, and brightly written details, are in the book for everyone to read. It is published by Sidgwick & Jackson, and the price is five shillings net. Granville-Barker thinks that to create a theater of this kind in proper pride and security, a million pounds will be needed. It seems a big sum of money. It would be a big sum, indeed, for Northern Ireland or for the Free State to spend on a theater, but what is such a sum to such a great, mighty, and glorious nation as England? A sixth of the cost of one of her capital ships. Less, I suppose, than what she pays her members of Parliament for a single year. The present Prime Minister, if I remember rightly, sang a song of praise recently to the glory of Mary Webb, but a million Mary Webbs wouldn't weigh down the glory of a Shakespeare. A grant of half a million with a subsidy of, say, twenty-five thousand pounds a year would set and keep the ball a-rolling. If England doesn't start soon to do the things she ought to do for art and litera- ture, her culture won't be worth the expense entailed by the keep of a corporal's guard. The thinly clad Irish Free State, with a few coppers jingling in her pocket, gives seven hun- dred and fifty pounds to the Abbey Theater, and gives more to the Hibernian Academy of Painting than the proud and stately England ever gave, though she gave twenty-five thousand pounds a year to her Viceroy to keep the poor man from starving. If the Irish Free State can see her way to give seven hundred and fifty pounds to the Abbey Theater (not counting the grant to the Gaelic Theater) surely noble Eng- land ought to be able to give a thousand times more for the setting forth of the glory of her Shakespeare and his great companions, as well as a fair chance for the trying out of the work of her younger and more promising dramatists. A National Theater in London would mean, I'm sure, the crea- tion of one in Wales, of one in Scotland, and, maybe, one in Ulster to vie in a friendly way with her sister theater in Dublin. A National Theater may mean something greater to England than her army with banners or without them.

What is the Church doing for the drama? Damn all. The Church is hidden in the belly of timidity as Jonah was hidden in the belly of the whale. She is afraid of her life of the Theater. They do the brave bold boys when there is something to be seen that, they think, rubs them up the right way, as when in Boston the cardinal and the bishops next door commanded their flock to attend the performances of *The First Legion,* a play that made out the Order of Jesus to be a very mild collection of college boys. But the drama would be a pretty black thing if it consisted only of plays written around the Jesuits. Some time ago an Anglican bishop —the Bishop of Willesden, I think—rushed on to the stage after a performance of *The Tents of Israel* and told the audience that this particular play was a great play because it showed an entire nation prostrate in prayer and humiliation. A fat lot this head under a miter knew or cared about the drama. Recently a correspondent in *Time and Tide* makes us aware of the Bishop of London's declaration that "we are not prepared to tolerate any longer any exhibition of semi-nudity on the stage." Here come the clergy galloping straight to an interest in the stage as soon as they hear of a comely maid showing off a bit of a white thigh or giving a glimpse of those beauties so artfully mentioned in the Song of Songs. If the poor bishop only knew, this semi-nudity is running round everywhere. I see it every day in Battersea Park, and damn healthy and fine it looks on most occasions. Anyway, any man with a spark of life in him would far prefer to see a pretty girl stripping herself on the stage than listen to a soft, keeping-Heaven's-end-up, coaxy-woaxy sermon from a voice on the other end of the wireless. Always the stage and never the Theater. The cold, puritanical glare still trying to douse the footlights. Can't the clergy can this interest in semi-nudity on the stage for a while, and stretch out a hand to help those who are working to create and endow a National Theater for England? Let them speak about it from their pulpits. They could mention the need for a greater drama, and the need for the means by which that greater drama can be worthily displayed. And the Church can even do something more tangible than speaking about the Theater. She could easily spare a good and valuable site for the building of the temple. The Church has thousands of buildings, and can well spare one. A grand site and building would be St. Martin's-in-the-Fields. Here the National Gallery would be right opposite the National Theater and underneath the dust of Farquhar and Nell Gwyn to consecrate it. Here's a grand place for a first home for a National Theater. It can be spared, and Shakespeare needs it. Some time ago an anniversary service for Shakespeare was held in a church in Bishopsgate, and hymns were sung in honor of the master. Here's a chance of doing something more tangible for Shakespeare than singing hymns about him—he can do all the singing himself. If not St. Martin's, then St. James's in Piccadilly; if not St. James's, then St. Anne's of Soho.

Granville-Barker's plan, with its two theaters, its factory for scenery and costumes, its library of works dealing with the Theater, and its space for the thousand things that ought to make certain the success and comfort of the venture, deserves the support of every Englishman and Englishwoman. The Jubilee of his late Majesty is to be kindly and wisely commemorated by the provision of playing-grounds for the young. The coronation year of the present King should not be permitted to pass away without the laying of the first stone of a National Theater. Well, England, when is it going to be done? Never—sometime—next year—this year? Come along, England, say when.

Murdher in the Theater

Lizzie Borden took an axe
And gave her mother forty whacks;
When she saw what she had done,
She gave her father forty-one.

THE ENGLISH, OR I SHOULD SAY THE LONDON,
Theater is going gay. And the critics are going gay with it.
They are having the happiest time of their life, and the English drama now gives the critics the enjoyable exhilaration of
thinking out various murder crossword puzzles. Blood is
poured out as a rich libation under the noses of the gloating
critics. Men and women are made into nice mincemeat and
the critics sit spellbound, and then rejoice that the English
drama has made such a quick step towards greater things.
They wriggle in their seats with delight when a body lies in
a cellar, and all on the stage and off the stage are puzzling
their minor brains to guess who it was that put the body
there.

In the days made bright by the Elizabethans these horrors
were necessary to give a thrill to the groundlings, but they

were only part of the play; but now the horror incenses the play from beginning to end, and the critics are delighted. The critics usually put a murdher play with any touch of commonplace humanity, such as a geranium in the window or a kettle on the hob, into the category of what they spasmodically call "real life plays."

Now murdher has, as everyone knows, nothing whatever to do with life, and everything to do with death. And even if it had, murdher is such a rare thing (except, of course, when there's a war on) that it has no effect whatever on what we know to be real life. But from the point of view of murdher on the stage with which we are really dealing, let us have a peep at the "real life" that the critics hail as appearing jubilant in some of these plays, and let us see if the claim of showing off or up of things as they are in real life be a sober, true, and just one. J. G. B., in the *Evening News,* writing about *Love from a Stranger,* tells us that "this is one more play about a wife murderer (Plays Pleasant), and in spite of the quite extraordinary glut [glut, mind you!] of this particular plot, I think the audience would prefer to know from the first the true nature of Bruce Lovell, the breezy Colonial who steals the heroine's heart [and, possibly, J. G. B.'s as well]. If the author had seen fit to show his homicidal hand [the author acted in his own play] a little earlier, to let us all into the dreadful secret of Barkie Bellingham, we would have lost nothing of suspense and gained something in excitement."

* * *

Open-air charm and breezy manners of a murderer, stealing heroines' hearts, homicidal hands, and dreadful secrets may be, of course, common in real life, but we seem to have had these sorts of things in plays many, many, many times

before. Let J. G. B. go on again. "This piece is so outstandingly well written and done with so much of the brilliant
matter-of-factness of *Night Must Fall,* that I commend it
with very little reserve indeed." Curiously grand criticism of
plays of which we are told there is a glut. Outstandingly well
written and brilliantly matter-of-fact. Pretty good going even
for a London critic writing about a wife-murderer, and
little more could be said of Othello, who, though he wasn't a
wife-murderer, murdered his wife. And how can plain matter-
of-factness be brilliant? However, let us search a little for
the real life and the matter-of-factness that are to be found
in the play called *Night Must Fall,* so gallantly held up by
J. G. B. as an example of the realism the critics love and
cherish.

First the author, who is a young actor, plays the star part,
which in itself is against the portrayal of the substance and
the fact of life. In the play a young page-boy in a "modern
hotel" on the outskirts of a forest in Essex murders a flashy
blonde guest who has made up to him; he hacks the body
about, and after first cutting off the head, which he carries
about with him in a hatbox, hides the body in a rubbish
heap in the garden of a bungalow which forms the scene of
the play. The plays opens with the murdered woman missing.
The maid in the bungalow, owned by a Mrs. Bramson, is
with child by the young page-boy. He has an interview with
Mrs. B., who is a self-made invalid, miserly and contentious;
the boy impresses Mrs. B., so that he is employed by her, and
becomes her favorite "Danny Boy." A poor young niece,
Olivia, is being kept by Mrs. B. as a companion. She intui-
tively senses Dan to be the murderer, and falls in love with
him. He, at the end of the play, murders Mrs. B. for her
money. Accidental circumstances bring the police to the
bungalow, and he is carried away to be tried and hanged.

Now: the scene is the sitting-room of the bungalow. At the
back is a hall in which is the front door (door No. 1); on
the left, upstage, is a door leading to the kitchen (door
No. 2); on the right, upstage, is a door leading to Mrs. B.'s
bedroom (door No. 3); and, downstage, wide-open panel
doors leading to the sun-room (door No. 4). So we have four
doors in all.

*　　*　　*

Now, for a start, where's the true-to-life realism here? As
a matter-of-factness, is there a bungalow in England with a
room having four ways of getting in and out of it? They are
there because otherwise the author would be puzzled where
to move his figures when he wants them to go. And what is
a sun-room? Webster's Dictionary takes no notice of such a
thing. Many bungalows may have sunny rooms, but few have
a room specially put in to catch the sun. As a matter of fact-
ness, this room is there to get rid at certain moments of characters who can't go outdoors or into the kitchen or the bedroom. We are told that the bungalow is "built entirely of
wood, lighted by an oil-lamp fixed in the wall" (this to make
more plausible the attempt by Danny to burn the place down
after he has killed Mrs. B.), and yet this poor place has a sun-
room! The bungalow, we are told, is furnished in a Victorian
way, stuffed birds, wax fruit, Highland cattle in oils (funny
that—Highland cattle in oils), and antimacassars, and yet it
has a sun-room. Now the bungalow can't be built entirely of
wood, for we are told that the room has a fireplace, and you
can't burn coal in a fireplace without having a chimney
breast of brick or concrete. Then we are told that the room
has "a very solid cupboard built into the wall," which we discover in the second act to be "a small but very substantial
safe." Now will J. G. B. or any know-all about realism in

drama tell us how a solid and very substantial safe can be built into a wall of wood? We are told that Mrs. B. is a self-made invalid, fifty-five, old-fashioned in dress and coiffure, yet later on she lets us know she knows a thing or two about Marks & Spencers. And all this, according to the critics, is true-to-life realism and matter-of-factness! The dependent Olivia must be shown as a girl out of the ordinary, so she has written some poetry which her old aunt discovers and makes a mock of when she finds it reposing between the pages of *East Lynne*, which Olivia is reading to her. Now Olivia would never plant her verses there, and the planting of them there is just the dramatist's dodge, and has nothing to do with true-to-life realism. When the author wants to get rid of Mrs. B. he makes her row with the cook about the cutting of roses, and off she goes to cut them herself, which is just another theatrical dodge. Later on there is a glaring example of this true-to-life business of bringing people on and off the stage. Olivia, to get away, walks barefacedly into the celebrated sun-room; the cook comes in to tell Mrs. B. that there are men "ferreting in the garden," which sends Mrs. B. out to prevent them from injuring her pampas grass; and the cook, who has to get off to give Olivia (who strolls out of the sun-room) and Danny a chance to have a chat, suddenly sniffs, declares there's "something boiling over," and rushes out. This sort of thing is not only not true to life, but is really bad craftsmanship. After Danny has had a chat with Olivia, Mrs. B. comes back and Olivia flees out into the sun-room once again. Mrs. B. has a scene with Danny in which he bewitches her with a gentle word or two about his dead mother, goes off to the kitchen for some string to allow Olivia to come from the sun-room and have a chat with Mrs. B., and then to allow a curtain with Olivia and the young murderer on the stage, Mrs. B. hurries out once more to have a look at the pampas grass!

There is really no end to this sort of thing. In the last scene the cook and the maid leave for the night, though it is hardly likely that an old woman who thinks herself an invalid, who has hundreds and hundreds of pounds in a safe, who can afford to keep a cook, a maid, and a companion, would not have at least one living-in servant. But to leave the old lady alone with Danny they have to leave, and so they go and probability turns very pale. A particularly horrible murdher has been committed, and though the dramatist makes the maid afraid to cross the wood by herself, he sends a nurse, who has come to attend to the old lady, away as gay as a lark at dawn. Off the nurse bustles (the word the author uses) without a tremor though the darkness is falling, she has to go through a lonely wood, and she knows that a woman has been foully murdered by a man who is still at large. Before she goes the maid comes in dressed in her outdoor clothes, so the nurse would have guessed that the maid was leaving too and would, as a matter-of-factness, naturally have waited so that they might go together; but that wouldn't suit the play's movement, and off she goes on her lone. A knock comes at the front door; the cook answers it, and finds that it "is only the paraffin boy," whom she tells as she takes the can from him, to "bring the stuff on a Saturday night another time," but says nothing about bringing the stuff to the front door. Now there is a tradesmen's entrance, even to a bunga-low built entirely of wood, but the can is brought into the hall. Danny strikes a match, and the women get the jitters because of the paraffin, as if a can of paraffin was a keg of gunpowder! This is all done to sharpen the last scene when Danny begins to use the stuff to cover up his crime. But believe me, there isn't much danger in lighting a match in front of a little can of paraffin. Perhaps the critics know to the differ. Then Olivia comes in "dressed to go out and carries a suitcase in her hand," and she comes from her room through the kitchen, not the sun-room this time. She tries to warn Mrs. B., and her warning ends with the murmur of "Oh, won't you see?" and "The morning?" implying that morning will never come; so after "holding her breath, and trying to say something to Mrs. B.," off she pops. Then we have the great exodus so that Mrs. B. may be left secure for her murdher by Danny Boy. The cook and the maid go in spite of Mrs. B.'s "Everybody seems to be going. What *is* all this?" But no answer is given. Danny, saying that he is feeling funny, decides to go for a walk in spite of the maid warning him that Mrs. B. will scream the house down; which is exactly what is wanted, for Mrs. B., finding herself alone, gets frightened and screams like hell so that the maid and the cook hear her a quarter of a mile away, and come back with the detective to catch the murderer red-handed. Eventually, Danny smothers Mrs. B. with a black cushion as she sits in her invalid chair. The curtain rises again on the same scene though the wheel chair has been removed. Then Dan comes from the sun-room, does a few things about the room, and hurries back into the sun-room; then returns with the invalid chair which he liberally sprinkles with paraffin, and is about to smash the oil lamp over it when he suddenly hears the sound of a falling chair in the sun-room. This sun-room comes in mighty handy at times, doesn't it? Why he sprinkles the chair and doesn't sprinkle the body with paraffin I don't know. The noise in the sun-room was caused by Olivia, who has thrown off all the restraints of decency and moral sense to come to the arms of the boy she loves. And she arrives back by climbing in at the sun-room window. There's a tester for a clever soul to solve. Here is a house with hundreds of pounds waiting to be lifted, owned by a miserly old invalid, where a mangled body of a woman has been found at the bottom of the garden and the murderer still knocking about—and the window of the sun-room is left unshut! To use a word liked by the author—clumsy, I'd call it. Will J. G. B. tell us where the grand true-to-life realism and the pure matter-of-factness are to be found in this play?

The play has been praised for its psychological certainty, too. Well, let us have a glance at this claim and see if it has any sober justification. Is it true, or in any way important? Since Danny Boy attracts the love of the woman he kills and whose head he carries about in a hatbox, and the love of the maid that works in Mrs. B.'s bungalow, and the love of Mrs. B.'s young companion Olivia, the inference seems to be that women fall for insane young ruffians who take to murder as the only way of making a name in the world. Women are singular creatures I'll admit, but they aren't quite so singular as all that. That some poor women do, isn't a proof that women fall for the first or any murderer that may come along. Women do not worship the bodies (they can hardly worship the minds) of murderers who kill women and carry their victims' heads about with them in hatboxes (English uplift). That would be madness and not hero worship. The subsidiary psychology in the play seems to me to be just as cockeyed. Here's a tiny patch of the psychology:

OLIVIA (speaking to the Cook, the Maid, and him who wants to marry her): He's acting all the time [Danny]. I know he is! But he's acting pretty well, because I don't know *how* I know. He's walking about here all day, and talking a little, and smiling, and smoking cigarettes. . . . Impenetrable . . .

that's what it is! What's going on—in his mind? What's he thinking of? (*Vehemently*) He *is* thinking of something! . . . All the time! What is it?

Now quite a lot of us do a lot of acting—clergymen, politicians, kings and queens, poets, and workers; they walk about and smile and even smoke cigarettes, but few would think that any of them carried a human head in a hatbox. And each of us, big and small, rich and poor, is thinking of something all the time, but none of us, I hope, has made a woman into mincemeat. There is less of life and real people in this play than there is in Shakespeare's *Midsummer Night's Dream* or *The Dream Play* of Strindberg.

In an article appearing in the *Observer* for June the 7th, H. G. (this symbol, I understand, stands for a dramatic critic of long experience and for a playwright of some merit—the characters in *Youth at the Helm* [a translation] are more living and real than those in the play under discussion) tells us that, "dining in distinguished company the other night at the house of a Fellow of the Royal Society, I asked what was the best play in London, and received a unanimous shout of *Night Must Fall*" (I hope all the members of this gathering weren't Fellows of the Royal Society). "Agreed," said H. G.; "it is magnificent." Magnificent, mind you! So let us end the article as the author ends some of the acts of his play—with a blare of music as the lights dim out.

Critica Silentio Luna

The really dangerous people are the practitioners of the amusing trades of criticism, who can somehow or other persuade themselves that they are not ordinary rule-of-thumb workmen, but priests inspired direct from the oracle's mouth.
—Ernest Newman

THAT WAS A CRITIC SPEAKING, THAT WAS; A FINE one, too. It seems rather a mean thing for Mr. Newman to give the game away like this; but he is such a fine first-class critic himself that he can easily afford to be brave, and candidly face the music. But what on earth will his English colleagues in the dramatic wing of the Critics' Circle think of this disturbing humility? Isn't it true? Aren't there many rule-of-thumb men among the critics everywhere? The pity of it that so many seem to be with the English ones: fellas and damsels who dread drama with the heartbeat of life in it, saying it divides itself from the canons of good taste, and treat a play that has within it the sound of flutes as if it were a mendicant at a street corner begging a coin from cold pockets; fellas and damsels who are always yelling or wistfully whispering for new things in the theater, and, when they get them, are frightened, shrink away from them, and again long for such masterpieces as *Family Affairs* or *The Old Folks at Home*. Humility isn't a strong suit in the cards the English critics play; nor need it be, if even ten of a hundred of them had the gift every critic ought to have: a gift for criticism above those men or women of high intelligence, even with a love of the theater added to the intelligence. But to English critics humility seems to be one of the deadliest sins. Listen to what Mr. Agate, for many years dean of drama criticism, said: "For his reader's sake, the dramatic critic must have the arrogance to put himself in the position of the leading authority from which there can be no appeal. The reader of dramatic criticism must feel that his mentor is in no possible doubt whatever."

These remarks were addressed by Mr. Agate to Mr. Ivor Brown in the preface to *First Nights,* Mr. Agate having first smeared Mr. Brown with the honeyed remark that the world and Mr. Agate rate Mr. Brown "with the great critics of the past." Mr. Agate crowns Mr. Brown with a garland. Perhaps we ought to hope that Mr. Brown won't get lost among them, for his criticism seems to be ever as level as the lowlands low; humdrum and hoity-toity. No skirl from a pipe, no echo even of one, in any he writes. Odd, for Mr. Brown is a Scot, but a Scot in a coat of English mail, with the accent of a Scot and the fire of a Scot forever smothered within it. He seems to take no interest in the work of the younger poets of Scotland, who, in the spirit of a great time, call out "Not Burns—but Dunbar!"

But let the toast pass, lift up the glass, and drink to this critical water and gas. There is no appeal court or corner from which to challenge the opinion of these English critics.

Indeed, these chaps have gone on for so long unchallenged that a frozen silence encompasses them about, and all they say flows freely into the tide of infallibility. Well, well, here are a few examples of English drama criticism:

"Strip Millamant (*The Way of the World*) of her satins and laces and she ceases to exist."—Mr. Agate, Article 1.

"Wit of Millamant's order is imperishable, for the simple reason that her creator gave her a mind. There are more Millamants about town today than there are Hedda Gablers."—Mr. Agate, Article 2.

He has it both ways, but fails to tell his readers that there are damned few of either knocking about today on the English stage. Again:

"Mr. O'Casey has cut his characters too crudely for popular consumption [cannibalism?], however true to life they may be. Theater-goers in search of spiritual uplift do not wish to see a Bishop as the father of a Young Whore."—Critic of the *Theater World*.

"Now, if there is one thing the British public mistrusts it is edification, being in this respect the opposite of the American public, which adores uplift. The British public takes no interest in the Theater except as a way of getting through an evening and as an agreeable alternative of dancing, tennis, pillion-riding, drinking, gambling, dog-racing, the pictures and holding hands thereat, loafing at street corners, and mooning about the house."—Mr. Agate.

"It is still a pretty exciting thing to be English."—Noel Coward.

"When a nation is strongest, physically and spiritually, its people delight most in tragedy. When a nation is weakest, physically and spiritually, its people will not listen to tragedy, but demand what is called light entertainment, comic plays, and trivial shows."—St. John Ervine.

Well, I don't know; Shaw never wrote a tragedy, yet his comedy and his wit were a rushing mighty wind that swept through the theater, tearing the mantle of a false grandeur from the thousand trivialities that strutted on its stage; and today, now and again, at least, Shakespeare stands in the wings of the English Theater to the right, and Shaw stands in the wings as firmly to the left. Tragedy and comedy are co-partners in the glory of every theater, and no one can say either is greater than the other. And this without any help from the English critics. See what they have said about *Heartbreak House, The Dog Beneath the Skin, Draw the Fires, Strange Interlude,* Pirandello's *Henry the Fourth* (apart from what they said when Ibsen came to England), or any other play that showed the faintest sign of something these reporters hadn't seen before a thousand times, or voice a line an inch above (barring Shakespeare, whom they didn't dare to sneeze at) the grandeur of "The Boy Stood on the Burning Deck"; and one soon sees the kind of salute given when anything experimental ventures out on the English (or Irish) stage. But what's this about O'Neill?

"*Strange Interlude* is rotten and morbid with decay. There is no vitality, vigor, or anything approaching life in it, and no character has any preoccupation except sex."—Mr. Agate.

"*Musical Chairs* is the best first play written by any English dramatist during the last forty years [forty years in the wil-

derness for Agate—S. O'C.]. Here is the theme of the ring of serpents each swallowing the tail in front of it [swallow, swallow, swallow—S. O'C.]. The neurotic war-destroyed hero who loves, or has a bitter passion for, his stepbrother's wholly self-centered fiancée, but is loved by the family drudge, his stepsister. The hero's father, who loves his wife, is bored by her and indulges in a flirtation or worse with a mercenary little girl from the village. Everybody loves where he does not like and likes where he cannot love. A little masterpiece."
—James Agate.

A little masterpiece! So is a mouse. But a lion is a bigger masterpiece than a mouse, and, in comparison, O'Neill's *Strange Interlude* is a mighty well-maned lion mingling his great roar with the timid tiny squeal of the mouse-like *Musical Chairs*. And, as far as sex is concerned, there is little difference between the two plays, except that O'Neill deals with it in a soul-searching way, and the other playwright develops it out of a snigger. This was the fatal flaw in Agate's criticism—he couldn't tell a miserable play from a great one. He was frightened of any new idea in drama, and couldn't dare to face one, putting it away from him with an indifferent giggle as he lowered a glass of wine to give a glow to his cowardice. What most of the critics wanted and encouraged with bugle blare and drumbeat were good acting plays having nothing in them difficult to understand. A dramatist was expected to write down to the lowest common feeling of the crowd. Yet Shaw says about this point, "A good acting play is one that requires from the performers no qualifications beyond a plausible appearance and a little experience and address in stage business." Stage business, the highlight of drama, and that is what the English critics are almost always examining, and they are damned good judges. The poet

Dryden, himself no mean dramatist, says of this stage business: "I have both so just a diffidence of myself, and so great a reverence for my audience, that I dare venture nothing without a strict examination; and am as much ashamed to put a loose, undigested play upon the public, as I should be to offer brass money in a payment; for though it should be taken [as it is too often on the stage], yet it will be found in the second telling; and a judicious reader will discover in his closet that trashy stuff whose glittering deceived him in the action. I have often heard the stationer sighing in his shop, and wishing for those hands to take off his melancholy bargain which clapped its performance on the stage. In a playhouse, everything contributes to impose upon the judgment [here's where the sharp-minded critic is so important— S. O'C.]; the lights, the scenes, the habits, and, above all, the grace of action, which is commonly the best where there is the most need of it, surprise the audience, and cast a mist upon their understandings. But these false beauties of the stage are no more lasting than a rainbow; when the actor ceases to shine upon them, when he gilds them no longer with his reflection, they vanish in a twinkling. As 'tis my interest to please my audience, so 'tis my ambition to be read: that I am sure is the more lasting and the nobler design; for the propriety of thoughts and words, which are the hidden beauties of a play, are but confusedly judged in the vehemence of action: all things are there beheld as in a hasty motion, where the objects only glide before the eye and disappear."

The best where it is most needed—the best of acting, the finest of scenery, the brightest of lights to bedizen a miserable play; the hectic use of all art to give a play a goodness it has not; to create a glory that dies each time the curtain falls. "They talk of fine plays ruined by bad acting," says G. J.

Nathan, "yet what is more odious than a despicable play improved by good acting?" Well, any answer? If there is, tell us it then.

At times, some of the English critics seem to recreate themselves into arbiters of good taste; Beau Brummels of drama. Once, in reviewing Toller's *No More Peace*, G. W. B. said, "I emphasized two phrases in the lighter part of Toller's play. They and other remarks made by the angel at the switchboard in 'heaven' seemed to me to be in doubtful taste, and I said so." Nothing vulgar about an angel; even one at a switchboard. But how did G. W. B. know? Are they to be thought of as lords, ladies, and gentlemen? Certainly, what the soldier says to the lady and what the angel said at the switchboard are very interesting to the dramatist, and, surely, should be just as interesting to the critic. We shouldn't bury ourselves in our own dignity, but, now and again rise our heads over the tomb, and listen to what life in heaven, in hell, or on the earth, has to say: even bad taste may be very funny. There's bad taste in some of the remarks in Holy Scripture; in some of Strindberg's plays—where he sets a foundation of manure from which a castle grows; and many a Shakespearean play has a high temperature of bad taste. Some of our English critics are too damned fond of believing themselves to be always gentlemen, and it's bad for them when they sit down, in a taxi or at a desk, to write a review of what they have recently seen. Writing on this point, Bernard Shaw said, "Lewes had the rare gift of integrity as a critic. When he was at his business, he seldom remembered that he was a gentleman or a scholar. He never allowed himself to be distracted by the vanity of playing the elegant man of letters, or writing with perfect good taste, or hinting in every line that he was above his work." There is hardly a drama worth seeing that hasn't, in one way or another, hurt somebody or other with an example of "bad taste." In his *The Critic and the Drama,* Nathan says, "Good drama is anything that interests an intelligently emotional group of persons assembled together in an illuminated hall." That is, to my thinking, a drama as wide as the world feels, sees, hears, speaks, and rolls along from cradle to the grave. English critics would do well to follow Nathan's example— even afar off—and mingle the gentleman's mind with some of the emotions of a bum.

The playwrights, too; for if they haven't the emotions of a bum, sorra much they'll do in the way of stirring drama. We are the indifferent children of the world, unmindful of good manners, seeing life, however rough and tarnished, as selectable; this much we must be if we hope to become on drama's cap the very button. We can deck the muddiest things with dearest gold, and send down to trampled dust the hero and his plumes; laugh at virtue and crown dismay with courage; be one with those grieving in foulstrand as we are one with those dancing in fairhaven; admire a string of jewels round the lovely neck of a lovely girl, and admire the tarry rope taut in a sailor's brown-burnished fist; and the critic, if he be a critic, will never shrink from anything the playwright tries to do. So Irish and English critics, if not for God's sake, then for your own, give up trying to be gentle-men-critics; and listen, now, to what Nathan has to say to ye: "It is impossible for the true critic to be a gentleman. I use the word in its common meaning, to wit, a man who avoids offense against punctilio, who is averse to an indulgence in personalities, who is ready to sacrifice the truth to good manners and good form. The critic who is a gentleman is no critic. He is merely the dancing-master of an art." Put that in your pipes and smoke it.

And while the gentlemen among the critics are fixing

white ties to their collars, before they put on their tails, let them hear and hearken to what Bernard Shaw said about this terrified championship of "good taste": "It is contended by gentlemen who get their living by going to the theater and reporting or criticizing performances there, that Church ritual, or indeed anything of a sacred character, is out of place on the stage, and its dramatic representation a breach of good taste." Rather a kick in the pants for any fine old English gentleman among the drama critics. There's no more hypocrisy going on in the Church ritual on the stage than there is going on in that of the Church herself. Less. One of the most sacred things in life is life itself, and look how roughly life is handled. Look at the multitude of graves of the young and once hopeful dotted thickly over the whole of Europe, kept green and trim, all in good taste, a sweet recompense for the sacrifice of the kiss of youth and love, exchanging the liquid dew of youth for a bed with worms, and disappearing in dust and ashes. But yesterday, a Russian was here, one of the thousands who lost a foot in the war; a young man with one foot gone, and drama critics talk of good taste! After all that has been done, and with Governments blasting the heavens and the earth with poisoned outfalls from their atom bombs, it must make the angels sick to hear censors talking about bad books, and English drama critics thinking this or that on the stage to be in bad taste. Let us put what the English think to be, and call, "bad taste" into a thick glass case, and shove it into a minor museum in a faraway corner of the world.

These critics, too, seem to have an odd and rather barbarous idea of the critic's ambition, his ideals, and his work. We have been warned by James Agate that "The first function of a critic is to tell the public which plays are good and which bad [good enough, if he himself can tell which from which].

The second is to fulfil the duties of a public analyst. The third function is to entertain the Sunday-morning reader and, if possible, prevent him from turning over and going to sleep again. The fourth object is to keep the standard high." Yet this critic, to my knowledge, never said good morning, but always good evening, to any play that ventured beyond the trivial or the tame. He shrank away from every play that sounded a newer note. Not a single dramatist of first-class measure and material came to light by the critic-candle Agate carried on his forehead; it was a cold candle, never a candle of vision. Week after week, he trumpeted the glory of *Journey's End*, seeing in it the first fruits of a second Shakespeare; and, again, week after week, he trumpeted with the same resonance a play called *The Maze*, which has passed away into the haze of hades to gibber and bemoan among ten thousand companions as good or as bad as itself. Criticism has nothing to do with public analysis, and, unless I'm very much mistaken, it has nothing to do with lulling a soul to sleep at night, or rousing it up first thing in the morning. The fact is, far as I could see—not a short distance, by any means—James Agate didn't know a bad play from a good one. He was shocked into irritated bewilderment whenever he bumped against a play that shone with a light never seen on Agate's land or Agate's sea. In a hot and vehement retort to an article of mine "impugning the English Theater," Mr. Agate noted down in defense of England a number of dramatists who had held aloft her theatrical glory; but failing to point out that four of them were Scots, one (Somerset Maugham) a Cornishman, one (Emlyn Williams) a Welshman, two Irishmen, and another (Rudolf Besier), educated in Germany and born in Java. And these are most of the English contributors to England's theatrical happiness, hope, and glory!

This critic had a curious idea of the Theater when it suited him to consult his cuteness. When I had listed a number of plays that hardly added to England's pride, he came back with "What are the facts? The facts are that *Bitter-Sweet* and *Cavalcade*, being musical entertainments, are not strictly speaking within the category of the serious theater with which we are concerned." That, too, after this critic had clawed like a wildcat at anyone who had dared to say a cross word about the merits of *Cavalcade*; after the critic had to lie on a couch for weeks from the exhaustion of night-and-day praise of the tawdry show; after Mr. Coward, in a curtain call, had fulsomely announced, roused by the audience's delirious acceptance of the show's implications, that It Was a Proud Thing to Be an Englishman. Quite right, too, for England can claim as son a man called Shakespeare; but Mr. Coward was hardly thinking of Shakespeare: he was thinking of . . . another.

The serious theater—if there was ever at the time an idea of serious theater in the minds of the English critics, it was when this show swung itself like a gilded monkey from floor to ceiling of the Royal Theater, Drury Lane. But that doesn't count now, for we have travelled a welcome way from the tinselled midget aping the antics of a giant. It is Mr. Agate's gasping exclusion of the musical play from the serious theater that makes us laugh before we begin to sigh. What, rule out the music-dramas of Wagner from the serious theater because they are musical plays? Or even—to fall from the sublime to the commonplace—the musical plays of Gilbert and Sullivan? Are we to reckon out anything from the serious theater that isn't weighty, grave, given to deep thought, and free from laughter, even frivolous laughter? Are we ready to take down the mask of Comedy and fling it into the dustbin as a Face unworthy of the serious theater? Isn't *Twelfth Night* as

much a part of the serious theater as *Hamlet*; the frolics of
Liberty Hall in *She Stoops to Conquer* as much so, too, as
the dread prophecy in Bernard Shaw's *Heartbreak House*?

The critic was hedging on the show, spectacle, or paltry
pageant, that Agate thought so grand when it flooded and
floored the stage of Drury Lane Theater; that roused him to
rage at those who shyly mocked it, causing him to roar out,
"There's a nest of wasps that must be smoked out because it
is doing infinite harm to the theater." All this rile and rumpus
of adulation gone for nothing; for, later on, the critic gently
carries the play, spectacle, or pageant away to a lonely place
far from the ken of the "serious theater." The critic's rage with
the mockers was wasted, for their mockery did no harm,
utterly unable to make the pageant or spectacle a little
worse or better than it was.

It is surprising, when you look back over a few years of a
lifetime, to realize how many plays, shot through with praise
from the English critics, have been condemned to the outer
darkness of a lumber-limbo, the boosts and boasts that
bloated them turned to vapor.

It is odd and laughable to see how some English critics—
not the worst of them, either, by a long chalk—pine after
things dead and gone, and strew roses on what is no more
than a forgotten grave. Agate was always, openly or furtively,
hankering after *Letty* or *The Second Mrs. Tanqueray*;
couldn't let the poor dead ladies rest in peace. Pinero is still
their pin-up boy. The English critic, Archer, idyllized him.
Listen to my tale of worship:

NEVILLE: Yes, as Mr. Mandeville, who has been examining my
credentials, is brutal enough to remind me—yes, I am
married.
[There is a pause. Her cigarette drops from her fingers and
she carefully puts her foot on it.]

LETTY (*in a low voice*): You might have mentioned it before. You might have mentioned it before.

"Here we have in all its simplicity, without any melodramatic accessories, a tense and poignant moment in human experience," says Mr. Archer, the English critic. "We have no oratory; no lyric cry, but pure double-distilled dràma."

Isn't that good? No oratory, no lyric cry—why? Well, simply because Pinero wasn't capable of either. Double-distilled drama. Yes, indeed, if one takes it that anything worth the name or sound of drama had been double-distilled out of it. Pinero had turned the wine of drama into water. A miracle, a miracle!

"In that one line," goes on me bould Archer, " 'I am a single man; you ain't, bear in mind,' Mandeville reveals the whole tragedy of the situation."

Isn't that fine? Poor Neville, you ain't a single man, and there's the rub. Hamlet, Hamlet! Not this man, but Pinero! Archer isn't done yet. He goes on to say, "As far as any one can be called the regenerator of the English drama, that man is Arthur Pinero." From all accounts, Pinero was the regenerator, the accelerator, and prognosticator of the English Theater. He labored in the theatrical vineyard from the first hour, and carried off a rich booty, crowned with a king's accolade. He did his best, he worked hard and long, to enamor the Theater with his gifts—fifty-five plays all told, tripping close to each other's heels, longer than Banquo's issue, and crowned like them too. For years he was the theatrical maypole of England, and the English critics never got tired going round it; round and round in honor of him who came to take the oratory and the lyric cry out of drama, and gloriform it with the pure and double-distilled tragedy of "I am a single man; you ain't, bear in mind." He's gone now, and no one knows where Dandy Dick, the Second Mrs. Tanqueray, or the Notorious Mrs. Ebbsmith is buried. There isn't even a tablet in any church as a memorial to one of them. All gone.

> *What's not devoured by Time's devouring hand,*
> *Where's Troy, and where's the Maypole in the Strand?*

But some of the critics, when Pinero left home (as we all have to one day), said *au revoir* but not goodbye to him. His spirit haunts them still. Mr. Agate, before he went home, said with a sigh, "I personally should like to see revivals of Pinero's *Letty, Mid-Channel,* or *The Benefit of the Doubt.*" Carry me back to old Virginny. It wasn't that they were deceived, as Dryden was, by the cunning tricks of the stage, the fine acting, the bright scenery, the gay dresses; no, for they have had time to study Pinero, in performances, in books, and with the calm retrospective of memory; but they never rose from their knees, for was he not the regenerator and prognosticator of the English Theater? So, instead of giving him a paper cap, morned with a silver star, they pressed the crown of dominion on his head; circled him with the round and top of theatrical sovereignty.

Yet here is what an American critic, Nathan, said about Pinero plays, while worship went on in England, and the bells rang: "The Pinero plays, which originally seemed to the public to be great masterpieces, are intrinsically nothing but third-rate social melodramas. They have, assuredly, been effective at the box-office, and have also profoundly impressed the one-inch-deep emotionalism of two-feet-thick skulls, but so, too, have been effective in the same way *The White Heather,* Lew Morrison's *Faust,* and *Sawing a Woman in Two.* The man who still finds himself enchanted and moved by one of Sir Arthur's confections may be quickly put down as a very young man or as one who is somewhat deficient in the departments of wisdom and experience. For the Pinero drama today is as out-of-date as Stonewall Jackson's socks."

A shrill Last Post without a note of Reveille sounding after it. A depressed grave, and only the London critics throwing Chuckies there to try to make a cairn over it. But worse came smilingly after Pinero. A poorer playwright than even Pinero is held up as an example for better playwrights to follow. The eminent London critic, Mr. Ivor Brown, has this to say about a revival of *A Pair of Spectacles* by Sydney Grundy: "A happy revival, for we need to be reminded of the shapely, serene, and skillful formalities of the popular play of forty years ago. The current idea that form is irrelevant on the stage will pass, and the plays of Sydney Grundy, now viewed as charming curios, may once more be considered as examples." What are the popular plays of forty years ago? Can anyone living name a dozen of them? Can any young fellow or lass tell us the name of one from an echo that may have come into his ear? Only Ivor Brown left? Relevant or irrelevant, the younger playwright of any mind, and even a little imagination, won't sign his death warrant as a playwright by taking hold of Grundy's hand to guide him on to the English stage. Maybe Mr. Ivor Brown was joking. Anyway, beyond yea or nay, beyond good or evil, Pinero and Grundy, the two of them lie close together in the one theatrical churchyard, with, apparently, one poor mourner left to drop a tear and rosebud on their grave.

There is no artistic excuse for propping up dramatic rubbish, even by way of a joke; and a critic has no right, however popular a play may be, to lessen its littleness by nonchalant praise; to give a smoking straw an apotheosis into a flaming torch. Neither should he do this to keep the theaters going.

"*Cavalcade*," cried Agate, "has kept the wolf from the door of our nearest approach to a national theater!" That sort of thing. A cute dodge to boost a tawdry show and get away with a dishonest criticism. "Dramatic criticism has nothing to do with the prosperity of the theater," says Nathan. Dramatic criticism is or should be concerned solely with dramatic art, even at the expense of bankrupting every theater in the country." So it ought to be. Keeping the wolf from a theater door is no critical excuse for honoring a bad play. And there is no excuse, either, for a dramatist to write a bad play to keep the wolf away from his own.

Green Goddess of Realism

IN THE THEATER OF TODAY, REALISM IS THE
totem pole of the dramatic critics.

Matter-of-fact plays, true true-to-life arrangement, and real, live characters are the three gods the critics adore and saturate with the incense of their commonplace praise once a day and twice on Sundays in their trimly-dressed little articles. What the dramatic critics mean by the various terms they use for Realism is the yearly ton of rubbish that falls on the English stage and is swiftly swept away into the dustbins. The critics give a cordial welcome to the trivial plays because, in my opinion, they are, oh, so easy to understand, and gorge the critics with the ease of an easy explanation. It is very dangerous for a dramatist to be superior to the critics, to be a greater dramatist than the critic is a critic. They don't like it, and so most of them do all they can to discourage any attempt in the theater towards an imagination fancy-free, or an attempt to look on life and mold it into a form fit for the higher feeling and intelligence of the stage. They are those who compare Beaumont and Fletcher's *Philaster* with *Charley's Aunt,* and in their heart of hearts

vote for the farce and shove the poetic play out of their way
(a few spit the preference in our face, as Archer did).
Charley's Aunt is loved by Charley's uncles. They have grown
fat and lazy on triviality, so fat and so lazy that they are
hardly able to move. The curse is that these critics do their
best to prevent anyone else from moving either. They will
have simply to be roughly shunted out of the way, and these
few words are one of the first sharp prods to get them to
buzz off and do their sleeping somewhere else. Realism, or
what the critics childishly believe to be Realism, has had its
day, and has earned a rest. It began on a sunny autumn
evening in 1886, or thereabouts, as the lawyers say, at the
first production of *Ours* by Robertson, when the miracle took
place. "In reading the play today," says William Archer, the
world-famous dramatic critic, "we recognize in Robertson—
just what the stage wanted in its progress towards verisimilitude—the genius of the commonplace. The first act of *Ours*
was, in intention at any rate, steeped in an atmosphere quite
new to the theater. The scene was an avenue in Shendryn
Park which Robertson describes in the abhorrent prompt-
book jargon of the time. But one line had, I venture to say,
as yet appeared in no prompt-book in the world: '*Throughout
the act the autumn leaves fall from the trees.*' How this effect
was produced and whether it was successful, I cannot say.
Nor can I discuss the question whether it was a desirable
effect, or a mere trick of mechanical realism which the true
artist would despise." Now the falling of the leaves from the
trees was and could have been nothing but "a mere trick of
mechanical realism," because the trees couldn't have been
true-to-life trees, and, even if they were, the autumnal leaves
couldn't have fallen with the regularity and rhythm required
to create the desirable effect. And no true artist of the theater
would despise "a mere trick of mechanical realism" by which

to get a scenic or an emotional effect out of his play and over to his audience. We remember the fine effect that the first sound of the first fall of rain had as it fell in the first act of Obey's *Noah*; and this fall of rain was a mere trick of mechanical realism as it was also the opening of the floodgates of Heaven, swelling into a flood that destroyed all life that was in the world save only those who found safe shelter in the faith of Noah; or the sudden change in the wind in *Saint Joan* that set the pennon streaming eastward, and sent Dunois and Saint Joan hurrying out to make for the flash of the guns, and drive the English out of France. You see the artist in the theater never despises a mere trick of mechanical realism; but he knows how to keep it in its proper place. Let Archer open his mouth again: "Then as the act proceeds, *The patter of rain is heard upon the leaves,* and again, *The rain comes down more heavily and the stage darkens.*" The stage darkens, mind you, not the sky. "This effect of the rain falling and the stage darkening would," Archer tells us, "have been absolutely impossible in a candle-lit scene." Well, we have our floodlights, our spotlights, our baby-spots, our amber, blue, and pink footlights, but rarely do we get in our great progress towards verisimilitude the thunder, the lightning, and the rain that flashed and roared and fell on the heath scene in Shakespeare's *Macbeth*. Archer speaks again: "Then enter the sentimental hero and heroine, caught in the rain; and—conceive the daring novelty!—*Blanche carries the skirt of her dress over her head.* In the center of the stage was a large tree with a bench around it, and to get the best shelter possible, the hero and the heroine stand on the bench. Meanwhile Sir Alexander and Lady Shendryn, a middle-aged couple, hop in and sit down on the stump of a tree under another shelter. Unaware of each other's presence, the two couples talk in a sort of counterpoint, the romantic dialogue of the youthful pair contrasting with the weary snappiness of the elderly couple." And this is called an exact imitation of real life. Two couples, unknown to each other, carry on a counterpoint conversation on the same stage in the same scene at the same time, and Archer calls this "an exact imitation at any rate of the surfaces of life." Here's a bit of the dialogue:

ANGUS: What was the song you sang at the Sylvesters'?
BLANCHE: Oh!
ANGUS: I wish you'd hum it now.
BLANCHE: Without music?
ANGUS: It won't be without music.

—and Blanche croons over Offenbach's exquisite *Chanson de Fortunio*, and then we are told that we may search the Restoration and eighteenth-century comedy in vain for a piece of subtle truth like this. Where the subtle truth is in a girl under the rain holding her skirt over her head, standing on a bench, crooning Offenbach's *Chanson de Fortunio* or murmuring to her young man, "Cousin, do you know, I rather like to see you getting wet," only Archer or some other present-day critic-guardian angel of the theater could tell us. This arch-critical prate about verisimilitude, exact imitation of real life, and the unmistakable originality of the conception of this scene in Robertson's *Ours*, is an example of the commonplace genius of dramatic criticism. The incident of two couples taking their set times to say their say on the same stage in the same scene at the same time in full view of the audience is as true to life, is about as exact an imitation of real life, as the incident of Malvolio's soliloquy in full view of his tormentors and his audience. But the autumn leaves falling one by one and two by two, the sound of the rain pattering on the leaves, and the stage getting darker and darker and the rain getting heavier and heavier as the act proceeds, is all so sweet and all so simple to see and feel and follow that Archer and his fellow-follows-on hail this exact imitation of real life on the stage as a great and glorious godsend to them and their wives and children. They are so easy to manage in a weekly article; no beating about the bush, no humiliating strain on the mind or the emotions, no danger of giving a stupid judgment, for autumn leaves are autumn leaves, rain is rain, and the darkening night means the end of the day. And so we find that stuff like *Call It a Day* gets a rosy welcome from our regimental sergeant-major critics, while a work like *Strange Interlude* is pooh-bahed off the stage. And how quietly clever and exact this realism, or naturalism, or exact imitation of life has made the critics! Commenting on *Espionage*, Mr. Agate tells us that "the First Act is a corker, and readers will note my wideawakeness in the perception that whereas the draught in the railway carriage fritters the blinds, the passengers are able to put their heads out of window without a hair stirring." I'm sure all the readers felt an exaltation in the conscientiousness of criticism when they got sufficiently soaked in that wonderful bit of information. It gave them something to look forward to when they went to see the play. Not a hair stirring! Fancy that now. Strange that the same wideawakeness which saw a corker in *Espionage*, saw nothing, or very little, in O'Neill's *Strange Interlude*. But then O'Neill's great plays are "morbid masterpieces which have to be seen under the penalty of remaining mum in Bloomsbury," or, if the truth be told, of remaining mum in any civilized place where the drama is honored more in the observance than in the breach. And Mr. Ivor Brown, commenting on O'Neill's *Ah, Wilderness!* tells us that "The producers introduced the music of *The Merry Widow* to a Connecticut small town of 1906. In that case New England was well ahead of Old, for that operetta did not reach Daly's till a year later." Well, that is something worth knowing anyway, but it wouldn't have the faintest effect on the play or production even if the music hadn't yet reached the small town in Connecticut, or even if the music given in the play had been the first composition made on the first psaltery or sackbut, if the music fitted the theme. Is it a waste of time to hint in the ear of the critics that it is much harder for a dramatist to stir the heart than to stir the hair, and much harder to make music apt for the theme and the trend of a play than it is to bring the music in to the correct tick of the clock? These critics are like the tailors who visit an exhibition to see if the buttons are put in their proper places on the coats in the pictures that are hanging on the walls.

This headlong search or quiet scrutiny for realism, exact imitation of life in the drama, has outwitted the critics into being puzzled over everything in a play that doesn't fit calmly into their poor spirit level and timid thumb rule. The dramatist is told that he must see life steadily and see it whole; and a critic-at-arms (there are barons, knights, esquires, men-at-arms, and grooms among the critics) writing in the *Evening Standard* complained that a play he saw wasn't "a study of the whole seething brew of life"! He wasn't asking for much. The whole world, parallels of longitude and meridians of latitude and all, popped on to the stage in a flood of limelight, and the critics tossing it about like kids playing with a balloon. This critic-at-arms didn't (and doesn't still, I'm sure) realize that no one can view or understand the brew of life encased in an acorn cup; or holding this little miracle in the palm of the hand, no human pair of eyes can at any time see it steadily and see it whole. So the complaint about a play failing to show the whole seething brew of life is the complaint of a dodo critic.

Although the bone of realism in the theater has been picked pretty clean, the critics keep gnawing away at it, so that if a playwright as much as gets a character to blow his nose (preferably when "the autumn leaves are falling from the trees"), the critics delightedly nod to each other, and murmur, "An exact imitation of life, brothers." Commenting on *Call It a Day*, a play in which everything is attempted and nothing done, Mr. Agate tells us that "Miss Dodie Smith is never concerned whether 'it' is a play or not, but whether she has assembled on her stage characters so real that she might have gone into the street and compelled them into the theater," though these characters that might have been pulled in off the street are as tender and delicate and true as the tenderest and most delicate characters wistfully wandering about in the most wistful Barrie play. J. G. B., commenting on *Love from a Stranger*, tells us that "it is written with brilliant matter-of-factness, and is a real play about real people." Here our noses are shoved up against the image of realism in the theater. A real play about real people: here's a sentence that apparently punches home; but look well into it, and you'll find it empty of any real meaning. Week in and week out these commonplace plays are reducing the poor critics into more and more vague and vapid expressions that would give a sparkle to the mouth of a politician trying to cod his constituents—and very often succeeding. A real play about real people—what does it mean? This is something of a triumph—a real play with real people in a real theater before a real audience. But every play is a real play whether it be good or bad, just as a real lion is a real lion and a real mouse is a real mouse, and both are animals. But the real mouse isn't a real lion, nor is the real lion a real mouse, though both are animals. I wonder do the critics get this? There is a big difference between a lion and a mouse, though both are animals, and there is a bigger difference between a good and a bad play, though both are plays just the same. What is a "real play"? Answer, according to J. G. B., *Love from a Stranger* is a real play, therefore the nearer we get to this praised play, the nearer we get to a real play. Now is *The Dream Play* by Strindberg a real play? It certainly bears no resemblance to *Love from a Stranger*, but the imagination can handle *The Dream Play* just as well and with far fuller satisfaction. Apparently the critics think that a play to be a real play must have real people in it, though they never take breath to tell us what they mean by real people. Take people off the street or carry them out of a drawing-room, plonk them on the stage and make them speak as they speak in real, real life, and you will have the dullest thing imaginable. I suppose the critics will be shocked to hear that no real character can be put in a play unless some of the reality is taken out of him through the heightening, widening, and deepening of the character by the dramatist who creates him. Would the dramatic critics call the characters in *Hamlet* real people, or only the creations out of the mind of a poet, and isn't *Hamlet* all the better for its want of reality? Isn't it more of a play, and what has the word "play" got to do with reality? Is Caliban a real person, found in the street and compelled into the theater? If he isn't, then, isn't the character just as powerful as if he were? What peculiar quality does this term of "real people in a real play" give to a play, seeing that many plays, some of them in step with the greatest, have in them characters far removed from this critic-quality of matter-of-factness? Isn't Caliban as real a character as Gustav Bergmann in *Close Quarters*, or the ladies and gents in *Fallen Angels,* or *Night Must Fall,* or *Call It a Day,* the author of which, as Mr. Agate tells us, assembles on her stage characters so real (again this word "real"—the spyhole through which the critics view the stage) that she might have gone into the street and compelled them into the theater. (Though how a critic couples a play dealing with sex almost from the word "go" to the last lap, a play in which an accountant goes to the flat of an actress-client and nothing happens; in which the accountant's wife is entertained by a friend, and then entertains the friend alone in her house, and nothing happens; in which their daughter flings herself at an artist, and nothing happens; in which her brother falls for a young lassie that climbs over the garden wall to him, and nothing happens; in which the maid falls for the man-servant of the family a few doors down, and nothing happens; and the bitch brought out for a walk by the manservant rubs noses with the dog taken out by the maid, and nothing happens—how a critic couples all this sort of thing with characters hustled in off the streets, only a critic could know, and only a critic can tell.) If all that is in this play be life, then life is a mass of sentimentally holy hokum.

As a matter-of-factness no one, least of all a playwright, can go out into the streets and lanes of the city and compel the people to come on to the stage, for the people on the stage must be of the stage and not of the streets and lanes of the city or of the highways and hedges of the country. The most realistic characters in the most realistic play cannot be true to life. Perhaps the most real character in any play we know of is the character of Falstaff done by Shakespeare. Here is realism as large as life; but it is realism larger, and a lot larger, than life. Falstaff was never pulled off the streets into the theater by Shakespeare. God never created Falstaff—he sprang from Shakespeare's brain. God, if you like, created

Shakespeare, but Shakespeare created Falstaff. Falstaff is no more real, there is no more matter-of-factness in the character of Falstaff, than there is in Caliban or Puck or Ariel. He is a bigger creation than any of these three, and that is all. A play, says Dryden, ought to be a just image of human nature, and this is true of *Hamlet,* of *John Bull's Other Island,* of *Strange Interlude,* of *Six Characters in Search of an Author,* of *Peer Gynt,* of *The Dream Play*; but it is not true of the trivial tomtit-realism in the thousand and one entertainment plays patted and praised by the dramatic critics. Why, even the sawdust characters of the Moor, Petroushka, and the Ballerina are a more just image of human nature than the characters in the matter-of-fact, exact-imitation-of-life plays that flit about on the English stage.

As it is with the play, so it is with the dressed-up stage— the critics want to be doped into the belief that the scene on the stage is as real as life itself. The stirring of the hair is more to them than the stirring of the heart. But things as real as life itself on the stage they can never have; a room can never be a room, a tree a tree, or a death a death. These must take the nature of a child's toys and a child's play. Let me quote from Allardyce Nicoll's *British Drama*: "Illusion for the ordinary spectator is only partial at the best, and nearly all of us are aware, even at the moment of highest tension or of most hilarious laughter, that the battlements are not of Elsinore and the trees are not of Arden forest. The scene-painter's art allied to that of the electrician can now obtain effects undreamt of before. Our drawing-rooms can look like drawing-rooms now, our woods can look like woods, and our seas like seas. Those, too, who have witnessed some recent productions in which the new German lighting effects were employed will agree that it would be hard to tell the fictional clouds that flit over the painted sky from real clouds, or the fictional sunrise from real sunrise. The question is, however, not whether the semblance of actuality can be obtained, but whether it is precisely that which we desire. Would we not rather have the real drawing-room of Mrs. So-and-so, the real Epping Forest, the real Atlantic, rather than these feigned copies of them? Would we not choose to watch those beautiful clouds from an open moorland rather than from our seats in gallery or in stalls? It is precisely the same problem that arises in the consideration of drama itself. We do not want merely an excerpt from reality; it is the imaginative transformation of reality, as it is seen through the eyes of the poet, that we desire. The great art of the theater is to suggest, not to tell openly; to dilate the mind by symbols, not by actual things; to express in Lear a world's sorrow, and in Hamlet the grief of humanity. Many of our modern producers are striving in this direction, although it must be confessed that England here is well in the background." And what is the greatest obstacle the progressive producers have to face? In my opinion, the dramatic critics who prefer the stirring of the hair to the stirring of the heart; the death-or-drivel boys gunning with their gab from their pill-boxes in the theater those who take a step forward to enthrone imagination in the theater and make it more of a temple and less of a den of thieves.

This rage for real, real life on the stage has taken all the life out of the drama. If everything on the stage is to be a fake exact imitation (for fake realism it can only be), where is the chance for the original and imaginative artist? Less chance for him than there was for Jonah in the whale's belly. The beauty, fire, and poetry of drama have perished in the storm of fake realism. Let real birds fly through the air (not like Basil Dean's butterflies in *Midsummer Night's Dream*, fluttering over the stage and pinning themselves to trees), real animals roam through the jungle, real fish swim in the sea; but let us have the make-believe of the artist and the child in the theater. Less of what the critics call "life," and more of symbolism; for even in the most commonplace of realistic plays the symbol can never be absent. A house on a stage can never be a house, and that which represents it must always be a symbol. A room in a realistic play must always be a symbol for a room. There can never be any important actuality on the stage, except an actuality that is unnecessary and out of place. An actor representing a cavalier may come on the stage mounted on a real horse, but the horse will always look only a little less ridiculous than the "cavalier." The horse can have nothing to do with the drama. I remember a play written round Mr. Pepys, and in this play was used "the identical snuff-box used by him when he was head of the Admiralty in the reign of Charles the Second." So much was said about the snuff-box that I expected it to be carried in on a cushion preceded by a brass band, and hawked around for all to admire before the play began. Now this snuff-box added nothing to the play, and because of this commonplace spirit in the play, the play added nothing to the drama. It seems that the closer we move to actual life, the further we move away from the drama. Drama purely imitative of life isn't drama at all. Now the critics are beginning to use the word "theater" when they find themselves in a bit of a tangle over what they should say about a play that has a bad whiff of staleness in its theme, character, and form. For instance, Mr. Ivor Brown, writing of a recent play, said that "the play is not life, it is theater and might be allowed to wear its flamboyant colors"; "might be allowed," mind you—he, too, isn't sure. He doesn't tell us to what theater the play belonged. He left his readers to find that out for themselves. Was it the theater of Shakespeare, of

Shaw, of Strindberg, of Ibsen, of Goldsmith, of O'Neill, of Pirandello, or of Toller? Or the theater of Dan Leno, Marie Lloyd, George Robey, Charlie Chaplin, Sidney Howard, or Will Hay? These are all good theater and so they are all good life. But it is not the life that they imitate in their plays or in their actions that makes them good theater, but the unique and original life that is in themselves. They have the life that the present dramatic critics lack, for the critics cannot, or are afraid to, be lively. They wouldn't venture to give the plays they call "theater" their baptismal name of rubbish. Where would we see a criticism like unto the meet criticisms for such plays given by George Jean Nathan:

THE FIRST APPLE. Lynn Starling. Oh!
THE LAKE. A play that got a lot of praise in England. By Dorothy
    Massingham and Murray MacDonald. Badly confused effort
    to mix a little Chekhov with a lot of boiled-over Henry Arthur
    Jones, the result being even worse Massingham-MacDonald.
THE LOCKED ROOM. Junk.
THE GODS WE MAKE. Terrible!

The Government would probably go out of office if even one of the sharp sentences just quoted came out of the mouth of a London dramatic critic. We haven't a critic like Nathan in the English Theater, and it is time we had. We have only to read some of his works—*Testament of a Critic, Art of the Night, The House of Satan, Since Ibsen, The Critic and the Drama, Another Book on the Theater, The Theater of the Moment*—to realize that in the Theater of Nathan the curtain is always going up, while in the Theater of the critics here the curtain is always coming down. The critics here are afraid to be alive or alert. They take their timid thoughts out of a pouncet box. Every bare expression they use is carefully covered with a frill. They take the moaning echo of a shell to be the thunder of the sea. Their criticisms come to us on a pseudo-silver salver. Instead of knocking a bad play over the head with a stick, they flick it over the cheek with a kid glove. They are pew-openers in the temple of drama, nicely showing the people to their places. They are the modern groundlings in the theater—always waiting to be entertained. Shakespeare, of course, they are certain about, for tradition shoves them on to their knees the minute Shakespeare turns the corner. They often take a patch of flame-colored taffeta to be the burning sun. "Critics," says George Jean Nathan, "are artist-partners with the artist himself. The former creates, the latter recreates. Without criticism art would, of course, still be art, and so, with its windows walled in and its lights out, the Louvre would still be the Louvre." Quite right; but the weekly and daily purr of praise given by our critics to commonplace plays, packed with "matter-of-factness" and "exact imitation of life," like stuffed geese, is just unwalling the windows, opening wide the doors, and lighting a great gathering of lamps in a henhouse.

Coward Codology: I

CAVALCADE

A COUPLE OF YEARS AGO AN EMINENT MAN NAMED
Patrick Braybrooke, member of the Royal Society of Literature and Fellow of the Philosophical Society, wrote a book
about Mr. Noel Coward; and in that book that Braybrooke
wrote there was a nest, a rare nest, a rattling nest, and in
that nest there was an egg, and in that egg there was a boy,
and in that boy there was an actor, and in that actor there
was an author, and in that author there was a playwright,
and in that playwright there was a composer, all in that egg
that lay in the nest that lay in the book that Braybrooke
wrote. Mr. James Agate has since added things on to this
amazing evolution, telling us that in the actor, author, playwright, and composer there was a singer, and in the singer
there was a dancer, and that the reason why this fluttering
together of a cloud of geniuses into one mighty theatrical
avatar didn't further flutter into a conductor was that the
theatrical avatar "couldn't bear not to see himself acting on
the stage." This amazing infant phenomenon was called Mr.
Noel Coward, and today he acts, writes, composes, and
produces (doing other things in his spare time), so that

Mr. Agate, on the score of the irrepressibility of genius, coyly, if indirectly, connects the name of Mr. Coward with those of Napoleon, Hannibal, Horatio Nelson, Grace the cricketer, Isaac Newton, Abraham Lincoln, and Dan Leno. Braybrooke gaily and giddily starts the ball rolling by telling us that in thirty years the Theater has seen the rapid growth of a boy actor into a master dramatist. Not into a minor dramatist, not even into a mister dramatist, but into a master dramatist. And all this, mind you, from a Fellow of the Royal Society of Literature.

This Fellow of the Royal Society of Literature hails Noel Coward as a master dramatist. Glendower thought he could call spirits from the vasty deep, but here's a Fellow who can call a spirit out of a raindrop. Just imagine Sophocles, Euripides, Shakespeare, Jonson, Molière, Webster, Ford, Congreve, Sheridan, Ibsen, Strindberg, and a few others gathered together having a chinwag about the drama; and then imagine Patrick Braybrooke hurrying up to them, holding Noel Coward by the hand, and saying, " 'Scuse me, boys, but I want to introduce a master dramatist to you all. There you are; here he is: born in Teddington on the Thames, a boy whose genius is not only amazing, but harmonious, and few of you guys gathered together can say that of yourselves; a boy who in twelve years got to the very front of the front rank of dramatists: take off your hats, boys, and give him a chair!" The truth, of course, is that Noel Coward hasn't yet put even his nose into the front rank of second-class dramatists, let alone into the front rank of first-class dramatists. While forging to the front for the past twelve years he comes panting a hundred miles behind such dramatists as Maugham, Galsworthy, Brighouse, and many others. Comparing Coward to a first-class dramatist is comparing one of Beverley Nichols' dainty beech trees grown in a pot in a pantry to a full-grown

beech in a beechwood. That such a claim could be made
for him by a Fellow of the Royal Society of Literature is a
moving indication of England's progress towards higher
things in the drama.

* * *

Let us break away for a moment from Mr. Braybrooke
and take the arm of Mr. Agate. This critic says that in *Bitter-
Sweet* Noel Coward gave sustained entertainment throughout an entire evening to a critical and cultivated London
audience. Now, it is hardly likely that Mr. Agate was in a
position to go bail that the entire audience was critical and
cultivated, or that all who were in the critical and cultivated
audience relished the play, for if the audience was all that
Mr. Agate says it was, namely, cultivated and critical, then
it must have been intelligent *per se* perdy; and since the play
ran for two years, then it was likely that all the subsequent
audiences, or most of them, or a good and grand part of each
of them, were like the first audience—critical, cultivated, and
intelligent, too; a thing not to be thought of, for that would
certify that the capital city of the British Empire had a
critical, cultivated, and intelligent audience for the Theater
that numbered over a million people! Yet Mr. Agate in
another mood tells us that London has been beggared of such
a thing as an intelligent audience. Perhaps it is that Mr.
Coward, as well as playwrighting, producing, and perform-
ing, can also at will create for the proper enjoyment and
study of his plays a huge, battalioned mass of critical,
cultured, and intelligent people. To add a word to an Agatian
phrase—I don't believe a bloody word of it! Of course, the
feat becomes a little more practicable with Mr. Agate's help.
To entertain audiences that filled His Majesty's Theater for
two years may be a slick and clever thing to do, but it isn't

necessary to call God to witness that this achievement doesn't make this particular play a work of art, or place Mr. Coward in the very front rank of the foremost dramatists. *Chu Chin Chow* did that, but few will venture the opinion that this thing as art of the Theater was soundly and roundly to be praised. I have been told by men who ought to know that the music of *Bitter-Sweet* doesn't rank very high in the world of musical composition, and I know myself that its dialogue and songs rank pretty low in the world of dramatic literature. Not, of course, that Mr. Agate said that *Bitter-Sweet* is a great work of art, or even a great play; but it seems to me that what he says of the play in *My Theater Talks* gives the play a value so high—he seems so eager to make the most that can be made of it—that when he praises greater work his praise loses the power that praise ought to have. As a matter of fact art in the Theater, as fine art everywhere else, will always have a bitter fight for recognition. It has been well and truly said by someone that "great art" has to fight for success; it is the condition of great art that it shall rouse hostility. The writer should have said special and collective hostility; for bad art, just like great art, arouses hostility, hence the little swarm of wasps that stung Mr. Agate as he went in or came out of the theater. There is no doubt about the big opinion crowds of English people, at home and abroad, have of the greatness of Mr. Coward as a dramatist. In the loud hallelujah of praise the tiny buzz-buzz of a flying wasp will probably pass unnoticed, unheard, and unhonored in the din.

*   *   *

We have heard at the dawn, in the heat of the noonday, and in the cool of the evening, a large lot about the superb technique of Mr. Coward. A master of technique, say all, if he be master of nothing else. Let us, for a minute or two, look into the working of this wonderful technique, and let us begin with the play, pageant, or spectacle called *Cavalcade*. The impression was, as far as I know, at the time of its production, and still is, that this play, pageant, spectacle, or whatever it may have been, was a theatrical *Te Deum* to England, a precious pæan of patriotism. What is the central theme of the play or pageant? In spite of the hysterical scene of a woman kicking her little children's toy soldiers to pieces (a very foolish thing to do), the central theme, it seems to me, was the marching of a million of men to battle, murder, and to sudden death. From the beginning, when the bells were ringing the old year out and the new year in, till the singing by the massed community of "God Save the King" at the fall of the final curtain, that this was England, or all of her that mattered. Look at her, boys, and stand up and cheer. Is this play, or pageant, or spectacle, representative of England during the last thirty-five years? No, be God, it isn't, for England has something more to show for herself than war and sex. *Cavalcade* is but the march-past of the hinder parts of England, her backside draped with a Union Jack, the middle parts of England paraded with drum, trumpet, and colors. This is the play that floodlighted the minds of the critics and the people with exultation, and caused Mr. Agate to suffer agony when a few intellectuals said booh or bah to what they had seen and what they had heard in the play, pageant, or spectacle. Where is England's tip to science, and where is England's Order of Literature and Art? Not a mention, directly or indirectly, of England's creeds, Anglican, Nonconformist, or Catholic. Not a word about the white sheep of Capital or the red goats of Communism, or the red sheep of Communism or the white goats of Capitalism—whichever way you like to take it—though there is a picture in the book of the play of a frenzied-looking man speaking to a small crowd, and saying, "The —— world's gone broke" (one wonders what the empty space implies), but not a word about the picture in the play, pageant, or spectacle.

⁎ ⁎ ⁎

Now let us dig a little into the play proper. It starts with a bottle of champagne in a bucket of ice, and it ends (except for a theatrical coda called "Chaos") with a bottle of champagne in a bucket of ice. Its twenty-one scenes of drawing-room, dockside, theater, kitchen, park, ballroom, bar parlor, street, restaurant, seaside, ship, railway station, and Trafalgar Square, are propped up by four main characters, Robert and Jane Marryot—typical, presumably, of the well-to-do—and Ellen, the housemaid, and Bridges, the butler—typical, presumably, of the working class. An initial mistake, for the servants of the well-to-do represent the working class about as much as the toys on a Christmas tree do. These four characters drink out the old year and drink in the new. The well-to-do Robert Marryot goes out as an officer in the C.I.V. to the Boer War, comes homes again, says a few words, hears of a son's death on the *Titanic*, sees his second son go out to the Great War, says a few words, has another drink twenty-nine years after, and so ends his life's catechism. And so of his woman, too. They are two softly spoken town-criers for the play. The other characters are of the now-you-see-them-and-then-you-don't kind. They are like a tiny monogram on a huge bedspread, and the dialogue is so small and unimportant that, with a few cuts, the play might have made a silent film. We have a scene in which "the full splendor of a typical Edwardian Ball should burst upon the audience . . . with all the characters dumb, except the Major-Domo who

announces the guests in stentorian tones," ending up with
"Sir Robert and Lady Marryot" followed by the appearance
of "Robert with full decorations and Jane in an elaborate ball
gown."

From the front view of this ball, given in one of the
pictures in the book, the "burst of magnificence" seems to
be a very commonplace thing indeed. There is a scene called
"Kensington Gardens" in which, according to the book of the
play, not a word is spoken. In a dockside scene we have a
ship, a band that strikes up "Soldiers of the Queen" as the
ship and the soldiers sail away to South Africa; and again
a little chat cheers up the scene, like a bow on the tail of an
elephant. Later on we have a sketch in the bar parlor of a
pub. Bridges has left the employment of Sir Robert Marryot
and has opened a pub in a London working-class district.
Lady Jane, the wife of Sir Robert, pays a visit to the pub to
see her old employees. In the meantime, apparently, Bridges
has taken to drink. When the curtain rises high tea is just
over, and Lady Jane Marryot is watching Ellen's little girl
dancing. Two friends of Ellen's, Flo and George, are present.
Bridges hasn't been told of the visit, and is lying upstairs on
a bed drunk, so that later on he can burst in and make a
show of Ellen before Lady Jane. Ellen to excuse her husband's
absence tells Lady Jane that he is ill, to the surprise of her
two friends, who have heard nothing about it. Ellen then
adds that he has fallen off a bicycle, and has hurt his leg,
again to the surprise of her friends, who have heard nothing
about it. Now, Lady Jane would never jump in suddenly to
see her old employees—and no mention is made of the visit
being a surprise—and Bridges would have been on his best
behavior. Ellen would have told her husband, and had she
not been certain that everything would go off prim and perfect she would have prevented Lady Jane from coming.

Bridges would never have referred to his home as "a 'ovel," for the simple reason that it couldn't have been a hovel, and for the simple second fact that it would have been as near as possible in style and decoration to the home of the Marryots. Bridges would never have gone for Lady Jane, almost pushing her out of the parlor; even were he drunk—a most unlikely thing under the circumstances—the long habit of deference would have made him welcome what his heart would tell him was a great honor, and "her ladyship's visit" would have been the center of what he had to say to his friends for weeks afterwards.

In Part II, Scene Two, there are shown intersecting streets in, presumably, a coster district. People are at the windows of most of the houses. The center of the stage is crowded with people and barrows lit with naphtha flares. Two pubs are shown. From one come sailors with flashily dressed girls and roll across the street. (Always the poor sailors with the whores.) A German band and a Salvation Army band are playing, and costers start dancing to the music. Bridges comes reeling out of his pub and tries to grab hold of his little girl, who is dancing. He is pushed out, run over, and killed. A friend, Flo, rushes from the pub, runs out, runs back again, batters at the door of the pub (why doesn't she go right in?), and shouts, "Ellen, it's Alfred—'e's been run over—'e's dead! Ellen, Ellen!" The lights fade, as indeed they should.

Here we have streets, costers, people looking out of windows, bands, a policeman, barrows, crowds of shoppers, sailors with whores—enough of theatrical paraphernalia to make an East End Delhi durbar—and exactly twelve words of dialogue! Just enough for a minimum-worded telegram. And this sort of thing is looked upon as great technique, dramatic skill, and the quintessence of economy. This is,

I suppose, one of the works by which, as Mr. Braybrooke says, Mr. Coward will revolutionize the theater. The flash of realism isn't a flash of life, but a flash used by press photographers taking a picture. Mrs. Bridges would be as anxious as her husband to stop her girl from dancing in the public thoroughfare for the amusement of costers. Both of them would be moving all the earth they had and all the heaven they knew to make a little lady of her. The costers carrying on business in the street must have known Bridges, must have had many a drink in his pub, and would not have pushed him out, as the directions say they did. It is very difficult to run over and kill a drunken man. A trained eye will spot a drunken man immediately, and take precautions. Besides, in the quarter depicted in the play the drunkard would be watched, and all hands would be stretched out to save him. The accident would have been much more plausible had Bridges been represented as a sober man. Again, when the "shout and agonizing scream" had rung out, not Flo, but Mrs. Bridges herself would have run out to see what might have happened to her husband. But then the scene could not have ended with the news of Bridges' death. Oh yes, it could; Mrs. Bridges could have rushed out as Flo did, could have rushed back, could have battered at the door, and cried, "Flo, Flo, come down, it's Alfred—'e's been run over—'e's dead!"

*　　*　　*

The greatness of England here is symbolized by a cocked hat and a sword on a garnished coffin. This is the play, spectacle, or pageant that caused Mr. Agate to rush round in a rage, battleaxing the wasps that ventured to murmur against its tinselled triviality, saying as he smote with his battleaxe (or was it the jawbone of an ass?) that this buzzing coterie of highbrows considered the entertainment value of *Cavalcade* to be of no account, although it filled Drury Lane nine times a week for a year with an average of 2600 people at a performance; that it found work for a great number of actors, actresses, and stage hands; and that it kept the film wolf from the door of our nearest approach to a National Theater. These august fellows who think that cottage walls are better bare than that they should be hung with Friths and Landseers, goes on Mr. Agate, think it better that Drury Lane should be pulled down rather than that pieces like *Cavalcade* should succeed. These intellectual busybodies, shouts the critic, must be told that they number less than one per cent of the world's playgoers (ever heard of salt that hasn't yet lost its savor?), and that ninety-nine per cent of the dramatic criticism is not addressed to their superior selves, though the odd per cent is there if it is intelligently looked for. Evidently Mr. Agate's new theatrical policy of hush-hush harmony.

But this august fellow must be told that though there can be no objection to the austerity of a bare wall, there is a strong objection to one covered with Landseers and Friths; that *Cavalcade* did not succeed in even filling Drury Lane nine times a week for a year, for C. B. Cochran, the Manager, told us publicly that it tailed off after a few months, and those responsible faced a loss; that no one with the slightest reverence for English drama could be interested in the filling for a year of our nearest reproach to a National Theater; that *Cavalcade* is a tawdry piece of work, a halfpennyworth of bread to an intolerable deal of sack; and that the intellectual one per cent among the people have always and will always, whether Mr. Agate likes it or not, decide the fate of a play.

Coward Codology: II

DESIGN FOR DYING

MR. BRAYBROOKE, FELLOW OF THE ROYAL Society of Literature, tells that Mr. Coward's training as an actor sent him soaring into the art of dramatic writing. "Being an actor," says Mr. Braybrooke, "gives the coming dramatist a sense of the theater that nothing else can, and every dramatist should at least think it an ideal, if an impossible ideal, that he should have some practical experience of acting." The poor coming dramatist will swiftly get a practical experience of what acting on the English stage is like when he has the misfortune to get a play produced. The helplessness of most actors is pitiful when any one of them is asked to decide the merits of a play in book form or manuscript; and if one wanted advice on the merits of a play newly written, it would be wiser and better and safer to ask a policeman than it would be to ask an actor. There have been millions of actors, and I can tell Mr. Braybrooke that the fine plays written by actors wouldn't crowd up one shelf of a modern built-in bookcase. Shakespeare and Molière are, possibly, the only recorded instances of actors writing great plays, and, by all accounts, Shakespeare was a very bad actor indeed. If all the mechanical technique connected with a theater cannot be effectively learned and understood by a coming dramatist with a side glance from a half-closed eye, then, though he get runs of two or three years for the things he writes, he will never be able to write himself down a dramatist. (I do not write now about the glory and gallantry of an Edith Evans or a Cedric Hardwicke or a Sybil Thorndike: that glory and that gallantry is their own, and has nothing to do with the dramatist, came or coming, except to turn up the light of his effort to its greatest height and its fullest glow.) A feeling for life rather than a sense of the theater is the first thing a man must have if he wishes to become a dramatist, and no training as an actor or as a playwright can give him that if he hasn't got it before he sits down to write one word of his first play. If he has this feeling he can learn all things; if he hasn't, he can learn nothing. (This feeling for life isn't the real-life-characters or matter-of-factness, which are neither matter of fact nor real life, that the critics chatter and chirrup about; but the essences of life, its comedy, futility, grandeur, lust, envy, hatred, and malice, terror, irony, sad sincerity, and fascinating carelessness—all or some of these gathered together in a comely form of dramatic literature that is called a play.) And it seems to me that Mr. Coward hasn't yet shaken even a baby-rattle of life in the face of one watching audience. To him the stage is not a world nor is the world a stage, and he lights a little candle to let us see the sun. The kingdom of heaven in the theater is not the kingdom of technique but of passion, pathos, laughter, and satire, and these are not to be found in the building with its stage and ropes and lights. If the Theater is not in the heart of the author, the actor, and the producer, it is nowhere near, and all that is written and said and done outside of this mystery is but as another handful of dust added to the dust of the stage. It is curious the way most of the critics sidle around Mr. Coward's work and try to form a divinity like unto the divinity that doth hedge a king.

For the last number of years the critics have undergone a stage change, and have given out a softly lighted glow of praise, like so many critical glow-worms, for Mr. Coward's work, heightened into a fierce flame whenever any poor guy had the damned cheek to murmur a no against it. Mr. Agate seems to have become a hurdy-gurdy of praise perennial for almost everything that Mr. Coward does. After saying that "his best jokes are superb, but he has even more success with the poor ones," he rattles on to tell us that he "does not know whether Mr. Coward has genius [Why doesn't he? Mr. Coward has been working for ten years, has written nine plays, a multitude of songs and sketches, and yet Mr. Agate is unable to decide whether or not Mr. Coward is a genius], but is certainly possessed of *ingenium*." So Mr. Agate invests the playwright with the most rare and most illustrious order of the *ingenium*. Reviewing a book written recently by a publisher in which the author remarked with visionary reverence that "the philosophy of Mr. Coward was wonderful, and God alone knew what this accomplished playwright would achieve in the future," Mr. Ivor Brown tentatively and timidly remarks that he thought that "Mr. Coward was a very clever young man to have in the Theater." Mr. Ervine a little time ago reviewed the play *Design for Living* and quoted the following passage, seeing promise in it:

OTTO: It's true. Of course it's degrading according to a certain code; the situation's degrading and always has been. The Methodists wouldn't approve of us and the Catholics wouldn't either; and the Anglicans and the Episcopalians and the Christian Scientists. . . . I don't suppose even the Polynesians would highly approve of us. They could all club together and say with perfect truth, according to their lights, that we were loose-living, irreligious, unmoral degenerates, couldn't they?

GILDA (*meekly*): I expect so.

OTTO: But the whole point is it's none of their business. We're not doing any harm to anyone. We're not peppering the world with illegitimate children. The only people we could possibly mess up are ourselves, and that's our lookout. It's no use you trying to decide which you love best, Leo or me, because you don't know. At the moment it's me, because you've been living for a long time with Leo and I've been away. A gay, ironic chance threw the three of us together and tied our lives into a tight knot at the outset. To deny it would be ridiculous, and to unravel it impossible. Therefore, the only thing left is to enjoy it thoroughly, every rich moment of it, every thrilling second——

GILDA: Come off your soap-box, and stop ranting!

Read the play and see how they all enjoyed every rich moment, every thrilling second of it. There is no use of shouting out that it is nobody's business when things said and done are opposed by others. Everything said or done in this world has to justify itself or be destroyed by either force or neglect. Each has to fit himself in or go.

Let us look for a minute or two at the social, philosophic, and dramatic implications of this bit of dialogue quoted from *Design for Living*. The absolute, deep-down truths in the play are the facts that Leo loves Gilda, Gilda loves Leo, Gilda loves Otto, Otto loves Gilda, Leo loves Otto, and Otto loves Leo, Ernest loves Gilda and Gilda loves Ernest—for a while, and then goes back to the life that has a thrill in every second of it. There is no question of the approval or disapproval of these characters and their antics by Catholic, Episcopalian, Methodist, or Polynesian. Catholics disapprove of Methodists, and Methodists of Catholics; and Christian Scientists have

no great gradh for either. It is none of these religious bodies
that disapproves of this design for living. The absolute and
deep-down truth goes deeper than that: it isn't this Church
or that Church, but life itself that excommunicates these
persons. As the wasp tears the sickly grub from its cell and
casts it from the nest as a piece of rubbish, so life tears
such as these from the bowels of her companionship and
drops them down where death is standing. And let us realize
that not one of us can mess up his life without messing up the
life of another in one way or another. The saying "he did no
harm to anyone but himself" is out of the lower gospel. The
man who can do no harm to anyone but himself is dead.
But these characters aren't even alive enough to do harm.
None of them has lifted himself a foot to Heaven, or touched
a foot to earth. There is no red like crimson sin here that
might gather itself to greatness. They are but worms in a
winecup. The funniest line in this bit of dialogue (Mr.
Coward didn't mean it to be at all funny) is the line spoken
by Otto defending the tortured triplets, namely, "We're not
peppering the world with illegitimate children." (They
would be far closer to life if they were.) This is meant to be
a hit at life, who thrusts this sickly set out of her way and
beyond her ken. But it gives the show away. Here are a
couple whose lives "are diametrically opposed to ordinary
social conventions, who've jilted and eliminated these conventions out of their lives, and are finding solutions for their
own peculiar problems"; and yet they squeal out against
those who pepper the world with illegitimate children. What
have such free and daring-minded persons got to do with
illegitimate children? This line seems to show that they and
Mr. Coward, beneath all their daring and worldly wisdom,
are little more than "respectable little old women in jet
bonnets." Surely Mr. Coward and the characters in his play,

so much above the ordinary opinions and practices of ordinary life, should know that there are neither legitimate nor illegitimate children—there are only children.

Mr. St. John Ervine seems to see in this play a sign of deeper and better things to come. (The shape of things to come.) Well, these better and deeper things have appeared in *Conversation Piece* and *Point Valaine*. Recently, in an article called "Breathless Dialogue," Mr. Ervine quotes some of the latter play, and says, "This play, though not Mr. Coward's best, may be called a transition play. He still flips along, but he is flipping along to more purpose than formerly. My dearest belief is that Mr. Coward has his best play still in his head. *Point Valaine* is the finger-post pointing the way."

One damned finger-post after another. The critics are too kind to Mr. Coward. The best that is in Mr. Coward would, I imagine, have a better chance of popping out of his head if the critics cuddled him less, and showed more sharpness in the tide-it-over timidity of their criticism. They carry him along as the priests carried the ark and strike down with their critical staves (each carried like a caduceus) any hand stretched out to open the door and have a look at the emptiness inside.

The persons in the play are, I think, represented to be artists. Otto is a painter, Gilda is a decorator, Leo a playwright, and Ernest a connoisseur. It is amazing how many people know all there is to know about the game of love among the artists. (Artists wouldn't bother very much about peppering the world with illegitimate children.) It is very easy for anyone who botches cloth with color or any jibbering jack writing rubbish to set himself down an artist. We are told that Otto—he says so himself—painted a picture "unfalteringly true to life." We are told of a picture sold to

Americans by the connoisseur, a picture painted by Matisse, that "only three people could tell what it was supposed to be, and each told the buyer different." Now even those who spent their lives looking at the pictures painted by Mr. Agate's butties, Frith and Landseer, could easily identify the objects on a Matisse canvas. They might think a picture painted by one of the greatest modern decorative artists a daub, but a vase would be plainly a vase, an odalisque an odalisque, or a window a window. Picasso, Gleizes, Braque, perhaps; but Matisse, no. Mr. Coward should get to know Matisse a little more than he apparently does. In the Second Act we learn that Leo has written a play that has proved to be enormously successful, and many people are running after him. The following discussion takes place between Gilda and him:

LEO: It's inevitable that the more successful I become, the more people will run after me. I don't believe in their friendship, and I don't take them seriously, but I enjoy them. Probably a damn sight more than they enjoy me! I enjoy the whole thing. I've worked hard for it all my life. Let them all come! They'll drop me all right when they're tired of me; but maybe I shall get tired first.

GILDA: I hope you will.

LEO: What does it matter?

GILDA: It matters a lot.

LEO: I don't see why.

GILDA: They waste your time, these celebrity-hunters, and sap your vitality.

LEO: Let them! I've got lots of time and lots of vitality.

GILDA: That's bravado. You're far too much of an artist to mean that, really.

LEO: I'm far too much of an artist to be taken in by the old cliché of shutting out the world and living for my art alone. There's just as much bunk in that as there is in a cocktail in the Ritz.

The artist, you see, has worked hard all his life—for what? To write a fine play? Not at all: to have a lot of people running after him. And Leo (or Mr. Coward, for all these things said seem to proceed out of the mouth of the author) can't see that the most effective way for an artist to shut out the world is to have a crowd of people running after him! Mr. Coward may not live for his art alone, but he has succeeded in shutting the world out of his work. There is no bunk in an artist living for his work. He may neither wish nor want to, but he simply cannot help himself—if he be an artist. If Leo means by what he calls success the gathering in of a lot of money, he certainly will have a crowd after him; but if he means by it the creation of a fine work of art, then he will have more running away from him than he will have running after him. Epstein, for instance.

Later on in the play, Leo, the dramatist, who is "too much of an artist to be taken in," makes the following confession of his faith as an artist:

LEO: Let's make the most of the whole business, shall we? Let's be photographed and interviewed and pointed at in restaurants! Let's play the game for what it's worth, secretaries, fur coats, and de luxe suites in Transatlantic liners at minimum rates! Don't let's allow one shabby perquisite to slip through our fingers! It's what we dreamed many years ago and now it's within our reach.

There's a change from the confession of an artist made by the dying Dubedat: "I believe in the might of design, the mystery of color, the redemption of all things by beauty everlasting, and the message of art that has made these hands blessed." Leo would probably call this "bunk."

Let us look at, just for a second, a few of the jokes the best of which Mr. Agate calls "superb." Sixteen examples of this

superb wit in *Design for Living* are given by George Jean
Nathan in his book on the Theater, called *Passing Judgments*,
where he says, "One has been reading of Mr. Coward's wit in
the reviewing columns, and hearing of it by word of mouth,
threefold since his recent comedy *Design for Living* has been
made manifest. This enthusiastically applauded wit, it sad-
dens me to report, I cannot, for some reason or other, despite
painstaking hospitality, discover. I can discover, with no
effort at all, several amusing little wheezes, but all that I
am able to engage in the higher jocosity called wit is a suave
prestidigitation of what is really nothing more than commonplace vaudeville humor." Then follow the sixteen examples, two of which I give here:

GILDA: You've called me a jaguar and an ox within the last two
minutes. I wish you wouldn't be quite so zoölogical.
[In the old small-time vaudeville halls, it ran as follows:
"So I'm a goat and a jackass, huh? You talk like you was in
a zoo"!]
BIRBECK: What are your ideas on marriage?
LEO: Garbled.
[Old Poliversion: "How do you stand on marriage?—
Straddled."]

As well as these two and fourteen other examples of Mr.
Coward's wit, George Jean Nathan, in a consideration of
"Mr. Coward's broader humor," gives six examples from the
same play, one of which I give:

GILDA: After all, it [the London *Times*] is the organ of the
nation.
LEO: That sounds vaguely pornographic to me. (Regards to
Mae West.)

In the same comment are given nine samples of "the original
and profound philosophy underlying Mr. Coward's great

wit," all from the one play, *Design for Living,* each framed in a delicious comment showing up the foolish worship given to Mr. Coward as a wit and a philosopher by the dramatic critics of this country.

After Gilda has slept with Otto, then with Leo, then with Otto again, and has run off to sleep with Ernest (she apparently, at the end of the play, leaves Ernest to return to sleep with Otto and Leo again), Otto and Leo discuss Gilda's "escape," and the following talk takes place:

OTTO: What good would finding her do? We know why she's gone perfectly well.

LEO: Because she doesn't want us any more.

OTTO: Because she thinks she doesn't want us any more.

LEO: I suppose that's as good a reason as any.

OTTO: Quite.

LEO: All the same, I should like to see her just once—just to find out, really, in so many words——

OTTO (*with sudden fury*):   So many words! That's what's wrong with us! So many words—too many words, masses and masses of words, spewed out till we're choked with them. We've argued and probed and dragged our entrails out in front of one another for years! We've explained away the sea and the stars and life and death and our own peace of mind! I'm sick of this endless game of three-handed spiritual ping-pong— this batting of our little egos in one another's faces! Sick to death of it! Gilda's made a supreme gesture and got out. Good luck to her, I say good luck to the old girl—she knows her onions!

The principal persons in the play, whose "lives are diametrically opposed to ordinary social conventions," barge at each other in the most conventional way possible, without one curious twist of word or turn of phrase; when the three of them are fighting over Gilda passing a night with one of the men, these characters whose "lives are diametrically op-

posed to ordinary social conventions" are begged to "hold
on to reason for a moment, for the sake of all of us—hold on
to reason—it's our only chance," as if life would end because
Gilda slept with Leo instead of Otto; and, passing through
a period of four years, all the arguments, all the explaining
away of the sun and moon and life and death, have been the
screaming of Otto because Gilda went to bed with Leo, the
screaming of Leo because Gilda went to bed with Otto, and
the screaming of Ernest because Gilda decides to leave him,
and return to her orbital movements from Leo to Otto and
from Otto to Leo till the final curtain puts a veil over these
poor wincing worms in a winecup.

Coward Codology: III

EXCELSIOR INGENIUM

IN TELLING US ABOUT THE SPIRIT OF INGENIUM possessed by Mr. Coward, Mr. Agate informs us that to the Romans the word meant the power to attain success, for, he goes on, the capacity for genius and the capacity for getting that genius recognized are two quite different things. Now is Mr. Coward the startling and peculiar commercial success that many herald him to be? Has it been invariably on and on and up and up with him?

Bitter-Sweet and *Cavalcade* were two plays that had long runs, though *Cavalcade*, from what has been said about it, seems a little doubtful. *Hay Fever*, *The Vortex*, *The Marquise*, *Easy Virtue*, *The Queen Was in the Parlor*, and *Fallen Angels* enjoyed runs of from three hundred and thirty-seven to one hundred and twenty-seven performances. If anyone cares to glance at the list of long runs given by *Who's Who in the Theater*, they will find that *The Farmer's Wife* scored a far bigger success than *Bitter-Sweet*; that *Yellow Sands* and Mr. Ervine's *The First Mrs. Frazer* came very close to the run of *Bitter-Sweet*, with *Fanny's First Play*, Maugham's *Our Betters*, and *The Barretts of Wimpole Street* a step or two behind; and in the longer list of plays having more than one hundred performances, we find the plays of Mr. Coward privates in the ranks with 1500 others standing to attention, and without much chance of having the honor of another inspection. As well, we have to reckon the dead failure of *Home Chat* and *Sirocco* here in London, and the failure of *Conversation Piece* and *Point Valaine* in America, so that, it would seem, there is something of the will-o'-the-wisp in the spirit of *ingenium* received by Mr. Coward through the laying-on of the critical and apostolic hands of Mr. Agate.

How did this legend of *ingenium* arise, and what was the main reason for the mass acceptance by "duchesses, butchers, countesses, philosophers, lawyers, pantry-maids, soldiers, sailors," and all sorts of people, so that Mr. Coward stood with one slender leg crossed over the other "on the pinnacle of fame," eyes front and four-square, "a leader of the intellectuals," and "a dramatist of the very first rank"?

Mr. Patrick Braybrooke, member of the Royal Society of Literature, very obligingly points the way to a solution of the problem. He tells us that "Coward has been extraordinarily fortunate in his managers and producers. In the beginning he went touring under a master creator of touring companies—Mr. Basil Dean. Then his first important play was produced by Robert Courtneidge, who knows just a little more about producing than most other people. And then—but I anticipate. I will here write but one word, and I will write it in very big letters—COCHRAN." The most cunning hand in the theater today is the cunning hand of C. B. Cochran. He will conjure up a dazzling sky of limelight, and when the light flashes out, Cochran has vanished, and in his place stands a dancer, a singer, an actress, or a playwright, sunning himself in the pool of light that Cochran has created.

He can gild with no uncommon art the dull, dejected com-
monplaces of the stage, and when he gets it, gold holds all
its value. I seem to remember Mr. St. John Ervine telling us
that two outstanding creations in *This Year of Grace* were
first formed within the budding grove of Cochran's mind. Mr.
Braybrooke tells us, too, when he is writing of Mr. Coward's
first disappointing visit to New York, that "Broadway was
not impervious to loud shouting, but at present Coward could
not shout loud enough and there was no Cochran at hand to
shout for him." So, I think, we may take it that the Cochran-
Coward combination has, if not a lot, then something to
do with the hoisting of Mr. Coward into the minds of the
crowd as one who stood "in the front of the front rank of
dramatists."

There are some who think that Mr. Coward is not only a
first-class playwright, but that he is also a first-class philosopher. He means well, of course, but good intentions carry
few very far. Here are some examples given by Mr. Braybrooke, who calls them "Cowardisms" (Mr. Agate would call
them "Noelisms"), from *Hay Fever*. Judith Bliss soliloquizes
in this way as she goes upstairs to fetch some aspirins. "Ah!—
What a strange, mad muddle youth makes of things!" And
David Bliss, looking back over a few "amazing hours," remarks: "People do behave in the most extraordinary manner
these days!" Now, as touching philosophy, aren't these gems?
Age makes a mad muddle of things as well, and sometimes
better, than youth. Read Lloyd George's *Memoirs*. Wherever
youth may be making a mad muddle, you'll find a few with-
ered hands clapping approval. To pick out the phrase "People
do really extraordinary things these days" as a remarkable instance of observation is, to say the least of it, a little funny.
Extraordinary things were done in ancient Egypt, in Greece
and Rome, in the Middle Ages, and even in the days of

Queen Victoria. Indeed the most extraordinary thing done by people (including the critics) these days seems to be the crowning of Mr. Coward as a first-rate, first-class, front-rank dramatist. We are told by Mr. Braybrooke (how I'd love to meet him!) that in *Private Lives* Mr. Coward gives us a very clear insight into the marriage problem: "He did not say anything new, nor did he suggest any remedy. He was very original about a problem as old as original sin." Imagine a member of the Royal Society of Literature saying a writer was very original in discussing a problem about which he said nothing new! Something has been said before about Mr. Coward's wit. "*Vortex* shimmers with wit," says Mr. Agate. Mr. Braybrooke adds that "Mr. Coward was so dazzling that we could scarcely look at him." Another, that "he is the equal of Wycherly, Congreve, and Sheridan." Lord Lytton, another member, I understand, of the R.S.L., tells us that Mr. Coward "is the most representative exponent of the twentieth century," and compares him with Swift; R. Ifor Evans, commenting on this, says, "Surely there is something wrong here." Perhaps it's only Lord Lytton's little joke, or maybe the twentieth-century blues are beginning to get him down. Lord Lytton must surely have been thinking of something else when he compared Mr. Coward to Swift. Mr. Braybrooke dazzles our eyes with another superb gem from *The Young Idea*. He calls it a "Cowardism." It flashes from the bosom of Eustace, one of the hunting set:

EUSTACE: Most amusing, most amusing; I always said to Bessie that the only thing more expensive than hunting was virtue.

"These are lines," says Mr. Braybrooke, "that fulfil the essential requirement of smart lines. They do what they ought to do. They raise a good laugh and make playgoers nudge each other and whisper, 'clever, damn clever.' So they are—damn clever because Coward thought of them long before we did. In other words, Coward is a completely original thinker [Mother o' God!], a dramatist with a big punch, a playwright so versatile that it is difficult to think now of anything he cannot do." As a thinker, Mr. Braybrooke seems to be more original even than Mr. Coward. Both of them, like true Victorians, seem to have made the great discovery that virtue consists of sexual chastity only.

Mr. Ervine thinks that *Point Valaine* is a finger-post pointing towards better things to come. Here is an example of its humor. Two men have been fishing, and another is talking to them about it:

QUINN: Did you catch anything?
TED: Two groupers, a few little flat-looking things like skate, and a poor little bastard with frills on it.
GEORGE: We put him back, he looked kind of cissy.
QUINN: You mustn't be sexually intolerant.
TED: George would be sexually anything at the drop of a hat.

And here is George Jean Nathan's comment on the play, taken from his latest book, *The Theater of the Moment*: "*Point Valaine* is the kind of thing that W. Somerset Maugham might ironically write to order for Hollywood, provided that Hollywood paid him $100,000 in advance, plus agent's commission, and provided, in addition, that he was recovering from a prolonged jag and had a slight touch of the flu. . . . It is impossible to believe that Mr. Coward, a fellow of some humor, could have written such zymotic bilge with a straight face. Somebody was razzing somebody. The villainous barefoot Russian who crawled like a lecherous ape into the heroine's boudoir and made such grunts as had not been heard on a stage since Thompson and Dundy's elephants last appeared in the Hippodrome spectacles, the cynical literary gent who prowled the darkened stage (striking a match so the audience might duly identify him) and who shrank dramatically against the wall as the villain stole in to surprise the lovers, the heroine who 'had never known love' until the young aviator came into her life (the other thing, ugh! was vile, just animal passion)—no one, and surely not the sophisticated Mr. Coward, could offer whangdoodle like that seriously. What he unquestionably and deliberately set himself to write was a boob hot-pants version of *The Grand Duchess and the Waiter*. Or am I mistaken?"

We have seen that Mr. Coward's plays stand in a line with the plays of hundreds of other dramatists, and that even the longest run a play of his has had, has been beaten by the play of another dramatist, though this is no indication whatever of the merit that may be in his play or in that of another. The merit of a play is in the play and not in the length of its run. A long run, as the theater is at present, is wholly a matter of chance, and is as likely to come the way of a good play as a bad one. Commercial success carries the banner of pleasure, but there is no symbol of honor on the flag. It can add nothing to, as it can take nothing from, the intrinsic value of any work of art. A bad play that runs for years can be no better because of that run than a bad play that dies on the night of its production.

Several have written rebuking me for criticizing Mr. Coward's work, saying that "a sense of the theater and craftsmanship of the theater are not to be despised" (which is true, though they are not an end in themselves); that "Mr. Coward is fearless in his hatred of what he sees, the decay of the so-called 'pillars of Society, the pseudo-patricians'; and that in *Post Mortem* Mr. Coward queries, chastises, and denies acceptance of a system which permits warfare without reason, poverty without a sane cause, and misery that men cause themselves," but he spoils his plea by adding that Mr. Coward is afraid to put *Post Mortem* (in which appears his most fearless hatred) on the stage because, rest you merry, it would be unsuccessful in making money. Well, this odd mixing of Barrie, Maugham, Shaw, Coward, and Einstein's relativity, an effort, to say the least of it, has never been produced, as far as I know, and its queries, its chastisement, and its fearlessness seem to have been cancelled by the gorgeous recantation of *Cavalcade*. For some reason or another, we are not likely to see *Post Mortem* produced on any stage in our time.

I, for one, cannot see anything written on Lord Lytton's finger-post pointing out Mr. Coward as "the most representative exponent of the twentieth century," nor do I for a moment believe that the characters in his plays are true and lawful specimens of genuine or pseudo-patricians, or that they are representative of "the pillars of Society." Not one in every twenty thousand of our governors, teachers, spiritual pastors, and masters is quite so silly and cipherous as the characters put into the plays. The Bonar Laws, the Asquiths, the Baldwins, the MacDonalds, the Cecils, the Salisburys, the Chamberlains, or the Churchills never sprang from loins like these. Mr. Coward is as much an exponent of the twentieth century as Edgar Wallace was when he was here.

Mr. Coward is highly praised for his many gifts, and he is called, via Mr. Ivor Brown, "a clever young man to have about the theater." Well, as an actor, then, let us have a look at him doing one of the gallants in a Restoration play, or one of the young men in a Shakespeare play; as a composer let us hear something that can be taken seriously; as a lyric writer, something better than the words that we get in his songs; as a producer, let us see his work in an Elizabethan or a Restoration play; in other words, let him take more trouble over what he does, for we shall be well pleased to see his gifts grow greater. Finally, as a dramatist of superb theatrical technique and craftsmanship, let me quote the following: "The great problem for the young dramatist is whether to set out from the very first writing what managers require from him, or to concentrate on creating what he requires of himself. The latter is by far the more difficult course to pursue, but in the end, provided he is backed by genuine ability, infinitely more satisfactory. Financially the first holds greater possibilities, because he can accept, without offending his artistic conscience, hack jobs and rewriting the seedy farces which managers are always so eager to produce. Play agents will meet at lunch and discuss him jovially, telling each other that this young man 'will write a good play one day'! They are quite wrong, because he won't unless he changes his tactics. He may, of course, write a successful farce, but by that time he will have crushed down any literary or psychological impulses he may have had at the beginning, and become lost in a maze of 'situation,' 'technique,' and 'construction' from which escape is impossible."

This is written in the Preface to *Three Plays,* by Mr. Coward, and it is true for him as it is true for all of us: He that hath ears to hear, let him hear what the Spirit saith to the playwright.

Shakespeare Lives in London Lads

ON A FINE EVENING BUT A HAND'S-BREADTH AWAY
from the present, I roved out to see a performance of *Mid-summer Night's Dream* by the pupils of Sloane School standing in Hortensia Road in Chelsea. I have never seen a fresher or a more charming performance of a Shakespeare play than that given by these boys of Sloane School. Shakespeare came to life for once in a while and sang the music of his lovely lines and in his comic characters romped away to his heart's content (and to ours). Ranging from nineteen years of age down to nine, these boys plunged into the performance of the play with an enthusiasm that never lost dignity or grace. Each went straight to the part he had to play swifter than arrow from a Tartar's bow. Here in the great West End we have actors who have stepped the stage for years and years, that have learned and learned all the ins and outs of the actor's trade; actors that have been honored by public and by critic; and most of them are spilling out the little time left to them in this world in acting parts that all in all will never leave behind one thing as good as this performance of this play by these boys of Sloane School. With one or two exceptions, in all performances of Shakespeare by profes-

sional actors we see him through a glass darkly; here, for once in a while, we met him face to face. In professional perform-ances of Shakespeare plays the merit is mostly in a royal rally round a leading actor. I have seen a company long ago rallying round Benson; later I've seen a company rally round Forbes-Robertson; today a performance of a Shakespeare play would be a rally largely round Charles Laughton or some other well-known busker; in the performance given in Sloane School we had a company rallying round Shakespeare. These youngsters sailed in where experienced and well-dead actors would fear to go. They caught hold of Shakespeare's skirts with the same assurance that children once caught hold of the skirts of Christ. Shakespeare's mighty name didn't frighten them; they weren't thinking of their names in glow-ing lights over the door in the street. They gave Shakespeare the only honor worth anything to him by acting his play as it ought to be acted, and as Shakespeare would like it to be acted. They shamed the strutting professionals by giving a simple, high-minded, and graceful performance, grandly dif-ferent from the most of those which change Shakespeare's majesty and charm into the puffing pomp of a Lord Mayor's Show.

So in a dingy schoolroom (when is the great English Gov-ernment going to brighten the places in which the English children pass a lot of their life?) with its tired look, its maps, its hardy benches eked out here and there with a wicker-work chair, stole kings and queens, gallant courtiers with their lady-loves, all dreaming away an hour or two with Oberon and Titania and their fairy train round a bank

> *Where the wild thyme blows,*
> *Where oxlips and the nodding violet grows;*
> *Quite over-canopied with luscious woodbine,*
> *With sweet musk-roses, and with eglantine,*

where Bully Bottom (fell symbol of a bully-bottom actor or critic whose swelling head changes to the head of an ass to be fretted and fondled by his fans) and his men played their pranks, with a charming little Puck to halloo them astray, and to lead them back at the end of the revels to that little happiness so much sought after by so many foolish mortals.

Here were no stale mannerisms of the professional stage; no sudden entry of some big-named person expecting all things to stand still and breathless when he moved a foot; no spoiler of pure poetry speaking it as a Bottom would read the racing news in a daily paper. The poetry came to us like the fearless flow of a brook; the little fairies danced their dances with precision and charm. All the acting was remarkably fine, and the comic characters lashed into their comedy with spirit and success.

Were there any faults in the performance? Ay, marry, were there; but they marred the play as much as the ruby spots mar the blossom of a cowslip, or a few golden freckles mar the white forehead of a most beautiful lady.

The critic of the *Times* said that "the idea of performance given this time by Mr. de la Mare was by no means strongly individualized; it was merely intelligent." Merely intelligent! The word doesn't seem to go with intelligence. We can say that a fellow is a mere ignorant ass, but hardly that a fellow is a mere intelligent man. There are bound to be strong characteristics in every intelligent being. But when is our critic going to carry on a fight for the lifting of the London professional stage to the high plane of mere intelligence? To be fair, however, the critic, later on in his article, gives the production its due, as also does the critic of the *Morning Post*. They are not all dead yet. But the papers might have given the venture a more generous piece of space, for the production of this play was of more importance to the greatness of the English nation than the breaking of a poor horse's neck in the Grand National. So capitalistic England judges the importance of things. Communism could never fall so low.

The designer of the scenery, G. B. Alexander, the property man, A. T. Goodborn, and she who arranged the dances, Anny Boalth, are to be highly praised. And so are the producers, F. Allen and the Headmaster. The stage manager, too, is to be mentioned, for he did his work without a hitch, but his name is not given.

There must be a hundred schools in London like Sloane School in Chelsea; there may be hundreds and hundreds of lads able and willing to do what has been done by these boys. But are there hundreds of headmasters like Guy Boas? Ah, there's the rub! Look to it, Mister Minister of Education, for if your schools are to be but places where boys mumble addition and multiplication tables and sing out the letters in a thousand words, if the schools have nothing in which there is the making of a vision, then your defenses are in vain, for you are but plating in armor the pitiable shell of an ignorant shame.

If there be a God, and if Shakespeare be in Heaven, then God send him down to see this play performed by the London lads of Sloane School standing in Hortensia Street in the Borough of Chelsea.

Pro-Per Proscenium

NATURALISM, OR THE EXACT IMITATION OF LIFE,
or the cult of real plays for real people, has brought the
theater down very low in the plane of imagination. A playwright now is something of a real-estate agent. We can't pile
the Tyrolean Hills on the stage, but fresh autumn crocuses will
be planted for every performance. The pure stand-fast-to-
truth minds want illusion before everything else, and must
have it. Only today—the 4th of October, 1936—a critic
writing in one of the greater London weeklies about the
performance of *Oedipus Rex* tells us that "When I go to the
theater I want illusion, and whether the Greeks wanted it
or not, I just don't care." You see this great critic doesn't care
a damn about what the Greeks wanted. He knows what he
wants, and what he wants is a Watney. And yet this same
critic twenty-nine years ago wrote this: "If you insist upon
intellectual plays you must equally insist upon an audience
trained to think. If you are a Shakespeare or writer of uni-
versal plays—this class of author is not so small as you would
imagine if you go back far enough to include the Greeks—
any audience how ordinary soever will do." Buzz, buzz!

This play evidently made this particular critic go all whoopee and hot all over, for he goes on: "Oedipus putting out his eyes that they may no longer be offended is like a man with a cold cutting off his nose so that it may no longer be blown." (If thy right eye offend thee, pluck it out, and cast it from thee.) "The final exit through the audience is one of those colossal mistakes of which only your highbrow producer is capable. Keep Oedipus within his frame and he remains Oedipus. Send him among us, and those bleeding sockets are merely red paint on the countenance of a delightful actor with whom you remember chatting at the last Test Match. The Reinhardt gang has never realized that to venture one inch beyond the proscenium arch destroys the whole illusion so laboriously created. This is the age of the picture stage, and even if you are twelve German producers rolled into one, you cannot put the clock back. You may put something in illusion's place, but that isn't what I want."

Let us duly think deeply and try to get at what is in these great thoughts of the critic. How can it be said that the clock can't be put back when it has been put back right under the critic's nose? He saw Oedipus actually step outside of the picture-frame and go his way. In this way I myself have seen the poor clock put back in the Abbey Theater, in Sir Barry Jackson's production of *The Marvellous History of St. Bernard*, in the performance of *Murder in the Cathedral* in the Century Theater, and at several crazy-week performances in the Palladium. Hundreds and hundreds of other instances have taken place in the theater generally, and many theatrical hands have been busy putting the hands of the clock back. This unhappy critic will have to organize a corps of shock guards to keep Oedipus within the picture-frame, and "thou shalt not pass" shall be their slogan. And isn't the "this is the age of the picture stage" a funny thing to say?

One could say that this is the age of the aeroplane, the motor car, of concrete and steel, and of poison gas; but the age of the picture stage (maybe he means the films) is a funny, very funny thing to say. But let us be fair, and realize that the critic means, of course, the term in reference to the mechanical technique of the theater.

Twenty golden years ago the same critic received his first communion in the faith of the picture-frame stage, for he tells us in *Buzz, Buzz* that "All stage plays are pictures of a world removed from the spectator, cut off from and presented to his consciousness by the gilt and molding of the proscenium." (Just imagine any play being presented to any consciousness by the gilt and molding of any proscenium!) "It is vital to the art of the actor that he shall keep his frame, and that there shall be no point of contact between him and the spectator." (This isolation and setting-back of the player is admirably insisted upon by the use of a gauze for the production of fairy plays.) "A hair's-breadth advance by an actor into the breathing world is utter annihilation." Shakespeare knew better when he annihilated the theater, and made the world a stage and all the men and women merely players. He came out a little beyond the picture-frame. But the best thing is to leave these sayings as they stand, the consciousness awakened by the gilt and molding, the no point of contact between actor and spectator, the hair's-breadth advance, the frame, and the fairy dance behind the gauze curtain—all wonderful things from the mouth of a Buzz-Buzz Boy.

But is he certain that the age of the picture-frame is not passing away? Does he think that this age will last for ever? For ever and for aye. Ages may come and ages may go, the picture-frame will stay! When this critic says that "The Reinhardt gang has never realized that to venture one inch beyond the proscenium arch destroys the whole illusion so laboriously created," what does the fellow mean? The whole play, or only just the character of Oedipus? Or does he mean that at no time, in no theater, must any character in any play take a step that will land him as much as an inch outside the proscenium arch? Is there something sacred about the borderline of the picture-frame? Is the picture-frame to come before the play? Is the picture-frame to become the *ne plus ultra* of the drama? Are not the intervals when many of the audience and some of the critics hurry out to the forum to smoke, or into the bar to have a drink, more likely to interfere with the keeping up of an illusion in a play than any little step made by a character over the border of the picture-frame? Surely an illusion must be loosely held for a vision to fall and break when a character ventures to step an inch beyond the borderline of the picture-frame. A critic is no critic who makes the frame more important than the picture. And when this critic says "keep Oedipus within his frame and he remains Oedipus. Send him among us and he becomes an actor with whom you remember chatting at the last Test Match," how does he know that within his frame he remains Oedipus? Will this not depend on the acting of the part? He probably means that, no matter how splendidly the part may be acted, the moment a step is taken outside the proscenium arch the illusion of the character as that particular character is broken or altogether lost. But isn't he here describing his own personal, one-man reaction to the stepping of the character over the proscenium arch? What right has he to say that the rest of the audience lost the illusion with him—unless he stopped and took a vote man for man and woman for woman as the audience were hurrying off to their homes. It is a cheeky thing to think that because this critic reacted in a certain way to an action in a

play the reaction of all the other (or any) members of the
audience must have been identical with his own. But in
implication, a cheekier statement follows. The critic tells us
that "Production may put something in illusion's place, but
that isn't what I want. When I go to the theater I want
illusion, and whether the Greeks wanted it or not I just don't
care. Perhaps they were too High-Minded. So be it." Perhaps
to this critic the highest form of dramatic art is the "Maskelyne Mysteries," the shutting-up of a woman in a wooden
case, the piercing of the case with many sharp swords, the
opening of the case showing the sight of the sharp swords
piercing it in every direction, and the woman gone! For if
"illusion" be good, then the greater the illusion the greater
the play. And as the "Maskelyne Mysteries" are all illusion,
then they must be the greatest plays we have—which is
hardly true. The illusion that is anyway worth-while must
be in the imaginativeness of the drama first, and this power
of imagination in the play must be accepted by the imaginativeness of the audience assembled to see it. The imaginative power and emotion in a fine play will force itself out
to the audience even through the obstacles of bad acting and
poor production. And it is just as easy for the imaginative
power in a play to climb or creep out over the footlights to
an audience as it is for the imaginative power of an audience
to climb or creep over the footlights on to the stage. Unfortunately, at least on first nights, the imagination in a play,
as well as getting over the footlights, has to clamber over a
sandbag barricade of critics. But the picture-framed stage
is precisely the stage of the time of the sedan chair, the
stagecoach, the candle, the linkman, the silk- and satin-clad
ladies and gents that had become wholly separate from the
people. In aristocratic Greece the theater was the theater
of the people, high-minded and low-minded; in Shakespeare's

time the theater was the theater of the people, high-minded and low-minded; but when the picture-frame was lifted on to the stage the theater crept away from the people, and became the theater of the dandies—very clever dandies (some of them, at least), to be sure, but dandies that made it impossible for the play to serve any entertaining interest but their own. The dandies are here still, to be sure, but few of them are clever. And now the stage has become a picture-frame, a fourth wall, a lighted box in which the actors and actresses hide themselves as much as possible from the people. (All except the stars, who, most of them ignorant of acting, are always anxious to throw themselves on the bosoms of their admirers inside and outside of the theater. If they can't get a name through their acting, they get it through their dogs, their dresses, and their divorces.) Again, the picture-frame stage has driven speech from the stage, and the next step will bring the actors to the playing of a play in dumbshow. Already they are among the whisper-and-I-shall-hear boys. They have lost the power to raise their voices, and indeed, taking most of the plays we have on the stage now, it is just as well that the dialogue should be reduced to a mutter. But it is strange that man should be allowed to raise his voice, and should feel no self-consciousness when he does so at a street corner, on a public platform, in the solemn House of Parliament, or even in the House of God; but no man must be allowed to raise his voice on the stage. The picture-frame stage of the naturalists has frightened the actors almost into silence. The critics have said *ipso facto* that all on the stage must be an exact imitation of life, and so nothing spoken there must dare to be above a whisper. (As if there were no shouting in real life.) And most of the dialogue used isn't worth even a whisper; but when every word shall be heard, and passion raises her voice again on the stage, when a shout in its proper place shall have the importance of a silence in its proper place, then the dramatist will have to think more about the words he gives his characters to say, and more still about the way in which the actors say them.

In a book written by Mr. Frank Vernon and published thirteen years ago, the sword is drawn for the protection of the proscenium arch. We are told here that "Modern plays have retreated definitely behind the proscenium arch; and the attempts to bring the play amongst the audience have the effectiveness only of freakishness." The play, proscenium arch or no proscenium arch, *must* come amongst the audience to be effective. Again: "The apron stage does not bring the play nearer to the audience. It only brings nearer an actor whose make-up is increasingly obvious the nearer he comes to the audience. At close quarters he is no longer Antony, but a man with a painted face." He never could have been Antony, and always was a man with a painted face. He is a symbol, and as such is accepted by the audience just as a tin soldier, a metal cannon, and a cardboard fort is accepted by a boy, and a painted doll becomes the child of a little girl. Again: "My actor shall soliloquize behind the proscenium arch, where he looks like Hamlet or Macbeth, and not in front of it, showing the wrinkles in his tights and other aids to disillusionment." First it was paint on the face, now it is wrinkles in the tights. As if there weren't wrinkles in trousers in real life. The eye that fails to see Hamlet because there is a wrinkle in his tights is blind. This author suggests that the best way to overcome the need for an apron stage is to have a false proscenium behind the real one! He goes on: "I am for keeping the play where the play belongs—on the stage; and the stage is bounded by the proscenium arch. The theater is a box of tricks, and let us

beware of the exposure of our tricks." (Another vote for
Maskelyne.) Now the play does not "belong to the stage,"
for the stage is not the theater, and a play belongs to the
theater; and the audience is as important a part of the
theater as the stage or the actors on the stage. A theater cannot be divided up into parts—it is a unified whole, and what
takes place on the stage must also take place in the minds of
the audience, or, if not, then the unity is broken. And this
author must forgive us if we refuse to accept the theater as
"a box of tricks." The great men who have written for the
theater were more than a pack of conjurers.

When the critic quoted at the outset of this article tells
us that "when Oedipus stepped over the boundary of the
proscenium, the whole illusion so laboriously created was
destroyed," I wonder does he mean that the illusion so
laboriously created had to be created by the actors and
producer or by Sophocles, or if it had to be created by the
working up of his own mind? Possibly his own mind had to
labor, for he tells us that "To pretend that the concatenation
of miracles which is this play moves the modern mind to
anything other than a purely poetical emotion is the rankest
hypocrisy. It may interest or even excite. . . . Surely the
fellow [he means Oedipus] must begin to see. . . . Surely
after this he can't go on not knowing . . . and so the play
gets hotter and hotter, as the children say," as if Sophocles had
written the newest murdher mystery or a Shaftesbury Avenue
detective puzzle-play. So it seems that this critic, from all his
plaintive mutterings about the concatenations in the play,
the Oracle, the Sphinx, the many innuendoes, the failure of
Oedipus to see what fate had in store for him, lost the
illusion of the play long before Oedipus ventured to put a
foot across the proscenium arch. But what are we to think
of the alarmed bluster in the statement that because an

illusion is lost to a critic when a character in a play "ventures an inch beyond the proscenium arch," the illusion must necessarily be lost to every other member of the audience? There is no reason to believe that we all feel as the critics feel about this play or that play.

Commenting on the production of the same play, Mr. Ivor Brown says that "Today we are accustomed to the break-up of theatrical barriers and the irruption of actors from the back of the auditorium. Any young producer of a Left Wing Theater knows all these tricks now, a fact that proves Reinhardt to have been . . . a creator of tradition that has become part of our routine." Some critics evidently haven't got accustomed to it yet. Why is the bringing of the action of a play nearer to the audience emphasized as a "trick," while all the thousand and one tricks carried out in plays hiding behind the proscenium arch are looked upon (by the critics) as clever craftsmanship? And there is only one barrier in a theater, and that is the barrier of a bad play, though the terrible, vulgar, gaudily gilded thing called a proscenium arch is, in most of the theaters, the biggest barrier a play could have, and in the theater of the future will, in my opinion, have to be demolished. "This production," goes on Mr. Ivor Brown, "conforms to the Greek rather than to the English conception of theater." Well, the play was a Greek play anyhow. But what exactly is "the English conception of theater"? Are the ugly buildings strewn about Shaftesbury Avenue an English conception of theater? or the present mouse-like acting that goes on in naturalistic plays? or the frantic effort to make a building look like a law court when a trial-scene play was produced there? Or is the English conception of theater chained fast to the proscenium arch? There is no absolute English conception of theater, for the theater, like music, sculpture, or painting, is international, and when a great play is written, it belongs to all men.

The truth seems to be, nay, madam, it is, that the critics are still in the picture-frame age; they have lived all their life there, and they want to die on the old doorstep. But they mustn't object if we refuse to lie down and die with them. Perhaps some kindly manager will in some theater electrify the proscenium border so that any actor that steps over it will be immediately electrocuted; or, better still, put a sheet of Vita-glass into the picture-frame stage so that, to these poor people, all things done behind it may have a look of unalloyed illusion.

Sculpture, architecture, literature, poetry, and the domestic arts are actively walking about in new ways, and drama isn't going to stay quietly in her picture-frame gazing coyly out at changing life around her, like a languid invalid woman looking pensively out of a window in the fourth wall.

Bonfire Under a Black Sun

FIRE, FIRE, FIRE! WHERE? WHO DONE IT? WHO do you think done it? O'Casey done it. After thirty years of strenuous strain to keep him out, the agile interloper slidders in and kindles a fire, hot and hard to smother; kindles it right in the middle of our alley of sacred silent solus bolus. While we slept, little dreaming of what was to bee. Stung again! Stung again! Are we drama critics or are we not? Are we men or are we mice? Look out! Mind yourselves, or you'll be crumpled with these senseless droves of mental destitutes running to warn and warm themselves at O'Casey's bonfire!

The fire was blazing, the papers were full of it, the police were there, and the people flocking. The misery, *miserere mei,* of it all. Says one paper, "a queue began forming early at two p.m. outside the theater entrance. It grew and grew till it stretched down South King Street into South William Street, and an hour before the play began, the Civic Guards had a busy time keeping the streets free for traffic." Says another paper: "It was quite an occasion, this O'Casey first night. Seats weren't to be had for love or money. Even members of the Diplomatic Corps weren't able to get tickets. From Britain, America, and all over Ireland, the rich and titled, ministers of state, and theater critics fought their way through the crowds to see O'Casey's new play." What was it like? Well, the critic of the *Daily Mail* said: "O'Casey has exploded a stick of dramatic dynamite. An ugly play, beautifully written." Trumpeter, sound! The Irish paper goes on: "The critic of the *Times* said: 'O'Casey's best play for the last twenty-six years. Sean's best since *The Silver Tassie*. A little mellower, with a new kind of tenderness.' The *Daily Telegraph* said: 'I think it a much better play than anything O'Casey has written since his early masterpieces.' And now for our own *Irish Press* critic, who says, 'Each attempt at an eagle soar was brief and always ended in that swamp of prejudices and bitterness which have kept O'Casey so long in the dramatic wilderness. A grievous disappointment. In fairness to himself as a creative writer, he should return to Ireland without delay [next boat, lad]. At present he is completely out of touch with modern Irish life and thought. It seems to me that he was writing about the Ireland of fifty years ago. It had that old-fashioned air. Even the funniest scene in the play had the echo of the music hall.' "

Heigh ho! Fifty years ago,
We stroll'd along together, you and I, me old shako;
Faith, we didn't care a button if the odds were on the foe,
Ten, twenty, thirty, forty, fifty years ago!

And don't care now, either. But imagine condemning "the funniest scene in the play" because it had an "echo of the music hall"! Another of the silk-stockinged chaps. But, later on, we'll bring this toff near to the Ireland, not of fifty years ago, but the Ireland of today, and hold his lofty, snifty nose close down to the cracked mirror showing Ireland's figure and Ireland's face as it appears sad and shining in the play called *THE BISHOP'S BONFIRE*.

How mortified the Irish drama critics were to find that English and American critics happened to be interested in the new O'Casey play! It made them very resentful, for these foreign critics impeded and impaired the aim of the Irish ones so that their darts went wide away from what they aimed at; the foreign critics were damnably in the way. They were not only there, but there before them. So angry were they that they wouldn't let the sun go down upon their wrath.

Says one—a tip-top chap—says he, "When we went to the theater, we found before us such an intimidating array of the critical faculty of London and New York that we might well have questioned our right to be there at all. This was clearly an occasion. Thanks to Mr. Cusack's acumen the mountain was coming to Mohamet. It is true, of course, that the most notable applauders of the master's barren years were conspicuously absent (for if present, not publicly listed), the Cornish J. C. Trewin, and the redoubtable man-of-the-world, George Jean Nathan. (Perhaps, like the master, they have arranged to come over should the weather be favorable.)"

Not content with criticizing the play, this critic must attack "the master"; not only the master, but also those who think that "O'Casey's barren years" have borne some fruit, bitter fruit to this critic, setting his teeth on edge; for everything O'Casey has written for the last twenty-five years has been to this critic fruit from a forbidden tree, forbidden by the critic himself: in the day thou dost eat of the fruit of this tree, thou shalt surely die. A hot-war chappie, this, among the many Irish ones carrying on a cold war against O'Casey and all his works, the pomps and vanities of his

wicked nature, and all the sinful lusts of his laughter at
hypocrisy and humbug.

Of the play, this critic says, "Dramatically, it is a series
of not too bright music hall sketches [exactly what was said
of the "masterpieces" in the old time before him], strung on
an outlandish string and laced with the extraordinary encyclical pronouncements of Mr. O'Casey himself. A sad evening in the theater if ever there was one."

Three columns of this, and, boxed in the center, in tower-
ing type, the encyclical announcement that "Our critic will
have more to say about THE BISHOP'S BONFIRE in his
usual Saturday column."

No more, I pray thee! Oh yes, a lot more. Three more
columns in the evening edition, but not enough yet. What,
more? The critic has to sit down and set down four more
columns as "An Open Letter to O'Casey," plus angry replies
to correspondents who had written to oppose things he had
said in his previous criticism. The "Open Letter" opens with
a bang and ends with a simper. Now for it: "What in the
name of good fortune is the matter with you?"

> O'Casey, what ails you?
> Is the question that tails you;
> For years you have gone to the fair.
> To pose as a playwright
> Is to burn good daylight,
> And your books are but blasts of hot air.
> So we say and we shout out, beware!
> Beware!
> Take care!
> Are you there?
> To prevent you goin' quite quare,
> Our critics will flail you,
> Assoil and assail you,
> Till they bring you back whole from the fair.

After quoting some good things about O'Casey said by Brooks Atkinson, George Jean Nathan, and others, which so agitate the angry lad that he shouts the question, "What's wrong with you, man? Why can't you count your blessings and keep your mouth shut?" I don't really know, buttie; mine is a wide mouth, and hard to keep shut. I do count my blessings, though, and count your curse in as one of the best; for (whisper) I've gotten tired of counting blessings, so tired that a curse—especially if the curse be a comic one— is a new joy, always remembering blessed Blake's "damn braces; bless relaxes."

This critic has a pretty wide mouth himself, for he goes on—get back a little, reader; there's a bit of an explosion here—"I'll tell you what's wrong with you, Sean O'Casey; in the first place it is because your overweening vanity is severely hurt. You don't like criticism, Sean O'Casey; you only like praise."

Recovering speech after hours of unconsciousness from this blast, I faintly answer: Every man likes praise, and a fine thing, too, when it comes from those qualified to give it. This critic, who is something of a devotee, should know that to like praise isn't a mortal sin, or, far as I know, a venial one either. Christ Himself sanctions it with His hearty "Well done!" to His good and faithful servants. God likes it too, as this critic may discover if he reads almost any of the books of the Bible. The saints like it, though, according to accounts, they don't live for it, but relish their share of it when the Church puts them into the Gerontion elevator, and sends them up beyond the clouds; and can't I see Saint Patrick cocking his ears whenever he hears a Limerick Confraternity bawling out his praise! Another thing—however I may dislike criticism, I have to put up with it; even with this criticism which isn't criticism at all. "It is easy to confute, but impossible to silence," said Jefferson; so, since criticism, however stupid, can't be silenced, it must be borne. Though I have to put up with it, I'm not going to be put down with it, for that is a matter of salvation. We mustn't live for praise, neither must we work to gain praise; but, if it comes, there is no declension in giving it a welcome.

As a matter of fact, criticism is a part of my best-loved literature. I have read as much of it as I have of story, poem, or play. A big amount—Atkinson, Nathan, Watts, Gassner, Emerson, Matthiessen, Coulton, Coleridge, Dryden, Shaw, Yeats, Shelley, Read, Eliot—to mention a worthy few; criticism of philosophy, religion, of story, poem, and play; from Shakespeare's comments on life and love in the Sonnets to Yeats's sad comment on a young man's foolishness in his *Down in the Salley Gardens*; for every poem, play, and story enshrines its own comment. Criticism at its best is like well-chosen blossoms in a vase, showing off, adding to, and honoring, whatever grace and color the vase may have. Good criticism is at times mistaken, but it is invariably interesting, and always leaves us to follow our own judgment. "Take it or leave it" is always written on the brow of her bright face. To me, literature in its obscurity and reserve seems to be trying to hide from criticism; but succeeds only in getting deluged with more and more of it.

We must get back to our penance and the shouted rebuke of the Irish drama critic into the ears of the trembling O'Casey. So here we go again: "You choke with rage, O'Casey, because an insignificant handful of Irish drama critics find that they cannot see eye to eye with the world's view of you, and more particularly with your world view of yourself. . . . The British stage, for all its current guff, saw fit to neglect you for years; and Broadway, in spite of Nathan's panegyrics, turned its back on you."

Looks like he is using this neglect for years by the British stage, and the turning of its back by Broadway, as a full and triumphant justification for his previous statement that the last thirty years have been "barren years" for O'Casey. But for many years, the British stage turned its back on Shakespeare, but that doesn't say that Shakespeare's years were barren ones. Only now are the British drama critics beginning to discover something of the grace, the fantasy, and the deep feeling in the plays of Giraudoux. Broadway turned her back on him; but this dramatist throughout the time of this neglect was the first-class fellow that he is now when they are taking him out to have a look at him, and give him the bow he always deserved, though Nathan sang his praises many a time, many a year ago. No, buttie, you don't prove anything that way. To play this tune of shoving a dramatist away from life because Broadway turns her back, and the British stage ignores him, is just to show that The Strings, My Lord, Are False. Be sure, buttie, that though the British stage neglected the dramatist, the dramatist didn't neglect the British stage; though Broadway turned her back on him, the dramatist didn't, hasn't, won't turn his back on Broadway. You have me, have you not?—as Polonius says to Reynaldo.

The same drama critic (or is it another? They all write alike in thought and phrase; so many of them parade their criticisms before the saluting point of an initial, or another name) says, "Mr. Cusack's curtain speech made it only too clear that Mr. O'Casey had his support and blessing." Well, since Mr. Cusack took the play, put his money into the production, managed it, liked the part he played, liked the part his wife played; since the production was a great success, far exceeding expectations, it would have been hardly decent on the part of Mr. Cusack to refuse his support, or send a curse hurtling at O'Casey's head, instead of balancing a blessing over it.

To show the rapid run of his cordiality, this chap speeds from play to book, saying in another place, "Milton's Samson, 'eyeless in Gaza,' was tortured by the knowledge of his having misused the power with which he had been endowed. But there is a grim gaiety in the irascible, quirky authorship of the fifth of O'Casey's adventures in autobiography which suggests that he is now contented to labor 'at the mill with slaves.'" When, where, and how did this glittering simile come into his mind. I wonder? I wonder, is it a subconscious effort to transfer the torture of his own lot, of his own labor at the mill with slaves, to the wished-for picture of O'Casey doing it instead? Is the "mill" that part of Dublin which John Mitchel declared to be a city of "bellowing slaves and genteel dastards"? He knows and God knows, does this free and fetterless thing. I'm giving this lad's wise criticism a world-wide view so that he may reveal himself to the many rather than to the few:

> For to have a thing is nothing
> If you've not the chance to show it,
> And to know a thing is nothing,
> Unless others know you know it.

Another note from the eagle's whistle: "Deep down in you nags the possibility that the Irish critics may be right. Time was when you acknowledged one of them as your 'first friend in literature and drama,' when you claimed that 'his friendship and talent was, and is, a wonderful gift to his friend and buttie, Sean O'Casey.' Isn't there an awful possibility that such a fellow may not have lost his wits completely and that with a sparkle of that talent left he may, like his colleagues, be visionary enough to see what pride and willfulness can do to a greatly gifted writer?"

Hold me up, constable, hold me up! Wait till I get my breath back. Let me think, now, let me think. Tell this critic from me that I don't believe either this or those to be right, and I greatly doubt the honesty of some. Why? Well, the early O'Casey plays which present critics call "master-pieces" (not because they believe them to be such, but because it serves their purpose so to do), were condemned by critics past—a much more competent group than critics present—in similar phrases, almost identical in word, which critics present apply to the later O'Casey plays. Which be right? Critics present have been challenged on this question before, more than once, but have ever remained silent. They have never ventured to even whisper that the critics past were wrong. Again, if critics present were lads of judgment and sense, they would never have criticized the play, *THE BISHOP'S BONFIRE*, by comparing it with the earlier plays; for this play is of another method and manner, a different genre. They should have compared it with the play that went before which is of the same method, manner, and the same genre: the play called *Cockadoodle Dandy*. Instead of coming close to this play, they spurred away from it. They knew the play was there; they had read it; one of them saw it done; and it had been reviewed in the Irish papers; but they deliberately and dishonestly ignored it. The American drama critics, "venal" as some of the Irish critics think them to be, had the critical faculty of knowing what ought to be done, and immediately and inevitably compared the last play—not with the earlier ones—but with the play that had gone before it.

As for the time when time was I acknowledged this bird as "first friend in literature"—well, that's

A very long time ago, a very long time ago:
Just let me see, just let me see,
It's thirty years or so.
When bells began to chime,
And I began to go,
I knew this bird, and so,
It's a very long time, a very long time, a very long time ago!

As for his wail of "Isn't there an awful possibility that such a fellow may not have lost his wits completely?": there remains, too, the awful possibility that he has.

Another Irish critic, a tufted toff this time—Hush! Open your ear softly. This one is of the Committee, Cultural Conference, or Arts Commission which aims at making Ireland's finer ways of life known upon earth, her quaint and jewelled arts and crafts among all nations. So this drama critic is a most important person, for the Cultural Committee, of which he is an honored member, is part of Ireland's Department for External Affairs. This critic is one of Ireland's silver cops. We just must listen to him as he flicks a glove or makes a moue at any vulgarity that comes between the wind and his nobility. Are you all in a state of respectful repose and artistic grace?

He tells us in the *New Statesman and Nation* that on the first night of *THE BISHOP'S BONFIRE,* "The audience was crackling with excitement, delighted at the sense of a big occasion, ready to laugh or cry and, above all, ready to shout down the interruptions that were expected from militant pietists, maddened by the muezzins of a local paper. No other living dramatist could have created such an audience, ready to do half his work for him before ever the curtain went up. When the curtain went down on the last act there was a round of polite applause, matched by a little timid booing from the shock troops of the Right. Mr. Cusack made his curtain speech with the air of Ajax defying a damp Monday evening, and the great audience sagged sadly homewards. To achieve this effect [the sagging sadly homewards?], in such conditions, it took the exile of Totnes three maundering hours, twelve ventriloquists' [sic] dummies, and the kind of prose he puts into his autobiographies. Nothing less could have done it."

"Done it"—there's an echo here: Done it, dunnit, Donat O'Donnell abu! No disrespect; it isn't the critic's right name; only a num mum de plume, a kind of alter ego, as if 'twere one yet a different person, a concealment within a revelation. But brave, for so many veil themselves under initials that it is a stern one who pushes forward into a full name other than his own.

A little gnarled nut of ignorance peeps out among the leaves of this chap's critical cornucopay. He says, "We never see the Bishop, and we hear nothing about him except that he is of peasant origin, a fact which Mr. O'Casey—wobbling surely from the Party Line?—appears to consider regrettable."

Now a Bishop can make himself felt without showing himself, as Dunnit should know. And when O'Casey sits down to try to write a play, he doesn't allow himself to bother about any Line—Party Line, Mason and Dixon Line, Protestant or Papal Line, or even the line of least resistance, or the Line taken up by any member of the Cultural Staff in Ireland's Department of External Affairs. But in point of fact, there doesn't happen to be any "wobble" in the play. There are haves and have-nots among the peasants, and the peasant farmers—from whom almost all the priests come— look down upon the peasant laborers. I met it myself a year or two ago when on a visit to a farm some miles from Athlone (Ireland's center). There, when I suggested that the peasant taxi-driver who had brought us should receive some refreshment, I was met with the remark, "What, him? He's of no account. Such as us have no truck with him." Let this Donat read what Professor McDonald says about the class of peasant from which the priest comes. He himself was one, poor and struggling, carrying a basket of grub with him when he walked to boarding-school; poor but property owners, therefore not peasants in any common application of the term, but the gentry of the Irish countryside. Out of his scholarly enrichment surely this Donat should have read, in *John Bull's Other Island*, the contempt that Haffigan, the peasant-farmer, had for Patsy Farrell, the peasant-laborer.

Speaking as a critic over Radio Eireann, this same lad told his listeners what torments his delicate senses suffered, sitting out a performance of a dreadful shoddy vulgar play called *The End of the Beginning*, stirred and starred with slapstick! Oh, the beginning of it even was nearly the end of him. Oh, the shameful time for Ireland and for me! Shut your ears, and don't look; close your eyes, and don't listen. This sort of thing stretches out and deepens the natural agony of a silken soul. Oh, what a passionate relief it was when the curtain blotted it out—and the creatures round me laughing.

Oh, learned son of agony, this little boisterous, knock-about one-acter was born out of a folk-tale, known to children all over the world. Nearer home, too, it is known in Dublin and in the country places where the plow speeds and the corn is green or yellow. Bring it nearer still to the cultured member of the Irish Culture Committee of the Irish Department of External Affairs, for it is to be found clad in the merriest Gaelic in the book called *An Baile Seo 'gainne* (*In Our Townland*), among a crowd of other comics compiled by the well-known native speaker, An Seabhac;

the whole was edited by Seosamh Laoide, M.R.I.A., a scholar and leader of the Irish movement in the earlier nineties. These comics compiled by An Seabhac are redolent—not of Dublin or the music hall—but of Corca Dhuibhne. Oh, Donat, Donat, you've dunnit, you dunno everything!

Isn't it a wonder, now, that these great Irish eagles won't suffer a little bird to sing? These chaps are always seeking to cage O'Casey, spreading nets of advice behind and before him. One of them, at frequent intervals, tries to lead O'Casey back to where he was more than thirty years ago, urging him to say again what he then said to the Grand Old Dame of Coole, when he went, all dollied up, to see her for the first time: "I owe a great deal to you, Lady Gregory, to Mr. Yeats, and to Mr. Robinson, but to you above all. It was you said to me, 'Mr. O'Casey, your gift is characterization'; and so I threw away my theories, worked at characters, and *The Shadow of a Gunman* is the result."

The timid drama-postulant knocking at the temple door, ready to wear any habit offered to him, and take any vow required. The habit to be thrown off when it got too tight; the vow abandoned when it grew too narrow; a vow vainglorious as Jethro's vow that lost him his daughter. Both abandoned: the vow before it had been fully uttered, the habit before it had settled round the body. Certainly, Lady Gregory's importance to him had been nicely balanced by his importance to her; for, since she looked upon the Abbey as her "liddle theater," she was obliged to O'Casey who came to the theater when things were so bad that his plays saved the theater from closing (or so Yeats publicly declared). So he saved Lady Gregory from a bad heart-pain, and those who loved the theater from the shock of a bang from the closing door. The Irish drama critics, out of pure love only, are always chanting "Remember the advice of Yeats, remember the advice of Lady Gregory, and, oh, remember ours!" I remember, boys, only to forget. I remember the advice given by a lad named Bernard Shaw, and it shall be remembered forever. Bernard Shaw, when commenting on a book, *Advice to Young Musicians*, written by Schumann, said, "Decidedly, if I ever write a book of advice to young musicians, the first precept in it will be Don't Take Schumann's. Indeed, the beginning and end of it will be, Don't Take Anybody's." I stand beneath the shelter of the Prophet's beard.

More odd than these critics' strife to lead one into the wasteland of self-derivative art is the odder effort to lime his soul as well; for, incredible as it may appear, Ireland is dotted generously with leading and unkindly lights. One day, years ago, sitting chatting to two literary chaps, I vaguely became suspicious when I found that I was answering twenty questions about things that (it was hinted) belonged to my peace. The two friends discussed, even argued, between themselves as to what books I should be given to read: A poor thief between two saviors! "Most suitable, not suitable at all; I think so, I don't think so," and such murmurings were bandied about between them. One of the friends, wiser no doubt, left it there; but the other persevered, for there was a spiritual war on; and a few days after, a book (I've forgotten the name), written by a Kuhnelt-Leddihn, came to me, a calmly-hysterical tale of a devoted layman's surreptitious journey through the U.S.S.R. to get in touch with the underground movement there for the Preservation of the Faith. I was to turn again, turn twice, and make for the twilight kingdom where I might hide from the Big Bad Wolf, to become a spiritual effigy widely away from the world of man. No, sir, the big bad wolf was no more than a Big Good Brother. Totality of being doesn't begin with baptism, or with art; it begins in life when a babe sucks its first food from its mother's breast; and is confirmed each time we sit down at table to eat. For however man may soar, like Yeats, like Eliot, he has to come down to have a bite and sup when hunger takes him.

The suspicion of being followed deepened and strengthened as days went by; the shadow was at his heels; the voice whispered

> *"I will show you something different from either*
> *Your shadow at morning striding behind you*
> *Or your shadow at evening rising to meet you;*
> *I will show you fear in a handful of dust."*

But O'Casey goes on puddling and muddling through the winsome ways of the flesh, eating, drinking, and singing an occasional song; gratified at Wexford winning the All-Ireland Hurling Final, because when he was a young fellow he knew Wexford lads in a club called The Blues and Whites, and had played hurling with them many a time in the Phoenix Park; going about grieving for a while because Dublin had lost the All-Ireland Football Final to Kerry, but consoled somewhat by the happy fact that Dublin had made a grand fight of it.

Some time after, he got a new hint of solicitude from him who knoweth which is which in those things that pertaineth to the body's correctness and the soul's security in the world that is and in the world which is to come; a man: amen. A stimulating thought for a new focus of living came in the shape of a slender copy of the play *Everyman*, which O'Casey foolishly takes to be one of the dullest plays ever written; and later on still, came a copy of the poem, *The Hound of Heaven*, and to Sean a poem of one, who, to the sound of his own toy trumpet and drum, ran from heaven's pursuer through valley low and hill high, through versesays and the fooleries, till he was caught, and brought to where there was peace, a safe bed, and something to eat first thing in the morning.

Later still, came the flotsam and jetsam of a medal, a moony picture of Virgin and Child, backed by a sentimental prayer, and a catholic truth booklet, sent to the critic by a simple soul with a request that they be forwarded to Mr. O'Casey, with a prayer for his spiritual advancement; a request that the critic couldn't conscientiously refuse. Still O'Casey sauntered on among the colored lights, singing, even now in the evening of life when his shadow is always rising to meet him; watching many of the young leaning from magic casements, opening on the foam of perilous seas; for the poem was one which had never appealed to him, and the trinkets were but ephemeral wisps of emotion, in no way able to turn a sinner from his ways, even were he so declined; or, if it went to the push, wasn't he able to see for himself the words in green on the red streak of the rainbow, "I've got the cinch on you this time, amhic."

So shines forth some of the background to the comments made by Irish critics on O'Casey's biographies and his plays, up to and including THE BISHOP'S BONFIRE. One thing these critics shared in common: they were insistent that O'Casey had "lost touch with Ireland," that his play "was old-fashioned, representing things that lived fifty years ago, but were all dead now." Old things had passed away and all things had become new. Ha, ha, aha, let us see then; let us brood a bit.

"The priest is no longer a power in the land." A dead letter? Only yesterday, October the thirty-first, 1955, a Holy Ghost Father, speaking at a meeting of Regnum Christi, said, "Some well-educated Catholics think it fashionable to question and contradict in private—and even in public—the teaching and decisions of the Bishops, which clearly showed how ill-instructed many Catholics were in the elementary Christian duty—obedience. . . . To the Bishops alone it belongs to decide both where the limits of their authority extend, and when and in what measure to exercise it."

That's pretty sure going, and what makes it secure is the fact that it would be a brave laddie of any Irish Clan who would stand on any political platform to deny that this Holy Ghost Father hadn't spoken as he was moved by the Holy Ghost when he gave his listeners this mouthful of ipse-dixit dogma. Last week only, the Irish Football Association had arranged for an International Match between Ireland and Yugoslavia, and there were Great Expectations of a thrilling day. The President was to be there; the Army Band was to shake the Irish Air with melody, the Match was to be broadcast by Radio Eireann, and many distinguished personages were to be there. They didn't go. No? Divil a one of them. The Chancellor to the Roman Catholic Archbishop of Dublin spoke unto the children forming the Council of Ireland's Football Association, saying, "The Most Reverend Dr. McQuaid had heard with regret that the match had been arranged." Dublin's fut was in the fire. Take it out, take it out! The President will not attend; the Army Band will not be present. The head of the Army Athletic Association said, "He was in an awkward position. Without saying more, he must oppose the proposal to go on with the Match." The Radio Eireann Broadcaster said he wouldn't go near the microphone; and there were hot and hasty runnings around by many to get away from even the thought of it all. Here is a quotation from a letter in the *Irish Times*: "The saddest thing about the whole business was the spectacle of those who last week thought a match with the Yugo-Slavs all right, scurrying back to give the impression that this week they thought it all wrong. No doubt their excuse would be 'the Bishop said,' but that is simply not good enough. There is nothing in Catholicism that makes it necessary for the laity to retreat violently from reason whenever a Bishop expresses an opinion." A hardy little skiff launching out on a perilous sea, flanked by the Scylla of Regnum Christi on the one hand, and by the Charybdis of Duce Maria on the other; for has it not been reported that Dr. Lucey, Bishop of Cork, declared (not fifty years ago, but in nineteen hundred and fifty-five) that "the Hierarchy of Ireland were the final arbiters of right and wrong even in political matters"? Ay, and in football matters and mutters, too, apparently. Bona fide finis. What goes for the Bishop, goes for the Monsignor, goes for the Canon, goes for the Parish Priest; and the ordinary ones of the Order of Saint Peter, the Boheroes, have little chance of standing on their toes; as little as had Dr. O'Hickey, Fathers Sullivan, Flanagan, Dr. McDonald, and his old class-mate, Father Sheedy, exiled for giving evidence on behalf of a priest against a bishop. Twenty years ago, I myself chatted with Father Flanagan, desperately trying to hold on to a life of thought while prisoned in a Convalescent Home for Sisters of Charity within the lonely wilds of Wicklow; and no voice from Irish Ireland—which he had served, like Dr. Hickey, so well—raised itself even to a whisper to help him out, or give him hope.

More than thirty years ago, I caused a semi-ignorant character in *The Shadow of a Gunman* to say of a young girl, "All she thinks of is dancin', picture theaters, an' dhress." Today we hear its echo in what a Holy Ghost Father, Rev. Reginald Walker, said at a meeting of the Catholic Women's Federation of Secondary Schools: "The world has gone crooked. In the case of many Catholic women there was little or no difference between their standards of judgment and those of non-Catholics. They went to the same films, and followed the same fashions in dress, many of which emanated from non- and anti-Catholic salons." "Emanated" is good. Catholic girls dollying up in fancy dress; clerics dollying up in fancy words. But the clerics are butting their tonsured heads against a wall when they try to frighten football fans or threaten pretty girls away from the desire to dress in what the latest fashion may happen to be. Lawus Deo!

From a Gaelic article in the *Irish Press,* called *Going to School*: "In September, they flock back to the boarding-schools on bus and by train. Forty of them sleep together in a long room, and eat a meal in the company of two hundred others. Newcomers asking those who might know if the priests beat them as the teacher had in the local school at home; and told that the priest's blow was twice as heavy as that of the old schoolmaster. Fog and drizzle throughout seven weeks till Christmas; the dead chill of the morning drowsiness at seven o'clock, the towel hard as a blackboard with frost. But don't let on; pretend not to notice it all."

Don't let on; cry of the school-kids, cry of the Irish critics: don't let on.

From the same daily, same time: "The gentle glare of the green covered with the yellow of the ragwort—orange and green, the national colors blended together gracefully, a lovely sight till it is realized that ragwort is a poisonous plant, harming the grassy turf wherever it may be. It spreads rapidly and sets itself deep in the farm meadows and pastures through the seasons. It isn't seldom that a cow or a horse eats of this plant, and goes off in death from their owners forever." One can hear The Codger talking! From the same writer: "And our ruins, oh, our ruins! There they are, a source of shame to us: monasteries, castles and chapels, now covered with filth, mighty weeds boring into them, creeping over them, and burying within them forever the pavements once beaten by feet unafraid, sometimes holy, and always prominent in the world by knowledge, of battle, or of cunning creations in illuminated print. The weeds of the farm colliding with the weeds in the ruins of the old-time sacred places. All so stridently and impudently active that it is perilous for any to make an effort to go to see them [see *Time to Go*]."

Again, one month earlier, in the same Journal, an Agricultural Correspondent writes, "The amount of food matter produced by the average Irish pasture is very much lower than it should be. There is too high a proportion of our grazing land on what are called permanent pastures. Many of these are so old that they have not been ploughed within living memory." Listen to The Codger talking about Reiligan's grass and Reiligan's hay!

There are many things said about the sucker-hold fastened on the young by the old up to forty, fifty, and even sixty years of age. Wherever one goes, the withering man without a wife and the withering woman without a husband can be found, threatening many districts with the condition of being without chick or child within a generation or two. And all these things stated and quoted appeared in the papers years after *THE BISHOP'S BONFIRE* had been written. One Gaelic writer mocks at those wailing about the low marriage rate; for, says he, it will soon be in Ireland that there won't be any women to marry.

How did I know these things before these things were said? I know the red wind that comes from the east, the brown wind that comes from the west, the white wind that comes from the south, and the black wind that comes from the north; I know the mind of Ireland because I am within it; I know the heart of Ireland because I am one of its corners; I know the five senses of Ireland because I am within them and they are within me; they bid me look, and when I look, I see; they bid me listen, and when I listen, I hear. Tell us what you see, says Ireland, and tell us what you hear; you speak out, son, and break the silence; for so many of the others are so afraid of their damned souls that they can but mutter prayers no good to God.

Here's a limelight flash from the mouth of another Irish drama critic: "The Ireland of the young O'Casey is dead. The priest no longer is a power in the land, and the O'Casey tirades against him no longer provoke the 'heretics' to rebellion or the angels to anger. As Joseph Tomelty is currently pointing out in the Abbey, the people are no longer priest-ridden—it is the priest who is people-ridden"!

This in spite of the incidents that whirled round the Students' Debating Society only the other day; the ecclesiastical hand (bishop's ring on a finger) that stretched out from Maynooth, and tore the Mother and Child Bill straight in two; in spite of the fact that the children of elementary schools are not allowed to sit down to a hot meal in the middle of the day—for fear, the clerics say, it would mean the intrusion of the thick wedge of Communism into Irish common life; in spite of the censorship of books, of films— even though almost all films coming to Ireland have already been sifted and sorted and screened by the Production Code Authority of Hollywood, the American Catholic Legion of Decency, and the British Film Censorship, they have to get another look-over and rub down by the holier Censors of Ireland, heads tufted with fairy-lights symbolical of the Pentecostal fire; in spite of the hundreds of instances of clerical control given in *The Irish and Catholic Power*, three hundred pages of them all documented, and indisputable; in spite of a single Member of the Dail, who had written to the press questioning a declaration made by the Bishop of Cork, saying at his letter's end, that he didn't sign his name to it because he had "no wish to end his political career before he had well begun it."

In his play *Is the Priest at Home?* Mr. Tomelty is a safe rider, and sits the saddle well. But then, the steed is a rocking horse that goes gaily forward and as gaily backward, though always remaining in the same spot, to the tinkle of little tin bells attached to the bridle holding the wooden charger from bolting, preventing any foolish prance or dangerous caracol. Ironically, the playwright reveals a tiny community "in the back of beyond," unintentionally, of course, that hasn't yet come out of a primitive time earlier than even fifty years ago, what with splicing the name of Communist to anyone seeking piped water in the home and flush closets to go with it; and a young priest reminding his parishioners of the fine men and women that were once raised in Ireland on spuds and buttermilk. Even the "death offerings," according to the play, are flourishing still in this parish "in the back of beyond." This is the cultural custom of collecting money to show respect to a dead neighbor. At the ceremony, the priest, or the official collector, sings out the name of the donor and the amount given as the tribute is put on the plate resting on or beside the coffin; all making desperate assaults on themselves to give as much as they can so as to preserve a high standing within the community. In my young days, it was known as "canting the corpse," from the Irish word *cantail*, selling by auction. The playwright makes the young priest say, "That's another thing I'd like to put a stop to"; but behind Father Malan is the Canon—and what would he say! It brings in money, and money is always needed to deepen and outstretch the kingdom of God. The playwright passes this civilizing custom by with a pat on the back as a sensible and amiable Catholic practice; for, of course, it goes into the cleric's pocket. The question that is there and yet that is not there, is the genial practice throughout the whole play. The small souls here haven't even a chance of "curling up in a window seat behind the *Encyclopaedia Britannica*."

The placid assertion of the Irish drama critic that the clergy have little say in Ireland now, and the waving of Mr. Tomelty's play before the world as a proof, is barriered back by the quiet statement in the Introduction to *The Irish and Catholic Power*: "Although I am deeply grateful to the many Catholic and non-Catholic friends who helped me, I shall not thank them by name." Why not, why not? "Under the circumstances it is best to respect and preserve their anonymity. Ireland is not a place where men can express frank and unorthodox opinions on Church and State without penalty. Many of the men who gave me the most significant information are Catholics or non-Catholics living in an atmosphere approximating genteel terror in which any association with an outspoken critic of the hierarchy's policies might lead to the end of their professional careers."

A writer in the *Irish Times,* commenting on life in an Irish-speaking district, says: "Needless to say, there are no theaters, no race courses, virtually no cinemas, and there is a great shortage of dance halls. The latter is probably the greatest privation in the recreational life of the Irish-speaking districts, and also is most surprising. Formerly, there were dances on the crossroads and in private houses. It appears, however, that the clergy consider such functions to be 'occasions of sin,' and, in the majority of cases, have succeeded in ending them. There is no chance whatever of a dance hall controlled by a layman being allowed to remain in existence. In Rosmuc the Parish Priest used to run ceilidhes in the former Gaelic League College, but twelve years ago, he decided they were a danger to morals, and closed the hall. Since then, never a dance in the parish."

Bang! What's that? The door closing. What's that lightning-like flash crossing and re-crossing the way before the door? That's God's Angel with his sword of fire keeping the people from dancing. In one of my books, I gave an account of Gaels dancing on a crossroads four miles from Dublin; and how on the second evening the priest calmly came along, ordered all who were there to go home; and like children, home they went. Fifty years ago, and yet they're doing it still. The Ireland of the young O'Casey dead? It must have suffered a recent resurrection, and a perfect one, too. No; Mr. Tomelty's people-ridden-priest play (and Mr. Tomelty is an honorable man) is but a lipso facto; and the drama critic's (and he, too, is a most honorable man) belief that the Ireland of the young O'Casey is dead must be in the nature of a die-dream. It is worse than it was fifty years ago. Is there a single member of Ireland's Government, Dail, or Senate, any one member of the Irish Drama Critics' Circle, who would dare to stand up today, and say to the Bishop of Cork as Michael Davitt said fifty years or so ago to the Bishop of Limerick: "Make no mistake about it, my Lord Bishop of Limerick. Democracy is going to rule in these countries"? Come on, now, give us a shout, Comrades of the Great Scare!

But all this is little but here and there, and written only to show that even in common things, the Irish critics are ignorant of (they don't, apparently, read what is written in Gaelic; if they did, they would know more about Ireland than they do), indifferent to, the things happening around them; or they deliberately falsify their knowledge of things so that they may (as they think) injure what O'Casey tries to do and silence what he tries to say. It may be that they haven't the courage to look at anything other than what is shown in their own little cracked pocket looking-glasses.

It is a pleasant experience and a pleasanter sight, on another day, and at another hour, to look out of a window and watch the Irish drama critics on their way to enjoy and report upon the tick and chime of Lady Longford's *Stop the Clock*, produced by the Lord Longford Productions in the building known as The Gate Theater.

> *Look at them, look at them—there they go,*
> *Hidden away in their Sunday best;*
> *Peruke on head and cane in hand,*
> *Black soutane and plum-colored vest,*
> *Humming a Me So Do;*
> *Knowledge their armor, caution their crest;*
> *Profound, but bland, as born to command;*
> *Peruke on head and cane in hand,*
> *In soutane black and plum-colored vest,*
> *They go—a Jest.*

Then come the reviews, each a low bow and a kiss blown from the finger-tips. Madame, I am pleased with you. I protest, 'twas fine, it was, really. Like all mortals, some of the Irish drama critics are Called, and but a few are Chosen. One of the Chosen speaks first: "To the unitiated it ought to be sufficient to say that Christine Longford has done it again; working in her happiest vein she has produced yet another of her sparkling comedies. *Stop the Clock* may easily prove to be the best of them . . . What is it all about? Well what is any laughter-provoking life-rooted whimsy all about? . . . If the characters have touches of caricature, the fact is proper to her purpose. Is there anything more to it than that? I think there is. But you must go and find that out for yourself." Thanks, sir. Very nicely said. One of the Called speaks now: "Christine Longford again proved her mastery of witty dialogue. She skimmed lightly over the political and social antagonisms of an Irish village and handled them in a spirit of gay burlesque [singing willow, titwillow, titwillow]. . . . Lady Longford winds her characters up and sets them going and then lays them back in the box to the general satisfaction." Very nice and very proper. Thank you, too, sir. Let one more of the Chosen speak: "Christine Longford may be congratulated once more for her shrewd eye on what goes on in the country, and the comedy that offers in two of its three acts a laugh a line— and that is as much as one can reasonably be expected of any comedy nowadays."

Glory for Christine, glory for her! O Lord, give me a glory and a workman's pride; for you've got to get a glory, or you're dead inside.

Let us read quickly and then slip away from a few remarks made in a general way about the drama by our Irish critics. One: "Incalculable harm can be done to competitions and young writers by an adjudicator making a wrong selection or giving uninformed criticism." "Uninformed criticism" is good, but he leaves out the selections given and the selections made by him and his critic-comrades. Another, writing of Irish drama of the future, says, "Irish drama should have some amalgam of the fundamentals of Greek, Mediaeval, and Elizabethan theater." Well, "amalgam of the fundamentals" is better even than "uninformed criticism." It's just lovely. One more: "Abbey plays dealt in general with superficial things that did not set any deep thinking process moving in the public mind." Would it be good for Ireland and her Theater if some miracle would set this "deep thinking process" moving in the private minds of the Irish critics themselves! For all the glory of Christine's comedies doing it over again, there is no vision in the Irish Theater of today. This year no prize was awarded for a three-act play in Gaelic, and last year—though prompted by a prize of two hundred and fifty pounds—forty-seven plays were sent into the Abbey, but not a single one of them, it was said, was good enough to be produced. The gap of brightness has darkened since Yeats followed Lady Gregory to the grave, and Fred O'Higgins, Yeats's hope, followed after, far, far too soon. The theater-sense in Ireland today wouldn't stitch enough things together to make a shift for young and pretty Miss Mary Hynes. Indeed, there is no vision in Ireland herself, bar the one of "Who is to have the power and so hold the jobs," with Fianna Fail in one group, Fine Gaedheal in the other, and Labor sucking a thumb to try to decide on which side the jobs shine for the Union Bosses, prologued by hurried visits to the altar to light a candle and shove up a prayer for their holy intentions: a low state of social morality for the highest Christian State in all the world. In spite of the Radio Eireann Orchestra, Music as an Art is a one-eyed lass in a gloomy room, with a tiny skylight in the roof as a hope and a way to get out (more than thirty years ago, Dr. Larchet—then Leader of the Abbey Orchestra—started a Fund to build a Concert Hall in Dublin; I subscribed to the Fund, but some months later got the money back, because the response to the appeal had been negligible. The Concert Hall isn't there yet; though, to be fair, it does appear occasionally in a dream); Sculpture—bar, as it is connected with architecture, the Bus Station in Dublin, the Air Ports, a few factories, fewer hospitals, and a lonely Catholic church in County Cork—hasn't moved a step aside away from Victorian leaves and lollipops. The other day,

Dublin wouldn't touch a sculpture by Henry Moore, and thrust a *Reclining Woman* out in the cold; though before that, they had taken with tears of joy an atrocity of a *Pietà*, weighing a hundred tons or so, from Italy, and carefully set it down in the National Museum—"the Musey Room," as Joyce called it—without a single word of protest from artist, cleric, or layman. A picture by the Catholic painter, Rouault, was boohpoohed out of Dublin's Gallery, too, because of its blasphemous aspect, for the muddy eyes of ignorance couldn't see the penetrating pathos peering out from the stained-glass effects of this painter's art. The clergy, thank God, weren't to blame here, for the Authorities of Maynooth welcomed it, and, I understand, there it hangs today; but low and all as the meaning and enjoyment of these arts be in Ireland, the state of the Drama is lower than them all. The drama is hobbled here by fear of the clergy watching what is being done from the valleys below and from the hills above; by the Catholic Press who employ the angels to beat away the lovers who are coming thro' the rye; by the Abbey in a panic whenever the box-office shows a pound less than the week before; by the Maria Duce with her broom sweeping the cobwebs of contraperception off the Irish skies; and, worst of all, the drama critics hobbled fast to where they were before they listed; with a brilliant member of the group exploding the brilliant dictum, "Only a dramatist of ideas can offer any hope of leading the theater, astray in the commercial labyrinth, out into the light again. When he appears, all lovers of the theater ought to stand up and applaud him. But they should first be sure that he is the right man and has the right ideas." The right man with the right ideas—see the conquering hero comes! They also serve who only stand and prate.

No hope then for Ireland? A lot of it, for hope springs

infernal in the Irish breast. There are brave ones, thinking bravely, in Ireland's three Universities; there are brave men, thinking bravely, among the workers; all isn't a sing-song acceptance among the younger clerics; the Friends of our National Galleries stand by the artists who express new ideas in a right way or a wrong way with the medium wherein they work; there is a hospital ward to be named in honor of Nurse Quinn, who stood to the death beside her patients when big bombs fell on London; there are the gallant boat-men of Ballycotton who bullied their way out through fear-ful seas to save the lives of comrade sailors; there are those who had the courage to go to Moscow, turning a laughing back-o'-me-hand to the yelling yahoos of Maria Duce; there is the cheeky and gallant town of Wexford, a little less in size than Littlehampton in Sussex, holding its annual Festi-val of the Arts, with opera flourishing, the finest of film shows, chamber music, and an art exhibition, with Trinity College students flaunting themselves in the poetic plays of Yeats, Continental eminence present, and Glyndebourne giving the town a bow. The Boys (and Girls) of Wexford are beginning another Rising: and there are still young writers bending over the maze of making a drama; there is Molloy, there is Burns, with others, and that is good, for it is more than something. One day, the poor old woman will dance again.

And where's and how's O'Casey, after the flarum harum scarum of THE BISHOP'S BONFIRE? At home, thank ye, and safe. A bit broody, trying to think out if he be the right man with the wrong ideas, or the wrong man with the right ideas, in the hope that, taking thought, he may assume the right proportions, add a cupid to his stature, and so be able to come before the Irish drama critics with a right reverend song. Diverted he often is by the buzz of bees and the sound

of the wind in the trees; and watching the strut of the black-
bird or the thrush on the lawn-patch, or admiring the colored lights strung along the promenade from one end to the
other by Babbacombe Beach. He does not weep for himself
as the Irish critics say they weep for him. He laughs, lads,
he laughs. Laughs as Cuchulainn did, even when his shadow
rises up to meet him, showing that the day is far spent, and
the night is at hand. It is the right thing to do, for it is part
of man's right and part of God's pleasure.

Laugh, for the time is brief, a thread the length of a
span.

Laugh, and be proud to belong to the old proud pageant
of man.

On Diverse Subjects

The Arts Among the Multitude

TALENT EXISTS IN EACH HUMAN BEING, FOR ART
is an expression natural to all, says Saul Baizerman, the
sculptor. So it does and so it is, though you wouldn't think
so looking around; great talent in some, talents of many kinds
dispersed among all only waiting for the word Go. There are
many more than seven arts, including the way of talking—
the orator—and the way of walking—the mannequin—to
mention only two. They are most manifest in us when we are
kids, when we have courage and little shame, for all can hum
an air, draw a line or two to make a comic face, dance a
childish measure in a game, and walk like a king or queen
going to, or coming from, a coronation, or carve a comely
boat from a block of wood; equally possessed of him born
rich or of her born poor. Born in us, but doesn't stay long.
Expression of art, or even an interest in its manifestation by
others, dies young among the multitude of men. Why?
Homes and schools first of all, then the church says a prayer
over the dead: a prayer of thanksgiving. Any interest in art is
slowly and politely pressed out of the consciousness of the
young rich attending the superior schools, and roughly driven

from the consciousness of those crammed tight into the inferior ones; youngsters, who, later on, have to labor to let life provide a leisured class to whom the setting of a horse at a hedge, the downing of a pheasant, or the shooting of a snipe gives a more decided thrill than a Beethoven symphony, a painting by Rembrandt, or a play by Shakespeare (though there's an active beauty in a horse taking a hedge, a pathetic beauty in a falling snipe, or a pheasant fluttering into death; but little in the smoke from the guns, and little feeling for beauty in the thought of him who fires the gun, or in the mind of the fellow or female riding the horse).

With the bird shooters and horse leapers we have little to do; they won't matter much later—let them down their pheasants, jump their horses, and shoot their snipe. We have to do with the multitude of men and women who swing away with a cackling grunt of derision from anything in art or literature that doesn't at once flash a message or a sentimental thrill into their restricted understanding; the vital ones who have been made dense by rule, environment, and hard labor. How then are the seven arts to become the companions of the working multitude, for it is these alone who can give the encouragement the arts desire, and it is these who need their civilizing influence; it is the multitude that make life, decide how life shall go, and determine how life shall look. It is useless to say that the artist can sit safely in his ivory tower, looking scornfully down from a lancet window at the people below. He can't, for sooner or later sturdy shoulders pressing against it will send the ivory tower toppling. The artist may live on for a while, hearsed in honor from a few; but when the few go, the end of the artist comes.

How often is Art, in all its forms and fancies, going to make friends with the multitude? National galleries sheltering the best, or municipal ones sheltering the worst, aren't much good to the common man passing through the common hours. For the first, he rarely goes near them; or, if he does, he has to stiffen himself into another toilet, be a toff, which unmakes him into another being without flexibility or ease of mind; so that an other than himself goes tiptoe through the elegant halls to see the wonders. He sees little, feels nothing, and goes away tired. The things shown look stately and aloof, guarded by dumb attendants, and seem to shrink within themselves when he comes near, forcing him to imagine that he has no kin with them, and they have no kin with him. Indeed, the pictures on the walls and the bronze or marble figures on their stands seem to be cocking a snook at him. Intimidated, if he mutters a word to a wife or a companion, he mutters a whisper, as if the place were holy ground and there were gods in corners who would hear and be displeased at the sound of a human voice. I don't see much in that, or, I like that a little better, are all the whispers come to: the wolf that should suckle Romulus and Remus is beginning to growl.

This soul adventuring among masterpieces has had no introduction to them through print or book at home; caught ne'er a glance at them during school hours where he went to learn; nor did he see anything like them at church where he went to pray: in these places there were only the cheap illustrated papers, the dusty maps, the tawdry, misshapen images, and the gaudy prints of holy men and holy women.

The multiude will get no savvy from the philosophical, esthetic, analytical, and psychological articles crammed into magazine and journal, or from the treatises on art crowding the shelves of the world's libraries; for none can agree. Every phase of art has its warring judges; every artist has his applauding clique deafening the ears of them who pause to listen. Picasso himself had many phases, and each is living

only as concerning himself, for Picasso happens to be a very
great painter. Judgments! What damn good are they, bar
the judgment of time? Yet we are told by Gino Severini that
when Gide went to Russia, he afterwards "refused to express
a judgment on Russian literature, and that, to me, seems significant." How significant? Isn't it time for us to leave the
Soviet literature aside for a moment, and have a quiet, sensible gawk at our own? Is it any better? In a hundred years,
will Gide himself be significant or insignificant? Has what he
has written power to alter the shape of things to come? On
the whole (though there be no sign of a Tolstoy or even of a
Gorky), from my reading of it, I'd say that the Soviet literature with all its many faults, its spasmodic propaganda prop-
agating tediousness, is very much nearer to life living than
the best of our own, than the writing of Sartre, Faulkner,
Mauriac, Graham Greene, and the rest of them: it is life with
its head in the stars compared with life with its head among
the maggots. However feeble some of the Soviet novels may
be, and many of them are so, in each there is a welcome touch
of kindliness, a wave of energy; of the writers we know here,
all, or mostly all, plunge their readers into an inhumanity
worse, far worse, than man's common inhumanity to man.

Again the same writer says "Mayakovsky and Essenin could
for a while live and work by dint of a 'conformity' which with
the passage of time became impossible. In fact both ended
by committing suicide." There is no evidence whatever to
show that either committed suicide because he found this
"conformity" impossible. In fact, I can mention names of
artists who committed suicide, artists who not only didn't
live in the Soviet Union, but never even paid a flying visit
there: two painters and one composer here in England, and
a painter (Irish) and a dramatist in America. Van Gogh, as
far as I know, wasn't pressed towards suicide by any storm of

"conformity" blowing from the U.S.S.R. There is a "conformity" here as bitter, silent, and more sinister than the conformity we so often talk about, parade before pitying eyes; while all the time we forget, or ignore, the conforming pressure that tries to stifle the artist in his own country. And here it isn't the "proletarian" who imposes the pressure; it is imposed by those, who, because of a superior education and the use of a better life, should know better. There was, for instance, a roar that was near to a riot when Picasso's pictures were given an exhibition in the Tate Gallery. Stanley Baldwin, then Prime Minister of England, couldn't stand Epstein's *Rima*, to be followed in his opinion by most of those holding any kind of a post in the Government, the Civil Service, the Army and Navy, the Young Men's Christian Association, and the Yeomen of the Guard.

Of course, the Soviet Union makes mistakes, silly ones at times. For instance, the demand for the withdrawal of Picasso's simple portait of Stalin was a silly order; and the editor of the French journal which published the portrait should have told whatever Soviet emissary who sent the order to go to hell. The same kind of boycott is carried on here (in England), but quietly, with ne'er a shout during the transaction. For instance, a writer holding views displeasing to privilege and power may venture to comment on a review of his work; the editor of the paper in which the review appeared will politely acknowledge receipt of the comments, but they will never be published. A first-class national journal has said of myself that the people who count have decided to ignore O'Casey because of his lamentable judgments. What have lamentable judgments to do with plays, or any kind of literature? One would think that such enlightened folk would show an example to the lesser ones without the law, or those behind the Iron Curtain.

Of course, as Thomas Mann says, a brilliant and clever intellect may be inclined savagely, and maybe sagely, from the brilliant intellect's point of view, to the right, soaring over with style and wit the lesser intellects of the left; but surely the facts are, by and large, that almost all the brilliant and lofty intellects appearing among man have been, directly or indirectly, on the side of humanity. Marching humanity is surrounded with a great cloud of witnesses. As for Ezra Pound's prize—surely he deserved the Bollinger Award for his great contribution to literature, just as he deserved prison for support given to Hitler and Mussolini; just as the seaman who, at the risk of his life, in the novel *Ninety-three*, captured the gun that was rushing round the deck of his ship, threatening disaster, was rewarded with a star for his courage and devotion, and then hanged at the yardarm for his carelessness in not seeing that the gun had been securely lashed to its rings.

"The Christian should be everywhere, and be free everywhere," Maritain is quoted as saying. Let us have a decent laugh here. The poor fellow is free only where the big mass of people care little or nothing for Christianity. And this freedom should belong to the artist too, says Gino Severini. Why to the Christian and to the artist? Why not to all men? Artists and Christians seem to be forever claiming rights they deny to others. In a letter before me, sent by a poet from Argentina, with a play in verse for me to judge, I read: Modern society is complicated. A poet has to live, but he would rather take pen and paper and roam the woods, to pick bluebells and admire the yellow of a cornfield. So would many who make no claim to being poets—though one shouldn't pick the bluebells, but leave them where they grow to show their own beauty to themselves, if no one else be there to see it.

The Arts are for all, like the bluebells, and not for the few.

They should become, in some form or another, common in an uncommon way, in the home, in the school, in the church, in the street, and in the parks where man sits to think or look around. They must be brought among the people so that man may become familiar with them, for familiarity breeds, not contempt, but a liking. England began this task well during the Festival of Britain, when artists of all kinds brought before the people many new forms, startling designs—like the Skylon—and many new ways with color and line. Herbert Morrison, then a Cabinet Minister, initiated the event and took responsibility for it. In spite of the heavy and insistent opposition of conservative minds, the Festival was a tremendous success; and Morrison did, not only a good deed, but, possibly, the best deed of his life. Its influence is now being shown in the present Coronation decorations: designs never seen before; graceful and, at times, enchanting; doing away with the vulgar and commonplace bourgeois bunkum-art of past ceremonial. Only the parading peers and the minor nobility cling to their old habits, looking ridiculous under the graceful and novel decorations of a new mind with a new outlook.

No one can bind the Muses. Nor Sainte-Beuve, nor Gide, Proust, Zhdanov, nor anyone else can change to please himself what the Muses decide to say or sing.

Always the Plough and the Stars

THE ARTIST OCCUPIES A PERILOUS PLACE IN life, for he is the most expendable of men. Really, he hasn't a place in life, but spends most of his time in a nook. He is brought out occasionally, shy, but hopeful, to show a picture or two, a figure on a stand, or a book in a shop window; gets a pat on the back, and then is coldly shouldered back into his hidden nook again. No sadder sight than that of a painter in a gallery surrounded by his figures, with ne'er a red tab on one of them to signify a picture or a figure sold; or a writer carrying a bunch of manuscript from publisher to publisher, soliciting acceptance, convinced in his soul that, given publication, the work would amaze the world.

A comic sight, too, if one looked deeply into it, but never for the suspiring painter or the agitated writer convinced of his own worth. They rush to where these things seem to flourish, and are fronted with wide ditches they have to jump, and barbed wire that has to be climbed over or crawled through. Then, in most cases, effort is weakened, and instead of achievement, we hear an outcry. The aspirants have not been warned. On the contrary, correspondence schools and

[170]

art centers throw promises like roses at their feet so that before the artist settles down to do things, his thoughts are discommoded by the shower of checks he sees in his mind's eye falling sweetly onto his breakfast table.

They should be told in the first going off of the difficulties in front of them, besetting them, and often tumbling them into the fiery dust of rejection. Once, Shaw, answering a request of mine to write a preface for a wild thing I called "Three Shouts on a Hill," refused, saying, among other wise things, that I'd have "to go through the mill like the rest of us." Shaw went through the mill, and came out bouncing; Yeats went through it, and came out with a wide-brimmed hat, a great black cloak, and a flowing tie; I came out of it tattered and torn, like a man tossed by the cow with the crumpled horn, but still sparring, ready for defense and a forward blow. But it isn't a nice experience, and it leaves one wondering. I always warn beginners who write to me to get work in field, factory, or workshop, and stay there as long as they can. Beginners should be told the facts of life. In drama schools, they should be told that merely to step on a stage isn't the advent of a great actor or actress; that a brush in the hand and a beard on the chin doesn't compose a great painter; that everything has to be learned through years of work; that work, work to make an artist, is as arduous as the work that makes an editor or a stonemason; the one difference being that if either editor or stonemason wasn't excellent at his work he'd have to go; while the incompetent artist can go on forever and ever, deceiving himself, though he deceives very few others.

Along with the desperate struggle to get enough dough to live, there are two more subtle dangers before the artist—self-glorification and the glorification of the crowd. For some curious reason, it is thought that the one who writes a book or composes a play must be a very special kind of soul; a soul that has been admitted to knowledge denied to even very intelligent people. A chap I knew once wrote a Barrie-esque play which had a spook in it; he was almost immediately asked to speak from a Northern pulpit on The After Life. He did, but never preached again, and never wrote another play. He was one of the wise ones. The writer should not encourage the thought that his work is more important than the worker in wood, in metal, or the weaver of textiles from the spinning thread. Neither should the painter or artist who chisels form from the silent standing stone do it either. The delicate pencil and paintbrush, the sculptor's searching chisel, or the potent pen is no more than the plumb line and the spirit level, the jack-plane and saw, or the hammer beating out utilitarian shapes from metal. Emerson saw and recognized that not only paintings, statues, and great buildings should have grace and dignity, but common things as well:

> *Give to barrows, trays, and pans,*
> *Grace and glimmer of romance.*

Springing from Emerson's trays and pans, and reaching to more modern things, we are told by Sir Claude Gibb, F.R.S., in the *Atomic Scientists News*, November, 1952, that "Atomic power in its industrial application is changing from being a science to a science plus an art. Engineers who would shudder at being called artists must nevertheless make the major art-contribution to atomic power development." Why does the engineer shudder at the idea of being regarded as an artist? Because he is ashamed of, and embarrassed by, the exaggerated self-glorification with which those who profess and call themselves artists incense themselves.

This elegant glorification seems to induce one kind of

writer to go climbing into an ivory tower, sending a sturdier
kind scurrying down into a concrete shelter, and never the
twain shall meet. Both isolate themselves from the crowd
hurrying about the world's business; the crowd that can be
so colorful, so kind, so venomous, so comic. But the elegant
one above stays there looking contemptuously down on the
one below, the one below shaking his fist up at the laddo
above, making a comic sight, and sending us laughing away.
Both of them are condemned to go unrewarded by the tense
tinge of man's sorrow and the merry medley of man's comic
catch at life. Both of them are wasting their time, and are
burning the daylight of life in their own peculiar coffins.
Both are afraid of life's full-throated shouting; afraid of its
venom, suspicious of its gentleness, its valor, its pain, and its
rowdiness. The artist's place is to be where life is, active
life, found in neither ivory tower nor concrete shelter; he
must be out listening to everything, looking at everything,
and thinking it all out afterward.

Then there's the gift that goes, or should go, with what
we do; for, as well as going through the mill, we must have
the gift that brings us safely through and makes us fit to do
the things most desirable in the sight of, and for the needs of,
men; the gift to be a writer, painter, editor of newspaper or
magazine, or critic, just as one must have a gift for handling
metal if one wants to be a good metal-worker; for handling
wood, if one wants to be a good carpenter. A gifted carpenter
will want to make things finer than window sashes and
door frames; a metal-worker something finer than a tin kettle,
useful and necessary as these things be.

We should try not to leave the gift given, or the talent,
either, desolate. Too many metal-workers and carpenters
and grandee dilettantes want to be writers and painters, seeing with foolish eyes a glow around authorship that never

was on sea or land. Reading is now as necessary as food for
the people, but, like food, most of it is for immediate consumption. It is no less important for that, and should be the
best that mind can give for the moment. Only a few great
souls come out of time to live beyond it.

We shouldn't abandon a craft we can do well for one which
we shall do but badly; nor should we set aside our craft to
do trivial things. Only the other day, I got a letter from a
man who lives in Calumet City, Ill. He begged me to send
him used Irish stamps, adding as a hint to me, that, as well,
he collected coins, matchbox covers, beer-bottle caps, auto-
club emblems, catalogues, and buttons, of which he had five
hundred. Casually, he mentions that he is a carpenter. Abandoning the calm and really beautiful art of carpentry for the
feverish collection of rubbish.

The artist—painter and writer—has hardly a place in England here, and none at all in Ireland. The mystical aura is
around him still, but sweet damn all else. Poems penny each
have no market. Might as well ask for a thousand pounds as
a penny for a poem now. Lately, it was suggested that each
borrower from a public library should pay a levy of a penny
for each book borrowed, the sum collected to be divided
among the authors. The librarians would have none of it, and
the borrowers said it was an attack on the spirit of free reading. Painting materials have gone up high to heaven in price.
It now costs at least five pounds to frame a picture, and
artists are in a forlorn state as compared with the chances of
the metal-worker and the worker in wood. In the old days,
the church was the great standby of the painter. Not so now.
Recently, a Dominican Prior, in love with new art ideas, got
Matisse to design the interior of a newly built church.
Matisse did a lovely, austere, and gently colorful design, but
the upper clergy condemned it, so Matisse's lovely idea of

what a modern church should be like will fade out, decline, and fall into the dust of forgotten things.

There are thousands of other places calling for an artist's skill—state buildings, municipal buildings, railway stations, restaurants, school, hospitals, and even the places where our dead lie. Decoration of these would keep artists going for a hundred years. When I was in New York City I had to go to see the Federal taxing officer in Battery Park, to settle accounts before departing. I came into a big room filled with benches on which people were sitting, waiting their turn to interview the officer. A big flag of the United States, tacked to the back wall, almost stretched from side to side. Nailed, not to the mast, but to the wall. No place for a flag to be, for a flag should always fly. Attached to its halyard, secured to its staff, a flag is active, a flag is alive. Stretched alone, and tacked to a wall, it is a dead thing. A flag crucified.

Whitman's poet and child saw this, and knew this, when they listened to "Song of the Banner at Daybreak." It is not decorative, and it has lost the power of creating emotion. It is a patch. Far better to have there a portrait of Washington, a picture of the Signing of the Declaration of Independence, the Battle of Bunker Hill, or Franklin coaxing fire from heaven by kite and key. This would give work to artists, and, by display, help to ridicule a bad artist or encourage a good one; bringing, too, mighty figures and the mighty things done by them before the eyes of American people. If we can't or won't give the artists canvas, then, at least, we should give them walls.

The artist's way is a way of life like that of the butcher, the baker, and the candlestick-maker, only that these three find it easier to make a living than the artist or writer. But however great a genius one may be one can ask no more of life than a way in it. To make the way worth while we must add a will to it—no easy thing to do, and never repine if the things we do seem small. Little things can be exquisite—a brooch, a miniature, a bowl, a vase, an essay. Many a little thing within its own limited compass can entertain as much loveliness as any frieze on any Parthenon. To me, the main problem is to give the artist and writer as safe a living as the living of a butcher, baker, and candlestick-maker, so that he may keep fear and anxiety out of his work, and bring hope into it.

However forlorn the artist may be in his state of life, he must go on using the gift given to him, overcoming obstacles, even the hindering one of self-aura and the crowd-aura, so fascinating to some. "Those who think highly of me," says Newman, "feel a respect, not for me, but for some imagination of their own which bears my name." An artist should not permit himself to swoon away into the conception of him created by others. He must be himself. He must use his gift as best he can. On the whole, so he has done, and so, so help him God, he will go on doing, living on equal terms with time.

Tender Tears for Poor O'Casey

IT TOUCHES THE HEART TO THINK OF THE DEEP and lasting affection in which the critics of Dublin hold O'Casey tight, and the big, round tears they shed so sadly over his present irresponsible playwrighting. He is lost! they cry, and will be utterly so, if he doesn't amend his ways, and turn back to first principles. He refuses; he won't: weep on, weep on, his hour is past! Tinkling their one-stringed harps, they sit them down by the waters of Anna Livia Plurabelle, and weep for the lone, lost bard. They want him to go back to the writing of another *Juno and the Paycock*; to the period of the first three "great" or "fine" or "grand"—they always give an uplifting adjective to the noun when they mention them—plays; and, because, so far, he has declined, they are about to build a wailing wall in Dublin to commemorate the poor playwright who took the wrong turning. Am I exaggerating now, or what? I don't think so. Listen; and let us take these critics in the order of their disappearance.

In an issue of the *Irish Times* in 1940, a critic, whose name doesn't appear on his comments, moans dolefully (though I imagine I feel a thrill-thread of joy through the moaning) in a review of *The Star Turns Red*, saying: "This play drives us to the thought that in *The Plough and the Stars* O'Casey's star saw the last moment of its proper brightness. These early plays were loved for the fresh fun they made in the theater [evidently a fellow fond of a loud guffaw at anything], and for their vivid version of already 'familiar characters.' We liked these plays because they said things about our serio-comic warfare, which, all the time we had been enduring them, we wanted so fiercely to say ourselves, but just couldn't, because we were afraid. [See? This critic liked these plays, not because they were fine plays, but because they said things he was afraid to say—and that, in his opinion, goes for drama criticism.] Then Mr. O'Casey, blown sky-high above his audiences, began to write 'great' plays. The first was *The Silver Tassie*, which the Abbey Theater at first refused—in Mr. O'Casey's artistic interest only. The latter history of that play is linked closely with the decline of his star." That's Duine gan ainm for you.

A critic signing himself "K" quotes a critic named A. E. Malone as writing in 1929 in *The Irish Drama*: "For the moment the future of O'Casey is artistically a problem upon which no decided opinion can be given [and he giving a decided opinion all the time!]. It may be suggested that his basis [his basis!] is definitely localized and except his talent be greater than it at present appears to be, his future will be as much a part of Dublin as was his past." And "K" adds for himself, "How triumphantly true!" There is nothing true in it, for there is nothing decided in it. The man was afraid to decide anything. Every man is localized insofar as he can only be himself. I can tell "K" definitely, without the slightest reservation, that however "great" O'Casey's talent may be or may become, his "future" will be as much a part of Dublin as was his past; just as Joyce carried the city to the end of his life in his heart and in his soul. In the last play written the identity is as clear and unmistakable as it is in the first one.

T. C. Murray, the dramatist *de facto,* and critic *de jure,* is also very hot and bothered about O'Casey's way of play-wrighting. Says he, "O'Casey took a strange twist after he had written his earlier plays, a lamentable thing to most of us. To discern the lamentable thing that has happened, we have only to recall those earlier masterpieces of his. One hears again and again, What's wrong with O'Casey? This is the question his best friends have long been asking." That's the question, Joxer; that's the question. His best friends! And doesn't he know them well!

> *One early mornin' as I roved out,*
> *I heard a man singin' with grreat llaamentaation!*

Valentin Iremonger, a writer himself, commenting in the *Irish Times,* says, with hand on his troubled heart and a tear in his poetic eye, "I am still young enough to feel sorry— and a little angry—watching genius being squandered away and frittered away upon ephemeral concepts such as Mr. O'Casey has elected to promulgate." Imagine "electing to promulgate ephemeral concepts"! Still there's dignity and sorrow in the sentence. But comicality too. As if Father O'Flynn, putting his blackthorn in his pocket, said, suddenly, "Th' time for jokin's past—we must be sarious now." Mr. Iremonger is, presumably, a young fellow, so here's a bit of advice from an old one: Let him think a little longer before he writes some of his sentences. He is young enough to learn to write more clearly. I will give one instance of his thought-less commenting as a critic of the drama: He is nearly dis-traught because of the difference between the way in which

Feelim in one play receives news of the death of his son and that in which Juno, in another play, receives news of the death of hers. Treating the play with the mind of a pacifist, rather than with that of a critic, he fails to see the different circumstances, the different environment, the different psychological influences of friends and neighbors in the two plays, or the enormous effect they have on those who live among them. Mr. Iremonger—to give another instance of sleepy drama criticism—resents the fact that *Oakleaves and Lavender* doesn't follow the pattern of realism woven into "the early plays, that made O'Casey so secure"; yet when Feelim, the character in the play mentioned, reacts realistically to the killing of his son, and vows vengeance on the heads of those who did it, and their comrades who helped them to do it, Iremonger goes all white, and moans out a pacifistic sermon, reminding O'Casey that "two can play at that game," which O'Casey knows quite well—and more than two for that matter; but all this is beside the point, for here Iremonger is judging a play, not as a drama critic, but as a pacifist. This critic heads his commentary with the title of "Rude Mechanicals." What are "mechanicals," and when do they become"rude"? Conversely, what are gentle and good-natured mechanicals? No mechanicals are ruder than those of Shakespeare, but they are delightful, lasting, incensing the woes of life with immortal laughter. "Ghost Dancers," he says again, "are devices long since popular with amateur dramatists everywhere." Everywhere? What is an amateur dramatist? And where's the "everywhere" where these and their ghostly dancers are to be found? When a statement like this is made, the critic should give instances of the numerous plays by amateur dramatists in which these ghostly dancers have appeared.

A Mr. Gabriel Fallon, drama critic of the *Standard* (a

weekly journal whose editorial office is in the porchway of heaven's doorway), listens to this tale of woe, and adds the tears of middle age to the virgin ones of Mr. Iremonger. Ay, indeed: "Even middle age may drown an eye [why only one; why not the two?] unused to flow on being compelled to witness the incandescence of genius doused in an overflow of its own willfulness." Another dignified sentence. He isn't done yet: "Unless there is a return to first principles, we shall all be forced to join our young poet in his anger and tears." Tears, tidal tears! What, all of you to be forced to anger and tears? Unless O'Casey goes back to first principles. Really? All Eire in tears! Over O'Casey. That's too bad to be true. "How is it," Mr. Fallon asks, "that a number of English critics described *Red Roses For Me* as a magnificent piece of dramatic poetry?" O'Casey doesn't know, and isn't concerned very much about it. While reminding Mr. Fallon that all the English critics aren't English (Ivor Brown is a Scotsman; Mr. Trewin is a Cornishman; and Desmond MacCarthy must have come from somewhere out of Spain), it isn't the question of the goodness or badness of a play that is the more important thing; it is the going back on the idea that the drama must change and develop a new outlook, a broader scope, and a fresh style, if it is to live as an art alongside the art of architecture, of painting, and of music. In my opinion, the time has passed for a drama to devote its expression to one aspect of life alone, and to consider that aspect of life as dominant for the time the play takes to unfold itself; that in one play one aspect of life must be the beginning, the middle, and the end of it. Consistency of mood and of manner isn't always, indeed, not even often, found in life, and why should it then be demanded in a play? This new aspect of playwrighting which puzzled audiences here in 1929—and some of the critics too—is now puzzling

the Dublin critics in 1947, and provoking them to anger and
tears. What angers most of them, however, is that it hasn't
been altogether a failure. A jewel moved about in the hand
shows many flashes of light and color; and the human life,
moved about by circumstances of tragedy and comedy,
shows more than many flashes of diversity in the unity of
its many-sided human nature. Of course, a great play may
be written around one aspect of life, but it doesn't follow
that this must be the one way forever in which dramatists are
to show life on the stage to those interested in the theater.
Not of course that a fine play, or even a great play, may not
again be written by a newer dramatist in the "realistic" manner; but it will need to be a fine one to lift itself from the
sameness of the tens of thousands of realistic or naturalistic
plays that have gone before it. They are as numerous as the
shadowy, silvery pictures painted by Corot—hundreds of
them, with additional hundreds of perfect imitations, so beloved of so many, especially by Æ; though few words of
praise were given to the portraits he painted, the loveliest
things Corot did. Why? Because the portraits were what
only Corot could do, while the silvery landscapes could be
done by a hand holding a brush with a little craft and trick-
ery to aid it. Dramatists cannot go on imitating themselves,
and, when they get tired of that, imitating others. They must
change, must experiment, must develop their power, or try
to, if the drama is to live.

But are those earlier plays of O'Casey the "great works"
they are said to be by O'Casey's "best friends"? And is the
tear at this moment shed the genuine tear it is said to be?
When these "early masterpieces" appeared first on the stage,
did they get the applause they deserved from the eminent
Irish critics of the day? Were these plays, when they appeared, "loved for the fresh fun they made in the theater"?

Did the then lower lights and the higher lights of Dublin think that these plays made O'Casey "secure" in the highlight of the drama? Let us see.

Here's what A. E. Malone (then considered an authority on the drama), Malone with his pert mustache on his little, frightened face, here's what he said: *"The Plough and the Stars* isn't as good a play as *Juno.* It is a series of *tableaux vivants.* O'Casey is a photographic artist. In the *Plough* O'Casey strives after a literary quality of speech which is alien to Dublin slum dwellers. The play has the structure of the cinema and the revue. The Prostitute, Rosie Redmond, has no significance whatever [a touch of humor here]. The career of O'Casey induces fear for his future." As if afraid his readers might forget what he had said, he comes out again, a little stronger: "Is O'Casey a dramatist? Is he but a combination of the cinema and the dictaphone? His plays are phases of Dublin life under conditions as abnormal as they are transient. His humor is the humor of the music-hall without its skill, or the sharpened point of its wit." Well, O'Casey is in no way ashamed for anything of a music-hall nature appearing in his plays. Well, here's a lad who wrote a big, big book, a "book of great authority," on the Irish Theater, who couldn't, wouldn't make up his mind about poor O'Casey, and gave most of his criticisms in a series of questions because the thought was father to the wish.

Most people will remember the tremendous opposition the plays met from the Plain People; but was this worse than that of Liam O'Flaherty, who, in a letter denouncing Yeats's defense of the play, tersely informed Yeats and the world that "in my opinion, *The Plough and the Stars* is a bad play." At the same time, in the *Irish Statesman,* F. R. Higgins, the poet, came out with the revelation that "A new political quality, approved by the arrogance of the Gall, is the only quality for which O'Casey is offered applause. His is a technique based on the revue structure, in the quintessence of an all-Abbey burlesque, intensified by 'divarsions' and Handy Andy incidents, with somewhat more original settings. His plays are but a laborious bowing on a one-string fiddle, and 'Fluther' is but the successor of Boyle's more lively ragtime. O'Casey in his new play entirely lacks the sincerity of an artist."

Well, there's the stern, quiet testimony of a poet, doing away with all the praise and good report of the Iremongers, the Fallons, and the Murrays. But there's another—Austin Clarke, a poet, too. He said, with the same poise and quietness, that "Several writers of the new Irish school [himself included of course] believe that Mr. O'Casey's work is a crude exploitation of our poorer people in the Anglo-Irish tradition that is now moribund."

O'Casey exploiting the poor! And now they want him to go on with this nefarious practice. Pilfer the lot of them; take the last penny from them, then leave them to God! I wonder is it really O'Casey who does this bad thing? I shouldn't put anything past him, for he carries the Red Star in the lapel of his coat, emblazoned with those dangerous weapons—the hammer and the sickle.

But we haven't come to the end of the list yet. There are a few left still. There's Professor Daniel Corkery, the man who found the hidden Ireland. In an article praising Clifford Odets' *Golden Boy* he shows how this play far surpasses the "realistic" plays of O'Casey. And since *Golden Boy* is but a third-rate play, then O'Casey's realistic plays must be low down, deep, among the dead men. One more from others: R. M. Fox of Dublin, a writer, in the *New Statesman* in an issue of August, 1928, calls these plays "The Drama of the Dregs." He says, "Peasant drama in Ireland has been succeeded by slum drama, though such an authority as W. B. Yeats tells us that the peasant drama is done, and slum drama will have a very short reign. As entertainment, this kind of drama is permissible. Neither the peasant nor the slum play deals in any direct fashion with typical problems of a group of people. But group problems may not lend themselves to drama, certainly not to melodrama, and so on the stage they are neglected. Besides entertainment we need truth." Well, there's R. M. Fox for you, telling you and me about the drama; all about the drama. He seems to think truth should be entertaining, though I know an Irish proverb that says truth is always bitter.

It wouldn't be fair to forget the recent roar of Brinsley Macnamara about "the vulgarity of O'Casey's worthless plays that have always been given far too much honor and attention by the Abbey Theater." So there is heard a pretty fine chorus against these "masterpieces" that have made "O'Casey so secure in the theater," from the sparrow-like chirrup of Mr. Austin Clarke to the ready and heady roar of Brinsley Macnamara.

Now these who said these things are just as intelligent, just as important, as those who have come after them. Their criticism is as likely to be right as the criticism of the present-day complainers; so what is the playwright to do? Here we have a vociferous assembly, men of gifts, some of them intellectuals, declaiming against these early "masterpieces" as bad plays, bad art, exploitation of Eire's poorer people, and decisively declaring that O'Casey was equipped only with the technique of the revue, the quick eye of the camera, and the ready pickup mind of the dictaphone; having nothing at all of the dramatist in either heart or head. And yet the critics of today implore O'Casey, with tears in their eyes, to go back to "first principles." All this shows how stupid these Irish critics are; that they fear O'Casey only a little less than they fear themselves; it tells O'Casey that he mustn't pay any attention to these chiming bells of St. Mary's ordering him back to the land of beginning again.

It shows, too, that Eire needs critics more than she needs playwrights. She has had good plays, good actors, good producers, but always weak, timid, frustrated, and damned bad critics. We have had no drama critic since Yeats, who, with his hazel wand and the red berry tied to an end, tried to exorcise inanity and commercialism out of the Theater of his day. But Yeats was a critic only in his spare time, and then only of the theater insubstantial. He tried to change the Theater of the world through the few things done on the Abbey stage, and, though he failed, he gave Ireland a great beginning.

The Irish Theater needs a critic who will set down the comments of the chronicles of the stage with precision, knowledge, and above all, with courage; refusing to condemn the new because he does not understand it (like the later pictures of Picasso), or dislikes it; a critic able to enter all her halls with confidence, from the highest thing the Theater has ever done to the dialogue and diversions of a Jimmy O'Dea on the Olympia stage. A critic who will never be influenced by his paper's policy or profit; who will be unafraid of clique or cleric; who, in his criticism, will separate himself from the seduction of a friend, or from animosity towards an enemy; who will know the theater of the Continent as well as he knows his own, far back, and present achievement; a critic who will look upon a play as a play, indifferent to whether it hurts or heals. Where is there a critic like that in Eire? Is there one of them who isn't afraid of his paper boss; afraid of his clique of friends; afraid of his clerical consorts; half afraid of his own thoughts? No-where; not yet, anyhow.

Now look, young dramatists, you have a theater to de-velop and to defend, and it is for this reason that I appeal to the younger (and so braver) writers in Ireland today who still go in half fear of clerical and clique; a theater of which we can be proud and of which others who know speak in high praise. Now, this isn't mere rhetorical bounce on the part of O'Casey. Listen to what George Jean Nathan, the famous American drama critic, says of the Irish Theater: "I take it there is small critical question, save alone in the lands of dictated appraisal, that the modern Irish drama leads what is left of the European theater. Our own theater is quick and alive and in many ways admirable, but its plays come mainly out of galvanic impulse rather than deep medi-tation. And only out of deep meditation is true drama born. Surely in searching the stage of the world theater of the later years it is difficult to find a body possessed of the Celtic poetic pulse. Surely, except in sporadic instances, that quality which insinuates into the mind and emotion its peculiarly lingering after-image is rare in the plays of men nurtured in other soils. It isn't, certainly, that all the plays that are com-ing out of Eire soil are masterpieces. Very, very far from that. But, as I have written in the past, in even the poorest of them, one finds a probity, a passionate undertone, a brave resolve, and a hint of spiritual music that one all too infre-quently encounters in the present dramaturgy of other peoples. And in the finer plays there is a poetic sweep, a surge of human emotions, and a warm, golden glow that even the best drama of other countries most often lacks." This quotation forms part of a preface to a book published by Random House, New York; it is titled *Five Great Modern Irish Plays* and costs ninety-five cents. The sale of this book may run into many thousands of copies; so one can see how many will come to regard the Irish Theater as something to be held in honor, and spoken of with respect. Readers will accept the statement on the flap of the jacket which tells the buyer that "No nation has made a richer contribution to the recent literature of the Theater than Ireland." Than Ireland.

This is a big heraldry of Ireland's theatrical fame. It would be a shame to let the colors fade or the gold tarnish. We should try to keep the colors bright, or even make them brighter. It is an expansive shield, with room for many new designs and waxing symbols; and we can't afford to let any slinking, shrinking critic push a hand aside, eager to put a new one there.

In everything but politics, perhaps even in politics, Ireland is lagging behind—dragging her feet after her like a half-nourished child. In the novel and short story, Ireland holds her own; but in music, in painting (imagine a Dublin art critic having to rush to the National Library to search out a thing or two about Picasso!), we are still in the age of infancy. Let us, at least, hold on to our place in Drama. Ireland won't hold it long if the present-day drama critics have their way; if destructive criticism takes the form of condemning any new thought, every new style used to try to widen the achievement of the living theater; or if constructive criticism takes the form of Brinsley Macnamara's purification, when he advises that audiences should "receive a play that had no appeal, or was simply boring, in stony silence—just no applause at the end, no calls [not even catcalls?], the merciful fall of the curtain putting a finish to the matter." Finis, the end. No applause, no calls—just the fall of the curtain, and stony silence. Was there ever before such an example of telepathic regimentation suggested to save the Irish Theater? Never, and, let us hope, there never will be again; for the thing is impossible.

To O'Casey, these are but *saecula saeculorum* critics. What they said thirty years ago about *Juno* and the *Plough*, they say today about whatever play he may chance to write. Not a single good berry from the bunches on the tree. Of the horde of Irish critics, one only stood out to say a word for the playwright as he murmured, "One longed in recent weeks for an angry Yeats to castigate the Irish critics for their behavior over Cyril Cusack's production of O'Casey's latest play"; one erudite critic, Donat O'Donnell, mixing a murmur with a heart-breaking sigh, called it "this sorry business"; all of them running, not for pens, but for pokers. One of the tearful lads, mentioned earlier on, not content with a first-night review, ran into a corner to write an "Open Letter to Sean O'Casey," starting with a doleful roar of "What in the name of fortune is the matter with you?" Oh, dear, what can the matter be; oh, dear, what can the matter be—Seaneen has gone to the fair! "I'll tell you," he goes on. "In the first place it is because your overweening vanity is severely hurt. You don't like criticism, Sean O'Casey; you only like praise." Musta been vanity fair O'Casey went to. Vanity of vanities, saith this preacher, all is vanity, and O'Casey is gorgeous with it.

So, young Irish dramatists, go ahead, and don't bother about the critics. They are no use to you. They don't know their own minds. The most of them are influenced by their jobs. Wait till a good critic appears, and then stop awhile to listen. You'll soon get to know him when he (or she) comes, though with Ireland as she is, there'll be but a poor chance for the poor man to live or write. While the dramatists wait for the coming of a pure and proper critic, there is nothing to be done but to go on doing their best to keep Eire in the forefront of the world's drama. Should the shadow of Censorship steal over that deep meditation, mentioned by George Jean Nathan, let the dramatists turn their faces to London and New York; for, if there be fullness of merit in what they create, their work will find there, sooner or later, the fulfillment of production. Take ye no thought for the contempt these places are held in by some of the critics.

So go ahead, my hearties of Irish dramatists, for Eire, and for New York and London. Remember that every Irish dramatist, the oul' ones as well as the young, longs in his heart—and not in a corner either, but in the core—to have his play's name shine in the red, yellow, and blue lights of Broadway and the streets of London's West End. And to quote Nathan again, let every dramatist be modest enough to be "a pilgrim on the road to a Mecca that is ever just over the skyline."

No Flowers for Films

NOT FROM O'CASEY, ANYWAY. NEARLY FORTY years ago, in the first little cinema fixed up in Dublin, admission sixpence, I saw the film of *Silas Marner,* taken, of course, from the book by George Eliot.

The book was far finer than the film. To me, the film sang a song of insignificance, a slow, faint, and foolish echo of the book. When I came to London many years later, I saw *Metropolis* in a Chelsea cinema. Here was a gusty, excited effort of the camera to show, in an expressionistic way, the surge of an over-industrialized city, with its action as rapid as that in the former film was slow. To me, all had changed, yet all had remained the same: the song was still the song of insignificance. However cleverly the scenes were set, however quick the figures moved, they never came any closer to life; they remained forever shadows.

By this time, many were eager that I should become interested in the films. Write for the films, write for the films, was a slogan often ringing in my ears. Mr. Adrian Brunel and Mr. Ivor Montague, two intelligent fanatics for the movies, lured me down to Elstree one sunny morning, convinced that I had but to see in order to believe. There was hot haste and sonorous solemnity everywhere in the place. Producer, actor, actress, artisan, and their allies behaved as if they were gods creating a newer world. Great doors opened onto wide, imposing steps leading down to an imposing room where a crowd of grandees appeared to be enjoying a sumptuous meal. Down these steps came Betty Balfour, escorted by a beau to the sound of drum and trumpet. This was repeated whenever the left foot of the Betty Balfour was lifted too soon, or the right one came down too late. Hundreds of pounds were being spent to bring a Betty Balfour nicely down a flight of steps. I had had enough for the day. It was all furious and false.

The Stories They Might Have Told

In all that the film had done there was nothing to tell anyone of England; her life; her literature; her work in field, factory and workshop; nothing of her saints, sages, poets, rebels or workers—all were hidden away behind the Betty Balfour going up or coming down the stairs. No glimpse of the Globe Theater; no drinking of wine or smoking of pipes in the Mitre Tavern; no Piers Plowman yoking a scraggy ox to till his poor patch of land; no noisy children just let loose from school; no bleating of ten thousand sheep when wool was England's wealth; nothing about London's City when everything everyone needed was made within her walls, from the Mayor's robe, praying-beads, and pottery to long-sword and sturdy buckler; from things meant to save the soul, to things certain to destroy the body; no sign of Prentice with his club or gallant with his cloak and sword; no hint of the great Gordon willfully and wistfully vanishing forever among the fiery sands of dark Khartoum. Only some

Betty Balfour tripping up steps, wide and imposing, or tripping down them to the sound of drum and trumpet.

Adventure Unlimited

Following a brisk controversy about the art of the film with
Sydney Carroll, I started to think of the movies, not as an
art, but as a part of England's lighter side of culture, and I
longed to try to show how it could be more than what it
was—the glorification of insignificance. I thought of how
the film could at least be linked to moving shadows showing
the life of these islands, how it had grown and had colored
itself in hues that brightened to glory or darkened to shame.
What these sturdy islanders had done for or against man
by the book, the plow, the machine tool, and the gun. Se-
lecting a man from many, I pictured the great Gordon, his
rugged face first forming from the folds of his clan tartan,
weaving patterns of life the world over, carrying the silhou-
ettes of the Highlands to the Crimea, to Turkey, to China,
to Egypt, and then fading out in the sands of the Sudan.
Gordon among Irish hovels, in Chinese temples, at the door
of the Turkish mosques, passing the pyramids, turning aside
the Sphinx's question to ask one of his own, and answering it
himself. The lonely figure crossing the sands, the long hori-
zons of Kordofan shifting before the interminable "cushioned
footfalls of his camel." To picture in action and pattern, not
the life given by Strachey to Gordon, but the life given to
him by God or by his own great nature. Here would be life
more picturesque than a hundred Betty Balfours; here was
adventure unlimited, far finer, braver, than the hooligan
heroism of Dick Barton, Special Agent.

Again, I thought of the filming of Ireland's Cattle Raid of
Cooley, the finest saga of her aristocratic folklore, the film

to be founded on Paudraic Pearse's lovely pageant done by night on a football pitch only a step away from Dublin's center. It showed, in fair language, patterned movements, and shining colors, the battle for the Brown Bull of Cooley between Ulster and the Men of Eireann; the defense of the ford on the way to the north by Cuchulainn, the Ulster champion, fighting alone, for the rest of the chiefs were in a stupor as a punishment for injuring a woman who was with child. The darkness and light in the nature of man are shown there: man surrendering life for love of a woman, malice, envy, nobility, fortitude, the lure of glory, and the lifelong love of comrades.

The Idea Hitchcock Liked

And a third, which I actually set out to do: a film of Hyde Park, London, its life, its color, its pathos, its pattern; its meaning to the rest of England. All its patterns to form a unity—its football, displays, speakers, evangelists, idlers, summer community singers; its swans, birds, dogs, traffic, and trees were to mingle together forming a changing and varied pattern around the life of a few people. The beginning was to be the opening of the gates at the dawn of a winter's morning, changing to spring, passing through summer to arrive at autumn, and to end with the closing of the gates again on a winter's midnight as the chimes of Big Ben struck twelve.

But it wasn't to be—the things that didn't happen in Saragossa and Honolulu were more important to the film magnates than those which happened under their noses in Hyde Park. Mr. A. Hitchcock was good enough to come to my place to talk about the Hyde Park scheme and admired the idea so much that he said I must come to his place to go further into it. I waited for the invitation, but it never came;

and I have never laid eyes on Mr. Hitchcock since. So I turned the idea for a film into the idea for a play, and it appeared under the name of *Within the Gates*. So, too, I turned my back on the film forever, leaving it to its own ridiculous gallantry and fulsome insignificance.

An Invitation to Hollywood

There is no question of sour grapes here. I have had many offers of film work, and have refused them all. When in New York in the 'thirties, I was asked if I'd go to Hollywood at a big salary, and didn't even answer the inquiry. In 1944 I got a letter from the John McCormick Agency of Beverly Hills asking if I would take the job of turning Thomas Wolfe's *Look Homeward, Angel* into a film, the letter saying, "Mr. Arthur Ripley of David Selznick Productions [who made the pictures, *Rebecca, Gone With the Wind*, etc.] has purchased Wolfe's beautiful novel. To date, in his opinion he has been unable to obtain the services of a writer worthy of adapting this book. He states that he feels you are the right man to do it. If you are interested, and will contact me immediately by cablegram, we can get you anywhere from between Fifty Thousand to One Hundred Thousand Dollars to do this screenplay." I was interested in Wolfe's remarkable book—and the dollars. It was a temptation for more than an hour, but remembering what Hollywood was, and what Hollywood had done, I resisted the temptation and refused the offer.

In 1947 Paramount British Productions wrote saying that Mr. William Wyler (who had directed *The Best Years of Our Lives* and *Mrs. Miniver*) owned the rights to two plays by Marcel Pagnol; that they had Marseilles as a background, and dealt with the gay, witty people of that city; that Mr. Wyler wanted to set the film in Ireland with Irish characters, and wanted to make the film in Hollywood with some members of the Abbey Theater; that Mr. Wyler spoke at length about me; and said he "felt O'Casey would be the right man to do it." In reply to a formal and polite refusal, Mr. Wyler's soft and persuasive voice came on the telephone, asking to come to Devon to speak to me about the proposal. Having had experience of the persuasiveness of Americans, and realizing my danger if he came to see me, I resisted my inclinations, and refused to see him. There were other offers. Only a few months ago I refused to do the dialogue for a new film; and indeed, a few weeks before I refused an offer for the filming of *Juno*. My works wait there for any film company that may desire them—for an arranged price, of course; and I'm not concerned overmuch with what they may do to them. But when it was said that the figure of "Captain Boyle" was to be all important (probably to the great joy of Barry Fitzgerald), relegating the other characters to insignificance, it was high time for O'Casey to say ah, no, be God!

In spite of powers thrusting big money before an author for work he doesn't want to do, and little or nothing for what his own will wishes to create, it is better for him to go his own way, even if it be with a limp. It is not a happy way, but it is his only way if he wishes to remain true to himself and right with God.

A Whisper About Bernard Shaw

A WHISPER IS ALL A SHORT ARTICLE CAN BE
about such a one as Shaw. A wonderful man, he was born
ninety years ago in the wonderful city of Dublin, capital of
Eire. Seer, saint, and sage, he was usually to be found teaching through a laugh among the community of publicans and
sinners. A leader who carried a flag of rebellion against every
wrong, every pious fraud, every stupidity that institutional
and conventional interest used to keep themselves up and
the mass of the people down. A leader who went forward,
not with a threat, not even with a frown, but with a laugh
flying like a pennon from his pointed spear of thought. He
showed to the self-satisfied bourgeois the indecent pictures
of themselves, naked of every new thought or idea; he went
on dancing round the strongroom of a bank, as David had
done before the Ark of the Covenant, not as the Israelite did,
to worship, but as a sure and sensible man, to mock. He
showed how many of them got the money out of the corrup-
tion and degradation of the people, enabling them to be most
respectable, and to give a grandiloquent worship to their
God. The piercing barbs he hurled at the self-righteous

possessors of wealth, of inherited power, of superior education, prostrate before their gods of stale ideas and outworn
creeds, were half-hidden in the curled-up, colored tissue of a
mischievous laugh; but when the colored tissue fell away, the
barb was often deep in the resentful and quivering flesh of
the victim, forcing the placid, self-satisfied voice to yell; and
on the way Shaw laid many of the bourgeois low, saving the
best of them, when their wounds had healed, from their own
conceit, stupidity, and self-satisfaction, proving to them that
two birds in a bush are often more beautiful and more useful
to man than one bird in the hand.

Shaw's main fight, armed with all his logical art and wit,
was to force forward a system of bare thought that would,
in the long or short run, evolve a sane and sensible life for
all. Poverty was the gigantic foe, the black Apollyon, that
Shaw met on his long pilgrimage through life; and this demon
he set out to kill. Wounding him sorely, Shaw didn't succeed
in destroying him, though he may yet have the joy of seeing
him laid low forever; for on this demon, in this land, Shaw's
clenched fist has dealt the hardiest blows, and he has had no
small part in bringing a Labor Movement into power. The
Lady Poverty of St. Francis is a slovenly, unhandsome dame
to St. Bernard. So far from fondling her, or even honoring
her, he does not even stoop to pity her. Kick her out of the
house of life! He says himself, "In the guise of plays, I contended that poverty should be neither pitied as an inevitable
misfortune, nor tolerated as a just retribution for misconduct;
but resolutely stamped out and prevented from recurring as
a disease fatal to human society." Fatal to human society!
That slogan holds the highest lettering of all the slogans on
Shaw's banner. He found poverty to be in the way of an
honest religion, of a decent life, of sound politics, and the
creation of color and form and line in art. And now, after

ninety years of a laboring life, there are few intelligent people left in the world who will dare to disagree with him. That
is the main reason that made Shaw—a born communist, as he
calls himself—into a practical and energetic Socialist; "for
under Socialism no one would be allowed to be poor. You
would be forcibly fed, clothed, lodged, taught, and employed,
whether you liked it or not; and if it were discovered you
had neither character nor industry enough to deserve the
trouble taken with you, you might possibly be executed in
a kindly manner." In other words, while you lived, you'd be
made to live well, and made to work well to make the good
life last. All this to Shaw was a necessary postulate to permanent civilization; and the world seemed to be going his way
now. These major claims, supported with all their correla-
tions—freedom for thought, worship, or antagonism to belief,
self-expression, sex, and brotherhood—Shaw unceasingly
preached, and fought for them, too, on council, on platform,
and in play. He fought for education trimly at times, and
again with a laughing violence; education for all; not only
for instruction in reading, writing, and arithmetic—so long
the trinity of the working class—to make them fit for the toil
of field, factory, and workshop; but an education fitting them
to educate themselves, and become genial, civilized human
beings; education that gave them a grand chance of enjoying music, of scenting out the flowers of literature, of tracing
the line and feeling the color and form of painting, and of
hearing Shakespeare's voice speaking out loud.

Though Shaw spoke many times to meetings of the workers, influencing them powerfully and making them feel
proud of having such a fine mind as friend and leader, it was
the solid, respectable, serene middle class that Shaw reached
and affected most, by preface and play, by puzzling them, by
teasing them, and laughing at them, even by frightening

them; but eventually convincing influential numbers of them that Socialism was not only not dangerous, but acceptable to fine and intelligent minds, and a movement to be supported by intelligent and conscientious men and women. This was, indeed, a great achievement, for among the middle class were many fine and sensitive minds, writers, men of law and learning, officers of army and navy, managers in bank and business house, in factory and storehouse, with ministers of religion, forming a substantial group of thought and action, giving weight and importance to the Labor Movement and to progressive thought everywhere. This forward step of the big middle class helped greatly to bring about the decline of the great Liberal Party; and even those left of it, who elect still to cling to the old name, are being impelled to put forward stronger ideas of an active democracy than they had held before the great power of Shaw's ideas, in his writing and his talk, collided with their power and influence. It is now desperately trying to revive its disheartened remnants, to rally its scattered forces, and, if it is to succeed in any way, it must enfold ideas and recommend action, which would have frightened, if not appalled, the soft-stepping, sure-stepping Liberals of a generation ago; and the merciless hunter in the woodpile was the veteran, Bernard Shaw.

It is on the stage that Shaw's effective influence did most work, work, in a great way, for God (should God exist), work for man, and work for the Theater (though Shaw's influence cannot be measured anywhere or at any time). He set down a lamp in the Theater that has ever since been a light to our feet and a guide to our path. Long before he started to write plays, Shaw had been known to many as a Socialist preacher, and a damn good one, too; not quite so well known as a critic of music and of painting; but it is, I think, as a playwright that Shaw stands pre-eminent in the recognition of the people. Occasionally, he is quoted as a philosopher, a social reformer, a sage; but, first and foremost, in all talk about him, in fervent approval or cynical rejection, he appears in spirit before us all as a dramatist. As a critic of painting, he seems to be forgotten; as a critic of music, his reception of Brahms as a musical prodigy, but, compared with his great predecessors, an addlehead, is still resented by the old brahmins; and his criticism of Shakespeare, whom he knew by heart, in comparison with Ibsen, is quoted, not unreasonably, as outrageous; but the fact remains that his ephemeral weekly articles of fifty years ago, written to boil his pot, are still alive in seven fat volumes which sell freely and are taken as models by his latest successors. Though most of the plays mentioned are so old-fashioned as to be forgotten forever, the criticisms remain potent and vivid opinions of the drama of that day, and, at times, of the drama of the future; but it is his position as a playwright in the world of drama that is a never-ending delight and a frigid or fiery controversy.

And a hard fight he had to get on to the stage at all. He says himself, "I had to cut my own way into it at the point of the pen, and then throw some of its defenders into the moat." A fine fighter against enemies of the people, against enemies of the stage. With him, the Theater in England began to wear again the dignity and grandeur of a proper place for earnest and hilarious men and women. Shaw claims that the Theater "is as important today as the Church was in the Middle Ages; having its own apostolic succession, from Aeschylus onwards, as serious and as continuously inspired as that younger institution, the apostolic succession of the Christian Church." Even more important now, he goes on, "for in that Church you can no longer laugh, whereas in the church of the Theater the oftener you laugh the better, because by laughter only can you destroy evil without malice, and affirm good fellowship without mawkishness"; though, to me, the philosophy of regarding evil without hating it, even maliciously, must ever be without effective fulfillment of its destruction.

What kind of a dramatist is Shaw? To what other dramatist does he correspond? None of the eminent, save perhaps Ibsen in his first polemical plays; with Ibsen, the poet, he has little to do; and with the far less eminent Brieux—who wrote one fine play, *The Three Daughters of M. Dupont*—he but exchanges a handshake and a genial nod of the head. He is nearer the Russian than he is to the German or the Frenchman, I think. By some cynical critics, Shaw has been called "a poet without the poetry," but that remark isn't at all fair, and true only within its own pontifical cleverness; for a lot of his plays are musical, and gleams of a poetical imagination stream out of them for all sensitive eyes to see. After some argumentative dispute with Shaw, Yeats, the Irish poet, wrote to Lady Gregory, one of the founders of the Abbey Theater, saying, "Shaw seems to have no poetical sense. He is a logician, and a logician is a fool when life, which is a thing of emotion, is in question. It is as if a watch were to understand a bullock." Well, first, I'd say that Shaw understood more about a bullock than Yeats did. Emotion is part of life, but it isn't the whole of life; and logic comes well into life, too: the logic of growth, the infant, the child, the adolescent, the man; first the leaf, then the ear, then the corn in the ear. Christ was something of a logician, and something of a poet, too; and so was Shaw. Yeats was wrong, for it is poetical emotion to be sensitive to all the phases of life, its sorrow, its joy, success and failure, the wonder of children, the splendor of animated nature; all of which Shaw had in full, but Yeats only in part; for he thought as much of Sato's sword as he did of an evening full of the linnets' wings.

Undoubtedly, there is poetry in the scene showing the death of Dubedat, between the young poet and Candida; poetry in many parts of the prophetic *Heartbreak House,* in the banks of the Loire scene between the Page, Dunois, and Joan of Arc; a comical poetry in the ending of the first act of the same play; there is poetry in the greeting of the tumultuous Roman soldiers, falling into a dressed front, hailing Caesar, quietly dominant on the throne of Egypt; and think of the lovely lyrical philosophy of Father Keegan, the silenced priest in *John Bull's Other Island;* and many, many more poetical instances for those who have eyes to see and ears to hear them. Let those who write plays today throw a wider chest than Shaw's, in either poetry or prose—if they can!

He was a great playwright, but the shy, poetic urge in Shaw was often restrained by the dominant urge of the thinker; and it is as a thinker that Shaw takes his place, in the opinion of many, among the great men of the world. He is, to many more, an odd thinker—different from those who seem to sit at huge dark desks, poised on important purpose, elegantly posed, surrounded by candles of knowledge, who drop granite thoughts, polished like pearls, into the bemazed ear of life; like Herbert Read etching his esthetic and philosophic views on stylish tablets: no loud word, not a one; no snatch of a song, not a tap of a taradiddle on the desk; perfect serenity, pure candle light; not a flicker from the flame.

Shaw was a gay one, a demonic democrat; full of courage, vigor, animated by a buoyant wit, devastating to sham and humbug everywhere, thrusting hypocrisy and cruel conduct out of the doorway of life. Hardly a creed, no institution of thought or manners, no gilded nonsense on the stage, in pulpit or press escaped the pointed remarks of this amiable, lovable, fearless philosopher who loved and fought for, above all things, "the golden heresy of truth." Apart from Shaw's belief in Socialism, which is but a common-sense way of life, it would be hard to pin down Shaw to any decisive creed on what the activities of life should be, or may become; of what the stage should show in scene or say in dialogue; or what the manners of men should be in the deeper things concerning man; for he ventured as far as thought could reach, and looked further; and he, a communist, born one, he tells us himself, is the rarest and biggest individualist in the British Isles. But one not out for profits, but rather for the gain of his own integrity; a gain that is bound to grow into a wider display of the same grand virtue by the people who come into contact with his brave and pure ideas.

By many, too, Shaw was thought to be "an irresponsible joker"; but his kind of joking is a characteristic of the Irish; and Shaw in his temperament is Irish of the Irish. We Irish, when we think, and we often do this, are just as serious and sober as the Englishman; but we never hesitate to give a serious thought the benefit and halo of a laugh. That is why we are so often thought to be irresponsible, whereas, in point of fact, we are critical realists, while Englishmen often mistake sentimental mutterings for everlasting truths. This silvery thread of laughter runs through all of Shaw's plays, and most of his writing, weaving a delightful decoration into his keen thought and thrusting satire. This joking sage has been a godsend to England (and to Ireland, too), for his wisdom, his love of truth and freedom, his gay spirit and fearless conduct have been a banner before us, a banner and a bugle band leading the slow, the certain, the glorious ascent of man.

Bernard Shaw: An Appreciation of a Fighting Idealist

SHAW'S PLACE IS A LARGE ONE IN THE NATURAL world, and it is expanding, as a common-sense guide and seer in the way to live and move and have our being; holding, too, perhaps (certainly to me), a wide space in the spiritual world as a dramatist, a critic, and as a lover in the lonelier things of life.

Possibly the venerable figure of Bernard Shaw may some day appear in a panel of glass in an equally venerable cathedral as the lively saint of the machine age and the social revolution. Maybe he was in a glass panel in some big church nigh a hundred years ago as a young, red-headed warrior saint who had died in battle (for Shaw is a saint, the most original saint present, past, or to come); becoming a reincarnation of one impatient at the sleepiness of the church in whose window he stood; angrily watching those who came and went, listening to them chanting praises, not to God but

[205]

to their own canting imposition of a self-righteous respecta-
bility.

Borne out of all patience by indignation at the senseless
show, the figure faded from the glass panel and came to life
as a little boy running round the genteel slum of Synge Street
in Dublin City. Here but the breadth of a slender hand divided Shaw from some of the direct shapes and signs of the
poverty-stricken parts of Dublin. Here, as a young man, he
must have wandered through some of the corroding streets
grouped around St. Patrick's Cathedral, right along through
the Coombe, as far as the Tenters Fields (where old-time
Dublin's linen was bleached), where whitewashed hovels
gave a dangerous shelter to many of the hard-pressed Dublin
workers and their women. A panorama of dirt and drabness
enveloped him, itself enveloped by the enigma which Dub-
liners called "the will o' God."

Shaw saw that there was desperate disorder in poverty,
and he liked order; he saw that there was disease in poverty, and he loved health; he saw that there was death in
poverty, and he loved life. So, possibly, in these Dublin
streets, the resolve first set itself into the young mind to cir-
cumvent this satanic trinity of death, disease, and disorder by
a fight to abolish poverty for ever and a day; and not by being
meek and mild about it.

Shaw, a born fighter, will be known and remembered, first
as a man of unshakable courage (the rarest, maybe, virtue
in the world today). His courage, indeed daring, is shown by
his flinging aside a good and safe job in Dublin which he
had held for some years and his imperious rush to London,
which he knew he couldn't conquer in a day, but would have
to spend years before finding even a safe corner of life, enduring hunger and illness, and risking all (except his soul)
for the sake of the divine call to go forth and preach a sensible

gospel to the yearning, ignorant people, those milled in primary schools into the recollection of a load of unimportant facts, and those grassed and groomed in the heyday, high-toned universities of Oxford and Cambridge.

There was little or no audience for Shaw in Ireland, but England, packed with a proletarian population, foolish, prosperous England (the Englishman so clever in his foolishness), teeming with controversies, attracted Shaw, and he realized that the wide wave-length of London carried his voice far farther than would the narrower one of Dublin. So this crusader, armed with a grand equipment of qualities, set out to conquer, not Jerusalem, but London, to call, not the sinners, but the righteous, to repentance; to send out golden arrows of thought into hypocrisy's breast and humbug's side, each golden arrow tipped with a point of stinging steel; to show, as well, that man's petty and insignificant needs are related to the stars. He became the voice of common sense, the voice of the everlasting republican, the scientific and witty thinker about the needs of man.

As well as being a dramatist of the first rank, an enlightening critic of music and the theater, a philosopher by no means to be neglected, Shaw stands forth and upright as an original theologian. Like most intelligent men, I am interested in religion, in all religions, though, of course, what is called Christianity has been the one that touched me nearest. I have read a good many books about and around religion, but never anything to surpass, for originality and wit, the analyses of Christianity so deftly done by Shaw in the preface to *Androcles and the Lion.*

There he laughs at the belief that the world is packed with religious people, pointing out that those deeply interested in religion are only those who "are passionately affirming the established religion and those who are passionately attacking it. . . . You never have a nation of millions of Wesleys and one Paine. You have a million of Worldly Wisemans, one Wesley, with his small congregation, and one Tom Paine, with *his* smaller congregation . . . the people . . . hunger and thirst, not for righteousness, but for rich feeding and comfort and social position. . . . If Savonarola only tells the ladies of Florence that they ought to tear off their jewels and finery and sacrifice them to God, they offer him a Cardinal's hat, and praise him as a saint; but if he induces them to actually do it, they burn him as a public nuisance."

Shaw leads us very simply and very cleverly through a short history of the ways of man with God to an intelligible reading of the gospels. It is a delightful and stimulating tour, with the great man as guide, through the green pastures of Christian ethics, through the thickets of apostolic contradictions; always going forward, often climbing, but glimpsing clearly the sense, the order, and the ecstasy of the promised land within the changing conception and practice of modern life.

He presents Jesus as a capable, brave, great, and lovable man; one who is fully related to human life, and not a myth that has been changed into a jewel-encrusted painting of an icon. As Shaw says:

"You may doubt whether He ever existed; you may reject Christianity [for any other faith]; and the iconolaters, placidly contemptuous, will only classify you as a freethinker or a heathen. But if you venture to wonder how Christ would have looked if He had shaved and had His hair cut, or what size in shoes He took, or whether He swore when He stood on a nail in the carpenter's shop, or could not button His robe when He was in a hurry, or whether He laughed over the repartees by which He baffled the priests when they tried to entrap Him into sedition or blasphemy, you will produce an extraordinary dismay and horror among the iconolaters. You will have made the picture come out of its frame . . . the story becomes real, with all the incalculable consequences that may flow from this terrifying miracle. The moment it strikes you . . . that Christ is not the lifeless, harmless image He has hitherto been to you, but a rallying center for revolutionary influences which all established states and churches fight, you must look to yourselves; for you have brought the image to life; and the mob may not be able to bear that horror."

Perhaps the mob wouldn't be so startled now, and the awakening of man's conscience regarding his fellow man's right to work, leisure, and education, shown fitfully in some lands, vividly in others, is indicative that the image has left the frame to receive a warm welcome from the people actively engaged in the fight for a finer life and running more steadily in the pursuit of happiness. Not the happiness of mere enjoyment, of the lotus eater; but the happiness of an energetic and useful life. The preface gives us grand, questioning chats with Paul, with Matthew, Mark, Luke, and John, with everyone interested in life or religion, as long as Christianity lasts among the mass of men; he writes as a theologian deep in common sense, and deep in intuitive wisdom; and, if one adds his play *Blanco Posnet* and the preface to *Saint Joan*, he becomes a braver and finer theologian still.

Shaw, too, is a politician of the highest order—the order of the Holy Ghost. His party isn't Conservative, or Liberal, or even Labor (though he supports labor fervently); his party is the wide, teeming seas of all humanity. One has but to read his *The Intelligent Woman's Guide to Socialism and Capitalism* to see how wise and witty a politician he is. Everything the world knows of is commented upon and criticized in this remarkable book. The church, chamber-maids, kings and workers, conservatism, Uncle John Cobley and all, including even Marxism, are set down before us, examined, and commented upon without fear and without favor. He has never written a word for gain, nor has he done so to kindle any flash of fame, nor to buttress any party; but has been as critical of the Socialists as he has been of the Cardinals.

It is typical of him that when offered the Order of Merit, he replied that long ago he had given that order to himself. He would not be a greater Shaw if another stuck a ribbon in his coat. How constructive he can be even when he is most critical! Even the headings of his book on socialism are revealing; take but one: "The Study of Poverty." "Poverty does not produce unhappiness; it produces degradation; that is why it is dangerous to society. Its evils are infectious, and cannot be avoided by any possible isolation of the rich. We cannot afford to have the poor always with us." And the chapter gives, in exciting and salient phrases, the why and wherefore of the headings. Poverty must go. That is Shaw's first gospel, and he has delivered it well.

This man was a great critic of music—about which I know nothing, though I can whistle a tune with the best of them. Someone, writing of Shaw, said: "I fancy he has got more out of listening to Wagner and Mozart than from all the books he ever read"; to which Shaw replied, "Hooray!" For some time, he was an art critic, but, as far as I know, no remarks of his on the plastic arts have been published. Here, it seems to me, Shaw was uncertain: he does not seem to have had any sensuous appreciation of color, line, and form, in spite of his beautiful reference to them through Dubedat in *The Doctor's Dilemma*. It is odd that one so forward in most things should be bothered by painting and sculpture, and that in his one effort to be in step with modern art he called in the scratches of Topolski to enliven his later plays.

But Shaw excels everything (save, perhaps, his soul-searching social essays) in his plays. A lot of what he longed for, socially, will be fulfilled, and so his social gospels will fade; but in his plays Shaw stays to live.

Some critics have said that Shaw is no poet, and a man almost incapable of emotion, opinions that can only provoke in me a grand guffaw. There is poetry in a lot of them, emotion in most of them, and, of course, thought and laughter in all of them: a fine synopsis of life—tears, laughter, thought and song.

He will live in the life that follows his own for his grand plays, for his astounding social wisdom, for his courage, for his fine criticism of music and theater, for his uncanny knowledge of children, so far exceeding the Peter Panism of Barrie, for his fight for the fame of Ibsen, for his love of Wagner, and for his brilliant leadership of men.

A man who laughed in pain of body or pain of mind; a man whose loudest laugh was shot through with seriousness; for though some called him a jester—and he could and did jest well—when he jests, he is clad, not in the formal motley of the fool but in a brilliant tabard woven by the Holy Ghost Himself.

Shaw is one of those mentioned by Yeats who will be remembered forever; remembered for his rare and surprising gifts and for the gallant way he used them. In time these will blend together, and Shaw will shine forth in the cathedral of man's mind a sage standing in God's holy fire as in the gold mosaic of a wall.

"St. Pathrick's Day
in the Morning"

GLEAMING BOTTLES, RED-CAPPED, BLUE-CAPPED, with a few princely ones capped in gold or silver, the excited clatter of many voices, and the gurgle of drink flowing down a crowd of gullets, surrounded Sean and Mick McChree as they stood at the counter of The Four-Leaved Clover, drinking in Ireland's National Day, he with claret, McChree with a pint of double stout.

"Ay," said Mick, "St. Pathrick's Day in the morning, Sean. All of us are Irish for that day, anyhow; the holy-day and holiday of us Irish wherever we may be—at home, on the sea, in the deep Canadian woods, or pushing along the crowd-clusthered avenues of New York City; a sprig of the dear little plant in every cap, in every bodice, in every blouse. Symbol of our faith in the Holy Thrinity, and of—what's this Moore the poet said? Oh, yes: of love and valor, and of wit, too.

[212]

A type that blends
Three god-like friends—
Love, valor, wit forever!"

He drank the last of his pint, and ordered another. "The dear little shamrock has come into its own, and the wearing of the green has lost its kick. They no longer hang us for doing it. Not so long ago, Sean, one daren't sing a song about the shamrock in any loyal Protestant home; and didn't your own brother, when a sapper in the Royal Engineers, find himself undher arrest in the streets of Chatham for wearing a disloyal emblem, though it was proved that what he wore was wathercress?

"All the same, he got eight days confined to barracks, the adjutant saying that the intention behind the wathercress was a disloyal one. Sure, Irish soldiers were allowed to wear shamrock only a short time before the Irish regiments disappeared from the British Army. That's the way they done things through the tare and ages. All althered now, and Irish Protestants hang out bunches of shamrock big as any bush that had hung outside of a pub of the long ago. And near time too," and he held his pint between the light and his eyes to see the ruby shining in its center.

"A day for meditation, what? A bad thing, this thinking, Sean. We remember too much. Let Erin forget the days of old, says Mick McChree. Always scalding ourselves with remembering. D'ye know, I've taken a vow for life that I'll never thry to remember things again. I suppose tomorrow'll be same as usual—bitther cold, with maybe snarling showers of sleet, shearing all comfort away from us when we venture to step outside.

"Well, we've survived through the tare of things down the ages, but, listen, whisper, I'm afraid we're withering.

Even the shadow of what we once were is fading. What's our exports now to them of the time when we roofed the cathedral of Salisbury with our Irish oak? Someone or something is ruining us, Sean.

"What do we send out to the world now but woeful things—young lads and lassies, porther, greyhounds, sweep tickets, and the shamrock green. We've scatthered ourselves about too much. We've spread ourselves over the wide world, and left our own sweet land thin. We're just standing on our knees now. Ara, what's the use of talking: I'll talk no more.

"A dozen of your best, Pat," he said to the barman, and a dozen bottles of stout were lined up on the counter before him. Mick McChree opened his coat, showing a stout belt, garnished with strong little hooks fixed into the leather all around it. He took a dozen pieces of string from a pocket, fastened one to the neck of each bottle in the form of a loop, and then, very carefully, festooned his waist with them by looping a bottle over each of the hooks.

"Specially made for Sathurday nights when I worked in Glasgow," he said, "and very useful still. What was it you once said of that fella Yeats saying about seeing life through either the eye of a saint or the eye of a drunkard? Well, saint or sinner, McChree's not going to feel lonely and lost on St. Pathrick's Day for the want of a drink!

"Now, like a decent man, link me arm, lead me forth, bring me home, and plank me down in me basket-chair where I'll be safe from harm; and go steady, for to fall wearing this skirt of bottles would be a disaster. Hold me tighter in case I'd slip. I was going to say when the call of 'Time, gentlemen, please,' broke into me meditation, that St. Pathrick must be the bitther-feeling and disappointed man throughout this day of all the days in the revolving calendar of the year. For why?

"Why because this is the one sole day of the year that he's taken out, shoved about, and introduced to everyone. Every other day of the year, we offer honor and send our petitions to foreign saints who never did a hand's turn for this holy isle, never saw it even in dhream. Hidden away the rest of the year like his own little iron bell, shut up in its gorgeous case, and stuck away in the Dublin Museum to be noticed only by some poor, puzzled, wandhering American who has lost his way in Ireland. It's given out that St. Pathrick is to judge the Gaels, and not me St. Francis of Assisi, nor St. Anthony of Padua, nor St. Pether of Alcantara; so we'd betther give him more than just a touch of the cap on one day of the moving year.

"Aw, safe in the old armchair. Line the bottles up on the mantel-shelf, Sean, and give me two to hold close to me bosom. Yes, we Irish are too prone to exaggeration. It's a fault that's undeniable, and I don't hold with it. We're great enough, God knows, without thrying to be greater than we really are. Looking deeply into things, we're a wonderful lot. We've worn ourselves away doing things for others.

"Looka John of Ireland, the scholar who busied himself helping the English king, Alfred, to lay the foundations of Oxford University, with the king saying at every tick of the clock, 'You're a sound man, Jack, you're a great help, staying here for years to give us English our first taste of geometry and asthronomy, and leading us into admiration for the learning of the time.'

"To this day, you can see the handsome, intellectual gob of Scholar John, carved in the best of stone, solid stone, mind you, perched over one of the enthrances of Brazen Nose College, Oxford, and it looking as if it was wondhering why it wasn't rather stuck eminently up in Maynooth Col-

lege, or over the main enthrance to the University College
of Dublin.

"Let the scoffing world remember, too, that Feargus, the
great scholar and friend of Irish John, told all, quite casually,
he met in pub or street, seven hundhred years before Galileo
was born, that our earth was round as an apple, that it had
many lands, with people living in them hidden from sight
on the other side of it, so irritating the then Pope, Zachary,
that he took away Feargus' priesthood, and hunted him outa
sight as a heretic; hunted him from the grapevine and the
mulberries to seek a shelter among the wind-torn thorn
trees of Galway and Mayo; the old brown thorn trees that
break in two high over Cummin Strand. But they carried
the mayblossom on them, anyway, that O'Hanrahan blessed:
he called down a blessing on the blossom of the May, because it comes in beauty, and in beauty blows away.

"We're a tormented people. There are the Irish who say
little because they're afraid to say anything: these torment
themselves; there's the Irish who shout out everything they
have to say, indifferent to a blessing, unafraid of a curse:
these are tormented by others. Oh, how mighty we'd be if it
wasn't for the disturbers! They're always somewhere. However silent the world may become, there's always an Irishman
somewhere bawling out an opinion in play, poem, or speech,
embarrassing many, and raising a cry of woe. There they are,
dividing the sacred shamrock and breaking the golden
sthring from our one remaining harp.

"All through the tare and ages, down to now, never a
minute without some disturbing voice—MacConglinne,
Tone, Swift, Merriman, Parnell, Yeats, George Moore, Joyce,
and Shaw: no shutting them up, no shutting them in, stirring us to frenzy, laughing at us, and paring all the color
off our sweet images, leaving them woebegone, and plead-

ing for something to cover them from the cold eyes staring. A nice array in front of the curtain behind, embroidered with de Valera's declaration that Ireland's the foremost Christian land in all the world. In all the world, mind you, and all these playboys in front of it, making a laugh and a mock of the whole conscious conception."

"If I were you, McChree, I'd lie down for a little."

"What! And the night of St. Pathrick's Day in its infancy still?" He got up from his chair unsteadily, and gathered another bottle to his bosom.

"Yes," he went on, "we're too fond of the bottle-cry and the battle-cry; all of us. Oh, there's that fellow, Synge, among them I mentioned—I near forgot him.

"We're all fighters, anyway. They can't take that from us. Warriors all. What grander thing is there in this world of living than Home they brought her Warrior dead? We love all fighters without exception. Didn't we all cheer Robin Hood's comrade, Little John, when he drew a bow standing on the Liffey bridge opposite Church Street, and sent an arrow whizzing away over the skee to Skye? At the Battle of Crécy, hadn't the Black Prince the Welsh on his right hand, the Irish on his left, set out firm, in the very front of the fight? In every battle, if we hadn't an army there, or a regiment, we had a man or two; for it's well known that the one in front of Joanne of Arc, scaling the walls of old Orléans, was a man from sweet Mayo; and the man who swung at him with an axe to knock him on the head as he came tumbling over the wall, was a son of Mid-Armagh. Me own grandfather carried a musket in the Crimea, his son a rifle in the Boer War, and his son's son, meself, manned a gun in the First World War. And all for England! Polishing the silver to shine in everybody else's place, and leaving our own to sink into the dullness of lead."

"If I were you, Mick, I'd lie down."

"Lie down be damned—I'm talking! We're everywhere, fleeing through every gateway from our own corner, while we're young, content to wear a sprig of shamrock once a year, and think ourselves at home again. There's not a state of America that hasn't an Irish sod in its soil; or some Irish fellow, pale as ever, wandhering about its desert places, down to the time two hundred years ago, when Capt. John Pope of the American Army, exploring the Mississippi, tells us how 'An Irishman in his crew, on a St. Patrick's Day, stole the brandy, sugar, and eggs, to make a tub of eggnog, and, after lowering a lot of it, whilst at the helm, ran the vessel into a strong eddy, to get her out of which employed all hands in hard labor for the rest of the day.'

"Yes, and it was an Irishman who printed the first copy of America's Declaration of Independence; yes, the very expression of 'Lynch Law' came out of Galway. When Handel came to Dublin to play his *Oratorio,* and heard the melody of 'Eileen a Ruin,' didn't he exclaim, 'Would God I had composed that exquisite melody rather than the over-praised *Messiah!*' Aw, let me sleep, sleep, and dhream of the days that are gone, boys, gone."

Scalding dreams, thought Sean as he watched him dozing. The Irishman, most adaptable, least adaptable of men. Unique. So many of our greater ones living far from home, and dying there. So many. Darcy McGee, Canadian Member of Parliament, sinking down on the steps of a boardinghouse in Ottawa, with a bullet in his brain; Meagher of the Sword, knocked off, or falling from, the deck of a boat sailing the Missouri and never seen again; George Moore in London, Shaw in Hertfordshire, Moore, the poet, in Wiltshire, Yeats in the south of France, Joyce in Zurich—not counting the innumerable flocks of Wild Geese. Oh, what strange fate brought you to such strange shrines?

Well, we've hated and loved as others have; we have our share of valor and wit, and no more. One thing only we Irish have in full measure—a sardonic sense of humor. It is shared by all—the Irish docker has it as well as Shaw, Yeats, or Joyce. Even this seems to be going. Speeches in the Dail show that Ireland's nimble mind is growing dull. We are no longer clever in our foolishness.

"Eh! Are you there? Oh, I've had a terrible dhream, a terrible dhream!" And Mick started up, staring. "I saw the old saints of Ireland parading before the white curtain embroidered with Mr. de Valera's motto of Ireland is the Foremost Christian Land in all the World, with a voice behind them, saying These are some of me beloved Irish sons who were never bad fellows at all. There they were—miters, croziers, canonicals and all. There was Columba, but undher his miter was the turnip-head and staring eyes of George Moore, and St. Laurence O'Toole's face was the face of that Bernard Shaw, red hair and red beard flaming, and, worst of all, St. Benignus, second Bishop of Armagh, had the mocking, laughing kisser of James Joyce, and them all singing in harmony, We Don't Care a Damn for Anyone!"

"Aw, for God's sake, go asleep, McChree!"

The Flutter of Flags:
A Healthy Pride

I'VE ALWAYS HAD AN INTEREST IN FLAGS: THEIR color, their symbols, their slow flap or quick, nervous flutter. The one prize gained in my younger and youngest years was a flag. Though my eyes couldn't be used in any educative way, I had attended school for a year. I marched with a class, stood with it in a semicircle, sat in a desk with it, trying to dream myself away when the listening or the silence made me weary. The roll was all-important then, and even one more name on it made it brighter and better. The heads of my then-world, though I had won no prize, decided that I deserved one. What would I like? A flag. They demurred for some reason. Other boys had chosen a gun, a bugle, a book; couldn't I do the same? I wanted a flag. I was but eight or nine at the time, but I remained faithful to the flag.

I got it at a great children's tea party, a Union Jack, the Queen's Colors, I was told; a small strip attached to a thin black pole, topped with a gilded spear-point. It gave that boy great dreams of valor and resistance, and many and many a time I saved it at life's risk from the guns, the bugles, and the drums of the other boys, enemies ready and eager to tear it from its staff and defame with the flag the people it symbolized; but their mocking hands never seized it; I guarded it too well.

Everyone with eyes that see is interested, at least for some minute or two, in a flag. They are held high or they fly high, they flutter in the winds, they are brightly colored, and they symbolize a healthy pride in nationality and race. Here they are, and here we are under them. Salute!

Thomas Davis, the Irish patriot, in his verses called "Nationality," writes of the flag:

> A Nation's flag, a Nation's flag—
> If wickedly unrolled,
> May foes in adverse battle drag
> Its every fold from fold.
> But in the cause of Liberty,
> Guard it 'gainst earth and hell;
> Guard it till death or victory—
> Look you, you guard it well!
> No saint or king has tomb so proud
> As he whose flag becomes his shroud.

Many have guarded their flags as Davis counselled— Wolfe the flag of England, Montcalm the flag of France, and the National Song of the United States commemorates the shattering and obstinate flutter of the Stars and Stripes over the highest point of Fort McHenry when it was shown that no one nation could fly two national flags.

But it isn't from any warlike point of view that I want to write about the fluttering flag, but about it as a point of thought, of remembrance, of its color, line, and form; a patch of animated color, familiar to every eye, provoking high emotion on occasions of assembly, of a march, of rejoicing, and in hours of formal ceremonial. Flags form a bigger part in our life than common thoughts can think; and such a symbol should be as lovely as the sensible and sensuous nature of man can make it to be; since a flag of this nation or of that nation is seen by all sorts of people, then the flag we fly should be colorful and expressive, telling in a few words of fluttering its country's records and its country's dreams.

Recently in the *Canadian Military Journal* a letter approved of a design for a new, more modern flag, "a distinctive National flag for Canada," suggested by T. G. A. Henstridge. The design shown in the *Journal* gives the symbol ten horizontal stripes of alternating blue and white, symbolizing the ten provinces. In the fly towards the end farthest from the staff a stylized *fleur de lis* shines from the center of a representational maple leaf, and in the corner near the staff, at the top, is the device of the Union Jack, as it is in the present-day flag of the Nation. It is much more expressive of Canada, and the design much more charming, than the present one of a red field, with the Canadian Emblem in its center and the Union device in the top corner nearest the pole. The latter flag is too derivative, and, even were it original, too ugly, unformed, and unfinished; for Canada's Emblem in its center is so small that it says little or nothing about the country it symbolizes. Apart from the Emblem—which seems to have landed there by accident—it is merely a copy of the Red Ensign, or the "Red Duster," as the flag is familiarly called by the men of the Merchant Service. The important and living place that Canada holds in the world today not only deserves, but definitely needs, a finer and more distinctive national flag.

One thing spoils the suggested new design—the Union device in the upper corner nearest the flagpole. This device as a quarter or as a whole field is an ugly one. It is too crowded, too complex, with its three crosses clashing together and struggling for room on the flag. One cannot get the design at a glance or two, for it is so mixed that one would almost need a compass and square to follow the pattern correctly. Indeed, to me, there is but one flag flying uglier than the Union Flag, and that is the present-day symbol of my own country, Ireland. There is no political opinion in this dislike; it is merely a thought provoked by a sensitive eye at a representation in color and line and form. The Irish colors are said to be green, white, and orange, but the orange is usually yellow, and the flag is generally termed in popular verse to be the one of green, white, and gold.

Green and gold! Only a few years ago, Ireland periodically smothered herself in this green and gold, just as Socialist countries tend to smother themselves in red like crimson. Even today, the telegram envelopes are green in Ireland, and so are the mailboxes. The Speaker in the Dail wears a gown cuffed and collared with green and gold. If we in Ireland decide to cling to the green, it should be kept to the one and principal symbol—the old flag, a lovely one, of the green field with the harp in its center. It should replace the sickly-looking tricolor of green, white, and yellow. It is a unique flag. There are eagles, lions, stars, suns, moons, and crosses in great numbers on the flags of the world; there is but one that flies the symbol of music's silver sound and wild voluptuous swell—the flag of Ireland, now revealed only over the place where Ireland's President happens to be staying.

The ugliest flag conceived by the mind of man was, I think, the banner of the Nazis, not because of its villainous associations, but simply because of its ugly colors, lines, and form—the grim red field, with the black swastika jigging wildly about in a white circular center. It had on it no strength of the lion, no swiftness of the eagle, no gleam of a star, no ray from a sun. It seemed to blare out a deformed arrogance, and stared at the world through the eyes of a beset man violently trying to transform himself into a god. It swarmed everywhere, and the world's thought of other colors, other lines, other forms, was to be swept within the circle of white to be strangled by the wriggling, demented swastika.

Science has brought the world so close together (if Science, through the hydrogen bomb, doesn't blow the nations farther apart than ever) that it is advisable to bring into our life as much diversity as possible, that all our national characteristics, in all measures and means, should be, not only preserved, but developed and intensified to enable us to distinguish the one from the other, and to deliver us from a dull and merciless uniformity. Conservatism should have other colors besides blue, other flowers besides the primrose; Socialism other colors besides red, and other flowers besides the red carnation. These flowers, the one delightful in its lovely simplicity, the other rich in its color and its perfume, are flowers for all to enjoy: national emblems, all right, like the rose, the thistle, the daffodil, the shamrock, but not for a party sign. Diversity without disorder.

In the U.S.S.R., very recently, a fine effort has been made to deliver the eye from the glare of a crimson canopy. All of the various republics have added differing colors to their national banners. Yellows, bright and pale blues, blacks, greens, and whites have been striped into them, so that the general Socialist symbol of red has been modified in each one, relieving the eye, and adding a happier and more comfortable diversity to any fluttering assembly of flags.

We shouldn't be afraid to change things, even change our national flags if the mind's eye catches a glimpse of a more suitable and likelier symbol. The newest conception of a national flag for Canada is spoiled artistically to this eye by the inclusion of the Union Flag in the corner. It is ugly; it links Canada, not with a national, but with a political, past that is over forever. A much better and happier design would be the English Rose as a background to the Maple Leaf and the *fleur de lis,* or even a Lion *couchant* or *passant* under the leaf and the blossom. The Union Flag itself could be simplified, and so improved, by taking the Cross of Saint Patrick out of it. There is now neither logical nor national reason for leaving it there. Should anyone whisper: What about Ulster? the answer is that the vigilant Protestants of the north could hardly object to taking a cross from a banner.

It is odd, when one comes to think of it, to see among the banners of the world, that almost all the countries flying crosses on their ensigns are predominantly Protestant in belief. Sweden, Norway, Finland, Denmark, Iceland have them; old Germany had the Iron Cross on her flag, and Protestant England, not content with one, has three of them in her banner. With the exception of Orthodox Greece, Catholic Europe seems to have none flying. Catholic Belgium, Catholic Poland have no cross in their flags, and Catholic Ireland has either the Harp or the three Republican stripes of green, white, and orange. All Roman Catholic countries of America, from Mexico down, have ne'er a one showing: all the banners are emblazoned with secular symbols.

Well, there they are, all the flags of the world fluttering away, bright and lively, a long way from the first flag of a bunch of straw or a green branch tied to a tall pole as a rallying point for fighting armies. There they are fluttering away, and here we are under our own—Salute!

The Power of Laughter:

Weapon Against Evil

LAUGHTER IS WINE FOR THE SOUL—LAUGHTER
soft, or loud and deep, tinged through with seriousness.
Comedy and tragedy step through life together, arm in arm,
all along, out along, down along lea. A laugh is the loud
echo of a sigh; a sigh the faint echo of a laugh. A laugh is a
great natural stimulator, a pushful entry into life; and once
we can laugh, we can live. It is the hilarious declaration made
by man that life is worth living. Man is always hopeful of,
always pushing towards, better things; and to bring this
about, a change must be made in the actual way of life; so
laughter is brought in to mock at things as they are so that
they may topple down, and make room for better things
to come.

People are somewhat afraid of laughing. Many times, when
laughter abounded, I have heard the warning remark, "Oh,
give it a rest, or it'll end in a cry." It is odd how many seem
to be curiously envious of laughter, never of grief. You can

have more than your fill of grief, and nobody minds: they never grudge your grief to you. You are given the world to grieve in; laughter is more often confined to a corner. We are more afraid of laughter than we are of grief. The saying is all wrong—it should be "Grieve, and the world grieves with you; laugh, and you laugh alone." Laughter may be a bad thing; grief is invariably a good or a harmless one.

Laughter tends to mock the pompous and the pretentious; all man's boastful gadding about, all his pretty pomps, his hoary customs, his wornout creeds, changing the glitter of them into the dullest hue of lead. The bigger the subject, the sharper the laugh. No one can escape it: not the grave judge in his robe and threatening wig; the parson and his saw; the general full of his sword and his medals; the palled prelate, tripping about, a blessing in one hand, a curse in the other; the politician carrying his magic wand of Wendy windy words; they all fear laughter, for the quiet laugh or the loud one upends them, strips them of pretense, and leaves them naked to enemy and friend.

Laughter is allowed when it laughs at the foibles of ordinary men, but frowned on and thought unseemly when it makes fun of superstitions, creeds, customs, and the blown-up importance of brief authority of those going in velvet and fine linen. The ban on laughter stretches back to the day when man wore skins and defended himself with the stone hammer. Many enemies have always surrounded laughter, have tried to banish it from life; and many have perished on the high gallows tree because they laughed at those who had been given power over them. Hell-fire tried to burn it, and the weeping for sins committed did all that was possible to drown it; but laughter came safely through the ordeals of fire and water; came smiling through. The people clung to laughter, and held it safe, holding both its sides, in their midst; out in the field, at home in the mud hovel, under the castle wall, at the very gateway of the Abbey.

Every chance of leisure the medieval peasant and worker snatched from his fearsome and fiery labor was spent in low revelry, banned by the church, deprecated by the grandees; the hodden gray put on gay and colorful ribbons, and the hours went in making love, listening to and singing ditties mocking spiritual pastor and master, and whirling rapturously and riotously round the beribboned maypole. The bawl of the ballad came into the Abbey or Priory Church, and poured through the open windows of the Castle Hall, irritating and distracting the lord and his lady poring over the pictured book of hours. In story whispered from ear to ear, in song sung at peasant gatherings, they saw themselves as they were seen by their people, and they didn't like it; they weren't amused, for these things ate into their dignity, made them nearer to the common stature of common men, who learned that the grand and the distant ones were but a hand's span away from themselves.

Nothing could kill or stay laughter, or hold it fast in one place. It spread itself out all over the world, for, though men show their thoughts in many different manners and modes, they all laugh the same way.

When Christianity became a power, and took the place of the Roman Empire, they closed the theaters, deeming them places of surly rioting and brazen infamy, destroying souls, displeasing God, and hindering holiness on its dismal way. Bang, bang went the doors, shutting poor Satan in with the shadows. The dispersed actors became wandering minstrels, and whereas before they had been thorns in the Church's fingers, now, in songs of laughter, satire, and ridicule, they shot arrows into her breast and into her two thighs. A lot of the minor clergy joined them, and added their songs, too, to the ballads of the minstrels, ridiculing and damaging the rulers of both Church and State. Footsore, tired, hungry, and ragged, they laughed their way along the highway of lord and bishop; they put a laughable ban on everything they knew, all they had heard of, laughing on, though the end of many was a drear death in a ditch, with the curse of the Church as a hard pillow for a stiffening head.

Nothing seems too high or low for the humorist; he is above honor, above faith, preserving sense in religion and sanity in life. The minstrels thought (as we should think, too) that "The most completely lost of all days is that on which one hasn't laughed." So, if you get a chance in the hurry and complexity of life, laugh when the sun shines, when the rain falls, or even when the frost bites the skin or touches the heart with a chill.

Laughter has always been a puzzle to the thinker, a kind of a monkey-puzzle, a tree that doesn't look like a tree at all, but is as much a tree as any other one. Philosophers and sages have stopped up many and many a night, seeking an explanation, trying out a definition of comedy; but have gone to bed no wiser, and dead tired, while man kept on laughing, content to enjoy it, and never bothering his head as to what it was. Crowds of thinkers have set down big theories about laughter and comedy, among them the great Aristotle, Plato, Socrates, Jamblichus, and Kant; but though all of them were often blue in the face thinking it out, none of them got to the bottom of its mystery.

One American writer has connected laughter with Salvation; and maybe he isn't far wrong. He says: "The Church will prosper not through diminishing its requirements upon its members, nor in punishing them too severely for their delinquencies, but in showing mercy and kindness. Mercy is a flexible connective between the ideal and the real; it is a proper manifestation of the comic spirit. God, too, has a sense of humor: is He not revealed unto us as full of compassion, long-suffering, and merciful?" That is Dudley Zuver's opinion, and a new and odd one it will be to many. Not to David Lyndsay, the Scottish poet of the sixteenth century, who saw God near breaking his sides laughing at a rogue of an old woman who got past the indignant St. Peter by the use of her ready and tricky tongue.

It is high time and low time that we made a sense of humor an attribute of whatever God there may be. Why, at times, the whole earth must present a comic picture to whatever deity may be watching its antics. There's the United Nations, for instance, never more divided than now in conference, sub-conference, committee, sub-committee, this council and that council, trying out one question, and making a thousand more questions out of their discussions. What fools these mortals be!

It is odd—significant, too—that in any litany whatsoever, Catholic or Protestant, Methodist or Baptist, there isn't a single petition for a sense of humor. There are petitions for everything, ideal conditions and real conditions; for everything except a sense of humor. If they petitioned for this, and got it, then the other petitions wouldn't be so many, for they would understand themselves more clearly, and cease to pester God to do things for them that they could do in an easier and better way for themselves. They would become more tolerant, would priest and parson, more understanding, more sociable, and, in many ways, more worthy of heaven and of earth. So let all who pray ask for what most of them need badly, a sense of humor to lighten their way through life, making it merrier for themselves and easier for others.

Then there will be something in the carol's greeting—God rest you merry, gentlemen!

Even Shakespeare seems to be somewhat shy of laughter; even he. He rarely—save in the play, *Troilus and Cressida*—goes all out for the mockery of the heroic and the nobility. He often dismisses his clowns with a scornful gesture, as if half apologizing for their existence. He gives a semi-comic and partly-pathetic touch to the death of Falstaff, his supreme comic character, and makes poor Bardolph swing by the neck from the end of a rope for stealing a silver pyx out of a church during the campaign in France. Mistress Quickly and Doll Tearsheet suddenly become shadows; so does Poins. Only the ranting Pistol is left to eat the leek, and then creep away from life forever. Shakespeare kept ridicule warm for the lower class, recognizing in his middle-class way that to criticize the nobility by comic characterization might be dangerous, by letting the peasant and poor worker know what they really looked like. Yet, by and large, we can warmly feel how Shakespeare loved his rascals, a love so deep that, in their drawing, he made them live forever.

Where was laughter born, and when was it first heard? No one seems to know. We don't even know what it is. A baby knows how to cry before it learns to laugh. Its first smile is regarded as a miracle. So it is—the greatest and most valuable miracle born amongst men, though one thinker, Vico, says that "laughter is an attribute of second-rate minds." Let it be, then, for it is a lovely humor. It is so intensely human: however we may differ in color, in thought, in manners, in ideologies, we all laugh the same way; it is a golden chain binding us all together. The human mind will always be second-rate in the sense of still having to learn. To rise above humor is to rise above partiality, and no human being can do this; we are all partial, one way or another. We do not seek to be gods; we are content to be good men and good women; useful, neighborly, and fond of life, rounding it off with a big laugh and a little sleep.

The conscious humorist, said Vico, is a very low fellow. We're all very low fellows, for all of us, some time or another, are conscious humorists. And well we are, for our souls' sake, and for the sake of man's sanity. We couldn't live without comedy. Let us pray: Oh, Lord, give us a sense of humor with courage to manifest it forth, so that we may laugh to shame the pomps, the vanities, the sense of self-importance of the Big Fellows that the world sometimes sends among us, and who try to take our peace away. Amen.

Come to the Fair

WE ARE ALL IN THE FAIR OF HUMAN LIFE, COMING into it, or just leaving it forever. The Have a Good Time of the departing visitor has died down into the curse of Glad to Go. Lots don't like it; some seem to hate it, brain, belly, and bones. Most of the present-day poets, novelists, and even painters are bewailing it, moaning about it, mocking it all. Come on, cover the head of life in a cowl of gloom; keep her nose in, and don't let even the tip of it show: it might get sun-bitten. Some imagine the human race to be near its close, saying, oh, well, since we can never be better, let's welcome the end. We're worsted in the fight, sang Sean O'Dwyer of the Glen, and a large section of the poetic and educated world is singing the same song. They sing the sad song of our fall and decline in a lutey chorus, adding a death-tune to it to make it more lively. All together, lads! They're hell-bent on wailing. Let's face it that man isn't able to make life worth living, and go; for if we don't scram while there is time, we're in for the fearful forfeiture of whatever dignity may be remaining with us now; the blind leading the blind into the dreadful future prophesied unto life by George

Orwell within the declaration he made on venomed vellum before his death. If we hesitate to go by this, then we have the Kafkas, the Koestlers, and many others to guide us to where there is nothing but a blue light burning and a sad little wind murmuring among a weep of bleached bones. There is no prophet left to prophesy unto us good things, for, by all accounts, good things are all gone. The hoary old counsel to Lift up your Hearts has been changed to a plea to force them down; down till the emotion touches nothing, and all is gained through losing all we had. This is the heritage which a hundred thousand years of life have brought to man. Life's walk from the cradle to the grave has changed from an angel's pavement to a crazy one. No hand now writes "comfort ye, my people," even with a stump of chalk on a tottering wall. Mind your step as you go on life's path that provides no foothold. Hope has become a fossil, and probing minds are now wondering what she looked like when she lived among us, walked with us, and had a home in almost all our hearts. Up with the black flag!

The pursuit of happiness, so long a ray of light to a man, is now a vain thing, a dead will-o'-the-wisp, a wandering minstrel without a lyre, a band of pilgrims cloaked in a night of doubt and sorrow, without a staff of thought among them to steady their steps, without even a cockle-shell of a song to stick in a cap. The pursuit of happiness, still in the American Constitution, has been removed by novelist, poet, and priest from the constitution of life. Pursuing it, we but rush after our shadow; the more we long for it, the more it eludes us; the quicker we run for it, the quicker it goes away. Give it up; and don't imagine, either, that failure to catch up with it yourself may possibly beget a parent or purpose bringing happiness to others. Thoughtful life has almost ordered us to change this clause in life's constitution from the pursuit of

happiness to the pursuit of misery and despair. We have
lived too long thinking we were men. The way to progress
is not from ape to man, but from man to ape. Perfection,
sensible people, is impossible; and it isn't worth while for
life even to aim at it, to try to bring it nearer, to knit the
aim into the stress and fortitude of human life, or to bring it
more understandingly to the life that insistently and inevitably follows our own.

Poets, writers, and screamers are going to the fair with
implicit and explicit warnings of coming woe and present-day
despair. A strange gloom and a cursing come over the writers
whenever they mention life or anything to do with it. They
have rejected both Christ and Mithras, and have turned away
even from Yeats's earlier cry that "Where there is nothing,
there is God"; they have found nothing in nothing save a
sad blue light and a murmur of wind through a weep of
bleaching bones. The few who follow Christ totter away
from him; for those who lead them are busy now pinching the
gold the Kings gave Him. Oh, woe, woe to all who dwell in
the tents of Israel, and to those who don't! The struggle is
over, the boys are defeated. Our one sense of life left seems
to be that of violence of one man to another. There is violence in what is written, what is drawn, from the Space Man
in the Comic to the venomous and warring lassies of St.
Trinian's School. There is violence now surging into the
preaching of the gospel: if he won't walk, frogmarch him
into the way of the gospel. Bully for Billy Graham. Fling
your arm up, cry hello to heaven, and leave the rest to God.

The gentler ones are just as bad, oh, just the same; just
as sure of man's timeless imperfection. These gentler, sighing
ones fix us all squirming to the cross of original sin, declaring
that this begotten stigma makes man helpless to guard
against greed, cruelty, vanity, and the itching lust for power.

Oh, the kindly flowers below in bloom, the lark singing into a deaf ear, the stars at night wondering why such a shadow looms below. It began all very early: the heart is deceitful above all things, and desperately wicked, wailed David, when he had done something he shouldn't have done. Yet the harp was always well within his reach. But those who have followed David in prayer and exhortation couldn't play even do-me-so-do on a tin whistle. It's always Lent and never Christmas with these ones. We were born bad, we live badly, and we'll have a bad end. It isn't, either, because of the paganism of the people, or the secular outlook of those governing the Christian world; not even because of the massed heathen tarnishing holy life in other lands; for the Catholic writer, Mauriac, shows us, in book after book, that the Christian woman and the Christian man are no whit whiter than those who couldn't tell the difference between a bandmaster's staff and a bishop's crozier; and the Catholic writer, Graham Greene, in story and play, tells us the same thing, whether he shows us Christian life on the African coast or on our own in bonny-faced Brighton. According to these, wherever you may go, life is lousy. It's an old mood—though long ago, only intermittent—for even the gay Shakespeare fell into despair at times, and, later, Prior declared passionately that

Who breathes must suffer, and who thinks must mourn;
And he alone is bless'd who ne'er was born.

Of course we suffer; of course we mourn; but this doesn't cordon us off from the joys, the excitement, and the thrills of life; no fear. Life wouldn't be the grand thing it is, if we didn't suffer and we couldn't mourn. Of course we suffer, of course we mourn, but not always and not forever. Sorrow may endure for the night, but joy cometh in the morning. No, we won't live the life that will prompt us to die with a whimper; rather shall we, when the time comes to go, go like soldiers; or at least, die bravely and quietly like gentle-men.

Even the one-time ebullient Mr. Priestley is down in the dumps; a minor moper acting the part of a prophet in the wilderness; one without the sad music that breathed over the Waste Land of T. S. Eliot. Mr. Priestley has no song to sing, not even a sad come-all-ye to give a tone to his *Voice in the Wilderness*. To him scientists and politicians, in a number of ways, are to blame for what we bear in the way of anxiety and fear. So they are; so are we all, Mr. Priestley no less than all the others. In many ways, we have left un-done those things which we ought to have done. He refers to the scientists as "Gray Eminences," and deplores their hermetic seclusion within their own conceptions. Yet, the Atomic Scientists Association offers association to all who wish to join it, and issues a monthly Bulletin in which it tries to tell us about the tremendous power, with its many implications, of the new-discovered vitality of nuclear energy. I myself have been an Associate for many years. The scien-tists wish to reveal rather than to hide, and it is no fault of theirs that Mr. Priestley seems to know so little about what they are trying to do. Mr. Priestley places on them the responsibility for the creation of the atom bomb, but seems to forget that they are responsible, too, for the discovery of what bids fair to become a flaming substitute for coal and oil when we have wasted away these precious things, so great yesterday, so crude and clumsy today; forgotten, too, that nuclear energy will assuredly increase the world's supply of corn and wine, furnish other scientists with the means to conquer disease and fight back death coming before his time is due; and, most important of all Priestley has forgotten, they have conjured out of nuclear energy such a dreadful weapon of destruction that it has put the fear of hell into all our hearts and has made every state in the world tremble at any thought of using it.

Mr. Priestley has wandered from the beach, bathed and bothered with colored lights; from the sunlit street, into a tunnelled roadway that goes down and goes on without ever showing a sign of a sky, where all sweet and joyous sounds are muted into the sharp murmur of his own grumbling; where memory is lost of the almond tree and the crocus thrusting beauty up into cold winds, giving way, when their fragrance and color have faded, to the dance of the hardier daffodils and the clustering apple-blossom, dear canopy to the eager-probing bee.

Says Mr. Priestley: "The world we're living in is largely the creation of the politicians, with some help from the bureaucrats they command. The ordinary citizen wants, not power and glory, but a quiet life. He has less and less control over the world. It is one the citizen never made. But whatever the ordinary citizen may say, the careerist politician is completely and happily at home in it."

There you have a roll on the Priestley drum denoting a destiny of death; he beats loud as his arms can, but no one listens, for they are hurrying to where a livelier trumpet calls. And, says I, Mr. Priestley is wrong in a lot of places. Not the politicians, but many centuries of evolutionary life have created the world we're living in; even the politicians are part of life's evolution. It isn't the politician who makes the community, but the community that makes the politician: the politicians are but the looking-glass in which the citizen sees himself. It is men and women, with the help of nature, or, if you like, nature's God, who have made, and are making, what the world is and what the world may be. We want a quiet life from war, but not a quiet life in peace. We want to get going, to do things; not to stay still, within a calm damnation, without breath or motion, like painted ships upon a painted ocean.

Year by year, the way of the world grows worse, groans Mr. Priestley, as if where we lived and moved and had our being was changing to a gritty waste, with adders hissing round our feet, and hyenas laughing among shrubberies of burnt-brown cactuses and blackened rocks. The world has got going, and the world goes on. Look at what it was like when I was a chisiler, and look at it now when I'm an old man, and merrier now than I could be then. Then, where we lived, with thousands of others, the garbage of the ashpit with the filth from the jakes was tumbled into big wicker baskets that were carried on the backs of men whose cloth-ing had been soaked in the filth from a hundred homes; carried out from the tiny back yards, through the kitchen living-room, out by the hall, dumped in a horrid heap on the street outside, and left there, streaming out stench and venom, for a day, for two days, maybe for three, till open carts, sodden as the men who led the sodden horses, came to take the steaming mass away, leaving an odor in the narrow street that lingered till the wind and the rain carried trace and memory far into outer space or into the heaving sea. Hardly a one is left living now to remember how this was done, or the work remaining behind for the women to purify hall and kitchen so that the feet felt no crunching of the filth beneath them, and the sour and suffocating smell no longer blenched the nostrils.

As for the healing of the sick, I remember when life lay down before diphtheria and tuberculosis, then called "a de-cline"; when a saffron bun was thought to be a sovereign remedy against scarlet fever; when a door was opened at the first knock of death. I remember the exorcism of sulphur and brimstone, burned in sealed rooms after an infection, with those who were convalescent shivering outside on the sidewalk for hours till the rotten rooms had been purified by the healthy and holy fumes. Yes, I remember, at a certain hour, when learning the alphabet, *ah bee see dee eee eff gee*, at the certain hour of lunch, a hundred or more kids, hot and tired with effort, drinking water from the same tin mug, water that had been swished from a zinc bucket that never knew the necessity of a rinsing; when no one bothered about a deformity or a disease, unless either was fraught with such pain as to force the kid to become a nuisance around it. Yes, I remember the time when a stout-cutting cane was the means used to inject attention and response to learning when the young spirit grew jaded from the want of even common food.

Now? Ah, now, the kids have a brighter and a longer lease of life. Freedom for them is no longer a danger; laughter no longer a sin. Their ears are peered into, their eyes are watched, their limbs are felt. They have been brought out of the land of Egypt, out of the house of bondage. The kid of the future will be the father of a man, no longer the father of a mouse. The separateness of a child, its distinct identity, is recognized even by towel and toothbrush. The school is no longer grim, but grand; its windows wide enough to let the kid see the world; its desk no longer a narrow desk, but a wide table where it can outspan its whole life of vision or fancy; the walls of that room are blue, of this pink, of the further one a rich yellow; and what fine artists saw are pictured on them all. The seasons spin their way about in the fading of one flower and the budding of another; in the spring bud of a beech or elm, in its full spread, in its tinted change when the year gets older, and in the leaf's fall when the sun sets soon and the stars grow mighty. The children now have the right to the heritage of life. They prance about, leaving the Priestleys to moan in the wilderness as if adders hissed at their feet, and the hyena laughed behind a shrubbery of blackened and burnt-brown rock.

"The ordinary citizen," he says, "wants, not power or glory, but a quiet life." But he does, in his own limited and praiseworthy way. He seeks to show himself to the world in one way or another, innocently declaring himself to be of value to the world. We meet them everywhere, men and women; in the family, the town and country committees, in amateur societies of all kinds; demonstrating their gifts before all around them. Man tries to glorify himself even when he tries to glorify God. We can't escape the desire to show ourselves in what we can say, in what we do, in all we hope. Each of us, at one time or another, desires to have an hour of glory in his life; a day, a year, or a life of it. Most of us would prefer it to a long life. So Cuchulainn did; so did every one of the Irish heroes, known and unknown. If we haven't the gift of a great glory, then we seek a glory more moderate among those with gifts of similar range to our own. And, if we can come to no sign of coming glory, then we daydream ourselves into it. Those who shove aside the glory of the world do so but to seek what they consider to be a greater glory still. The playwright seeks his meed of glory when he puts a play onto the stage, Mr. Priestley no less than another; or when we send our cries from the platform or the pulpit, or at a street corner, or high among the passing people in London's Hyde Park. Let those who will, mock the people's plaudits; they but mock because the plaudits are not for them. Those who clap and cheer a good thing or a great thing share in the goodness and the greatness, and neither in

those who give and those who receive is there a skin or a
core of evil. Christ Himself suffered the huzzahs and the
hosannas as He rode through the streets of Jerusalem.

Criticize as we may, we can't deny the politicians life: we
cannot do without them, though among them there be those
who see life but as a career. There are as many careerists
among authors and playwrights as there are among politicians. We are all politicians when we listen to a political
broadcast; when we write an article mocking one or many;
or when we saunter or hurry to record a vote.

Bureaucrats, born of the politicians, aren't all bad beings.
They have to live and have to work as have we all; and the
State, you and I, can't do without them. They have to carry
out those duties that the politicians have imposed upon
them, which the people have imposed upon the politicians.
The voice of God, which is the voice of the people, is echoed
by the orders and demands of the bustling bureaucrats. We
may curse them, hate them, but we can't do without them.
The people, looking back or looking front, aren't going to
mold a state-life that will be entirely satisfactory to the needs
of Mr. Priestley, or any other son of Adam or daughter of
Eve.

Not all of them are vicious, or inclined to act as if they
were dressed in eternal authority. There are a few who play
such fantastic tricks as make stern angels weep, and force
on man profane emoluments of speech; but they are few,
and can be humbled with a shout of vigorous resistance. I
have had a share of the bad company of officials, looking as if
they were inhaling airs from heaven, but all the time blowing out blasts from hell: once when my mother was too ill to
sign a pension-form, I had done it for her; but when I took
the claim for ten shillings to a Mr. Gunn, Postmaster of
Dublin's Talbot St. Post Office, I was hotly and fiercely re-

buked for committing forgery; that if the authorities got to know, I'd be a goner; and I had to meekly return back home, miles of a journey, to guide her shaking hand into making the sign of a cross on the form; which good deed coaxed the ten shillings from the angry official, who, when the money nested in my pocket safely, suddenly looked stunned when a volley of Dublin's best high-balled curses had pierced and flattened out against the dull-carpeted mind of the bureaucrat; and again, long after, here, in England, when forty-seven pounds was owed in Income Tax on a year's assessment, the Collector called, accompanied by a pompous bailiff, strident, almost jaunty in his movements, halfway on his toes, squinting about the room, pawing the books, while he asked casually if any were precious, first editions, or what? A smiling, beguiling fellow, while the Collector stood still near the door, uneasy, looking like a schoolboy who, having a reputation, had been asked a question by a visitor that he couldn't answer.

They left at last, shaking hands good-naturedly, and they were well away before I caught sight of a paper I had never noticed before, lying, curious and queer, on the table among the books. It was a greenish slip, saying "Take notice that I have this day distrained the several goods and chattels specified in the inventory written on the back hereof, in the premises now in your possession, situated at Tingrith"; and the several goods and chattels were typewriter, sets of books, and table. The bugger had slipped the order onto the table almost while he was shaking my hand; and so is the way it is often done when on some Majesty's Service.

> *What shall we do with the bailiff prowling,*
> *What shall we do when the bailiff's scowling,*
> *Tie him up, tie him up—never heed his howling—*
> *Early in the morning!*

Hang him high on a branch unbending,
Then, when his soul is downward wending,
Bury him deep in his sleep unending,
Early in the morning!

He wasn't buried deep enough; he pushed his way up again; and early one other morning appeared again, and started his sly prowl around the room. But not for long. The hand pawing the books was knocked aside by a sharp blow; the smiling scowl changed to a look bewildered; the pompous body was shoved to the door; the room lit up with the lightning-like profanity of the Dublin laborer; and the bailiff fled away to wider spaces of peace and safety; majesty's troops had gone; but two days after, by post, came the second Restraining Order, listing everything in the room; all my worldly possessions and chattels were hooked to a majesty's wealth: typewriter, books, bookcases, desk, filing cabinets, table, chairs, carpet, rugs, and angle-poise lamp. All to be swept off to swell the mighty wealth of the Bank of England. Yet, the lot of them, excluding the typewriter, wouldn't have fetched a tenner. All that would be left was the bed to weep in. The servants of majesty didn't seem to realize that they were to take away what was necessary for me to have if I was ever to pay them.

A fiery letter to a high-placed bureaucrat brought an important official down to Tingrith with outspoken regrets for the inconvenience caused, garlanded with the promise that the bailiff wouldn't darken the door again; the bailiff's fee was restored. That evening the Irish rebel took tea with the calm and kind bureaucrat, chatting about a hundred things under the old apple tree in the sun-filled garden of the Tingrith house.

With this one diversion, thirty years of life have shown me that bureaucrats aren't worse than others; in many ways, they are often more reasonable, courteous, and, in most instances, ready to help as much as they are allowed. All of us have striven, in one way or another, to evolve the laws best suited for the way we live, for the climate that heartens or assails us, in the surge towards increase of life, already crowded into a small space, the things we work at, the conditions of wealth and comparative poverty, the various ideas, religious and political, that crowd our minds—a tremendous job, that, as yet, isn't half done and won't surge forward as it should till we have more civic valor in all walks of life; in the theater no less than in the House of Commons; in the church no less than in the office of the bureaucrat.

Never mind the bureaucrat—Come to the Fair!

The Fair of Life is a fine one, even though we may, at times, fall from the swing-boats, or grow dizzy and faint as we ride the galloping, scarlet and gold clad roundabout horses, or fail to win a thing at any of the booths; yea, though there be a bureaucrat at the gate to take our money, another near the swings to put the brakes on when we tend to soar too high; though there be committees of them to tell us when to speak and when to be silent; when to lie down and when to get up; how to live and how to die. Let them stick clerical or political labels on our backs, and issue a thousand orders; life can give a new color and write new words on any label, and mind-evolution can stamp a braver and a fairer way through any order, other than those which life herself may give.

Never mind the bureaucrat—Come to the Fair!

The snifflers who sit on the fence, buzzing complaints, fellows who won't come in or won't go out, are worse, more dangerous to the spirit of the Fair, than the bureaucrats: the best of them meteoric—a flash, another flash, but nothing save fine dust falls. Mr. Priestley buzzes at the political parties for their unconcern at the struggle of the middle class to survive, forgetting that never again can men and women become shadow gentlemen and ladies on six hundred pounds a year. Looka, he says, "I don't want to be freer than a Russian, but as free as my father and grandfather were. I want to have at least as much control over my own life at sixty as I had at eighteen." He wants to wear the hat his father wore, and hear again the tick of his grandfather's clock. He can't do either, for hats have changed and clocks are electronic. All very pleasant forty years ago for Mr. Priestley on his cushy way to Cambridge; but what about the tens of thousands of Irish men and women locked out on the streets of Dublin by the massed might of the united employers, chairmaned by Mr. Martin Murphy, as blindly brutal as a rhinoceros and as ignorant as a kish of brogues? What about the Welsh miners, the railway workers, laborers and craftsmen of the building trade, far from security, and far farther away from any cushy road to Cambridge? What about the millions in the Empire of the Russian Czar, and of the countless multitudes of slave-driven souls among Africa's sunny fountains, farthest away from a cushy road to Cambridge, or any other place even showing only a phantom shape? Are his father's hat and his grandfather's clock more important than any of these, or all of these put together?

Later on, he says, "We are now staking almost everything on our chance of using atomic power to replace coal. The changes that atomic power will bring about will be very great indeed. Are we ready for those changes?" Is he? Certainly not, if he is pining to go back to the time of his father's hat and his grandfather's clock. Again, he speaks: "Post-war Britain is quite different from pre-war Britain, and is still changing rapidly. We are living, in fact, in a new society.

And how many politicians will acknowledge that fact, and take these changes into account?" Will he? Does he? Willy nilly he? Not if he thinks that the changes should leave him alone; that the more things change the more Mr. Priestley remains the same. Not if he goes on longing to wear the hat his father wore, or to listen still, voluptuously, to the ticking of his grandfather's clock.

Another of the snifflers is Mr. Malcolm Muggeridge, editor of *Punch*. It is a trial to him to hear any opinion contrary to his own. He has said himself over the wireless that he is uncomfortable when he is forced to agree with any opinions of fellow humans. He says, "The great majority of our citizens get over the difficulty [analyses of politics] by simply attaching themselves to a party. They are Conservative or they are Labor, in the same way as, when I was young, children were Oxford or Cambridge." That last phrase shows him off, and shows him up. We are all either Oxford or Cambridge. The millions of children in England, Scotland, Wales, and Ireland, kids of the slum and kids of the little houses with their little doors, little rooms, little windows, and little lives, were all either Oxford or Cambridge! Of course, Mr. Muggeridge wasn't thinking of these; they were over the far horizon, lost to his view. Like Mr. Priestley, he saw and heard only the tidiness, and from the tidiness, the voices of the middle class of his day. That one-time tidiness can't be quite so tidy now; the polished voice has become a flicker of sound, and has had to give way to the guff, steady and demanding, of the workers' unions. From these, helped by the comradeship of intellectuals, not the snifflers, but those more like men who aren't afraid to combine "the mind of a gentleman with the emotions of a bum," must come the braver, more enlightened, generations of the future. It is these who create, control, and enliven all the jollity of the Fair. Never

mind the sniffler: Let him go, let him tarry, let him sink or
let him swim; he doesn't care for me, nor I don't care for
him: we who are among the flags are also under the stars.

The flags of all nations fly here, all colors, set with symbols
either gracious or courageous. Along the ways, rough or
level, go flowers scarlet with ones that are very pale. Away
in the quiet corners are the hospitals where suffering abides
for a moment or two, unafraid now of facing the sun, and
showing that even illness can be gay. That airy building's a
school, wide-windowed, rooms of differing colors, and tables
topped to show the shining of a rainbow; rooms surrounded
by what can show the children how the seasons change. In
quieter corners still, sit those who find favor with books, or
those who seek to manage in thought the self-conjuring
world of an atom; but none of them so far that they do not
get the touch and tease of the world away from them.

Come to the Fair!

Never mind the organ with its breezy, brassy blare and its
thumping drum. It sounds good to the deafer ears, and,
remember, the instrument that blasts out Yip Hi Addy Hi Ay
Hi Ay may one day change into one that can work at a
Bach Cantata. It is the pipe of the crowd, determined that
every ear shall hear it, a boisterous nursery rhyme for the
elders, having its place, its own manner, and its own sway
over many good hearts and true.

Let the children who are beginning to learn among God's
bright colors come back home to a brighter look on door and
wall, and on the things the family wears and the family uses.
Let illness even be covered with a colored quilt. Let some of
the glow from a long-gone childhood linger on to show the
youngsters growing up that their elders have still a bright
share in life's resolution and life's hope. Let the young live,

and live you as if you wished no brighter thing than that children might play upon your grave, weaving daisy-chains there, or blow a dandelion's plumes away to see what it is o'clock. Let the young weave round them brighter colors than we, in our day, have woven round ourselves. What is called Western Civilization, born of Christianity, is too deeply edged with a merry or a gloomy humbug; too set to fill up life with common souls; too busy sheltering life under blackest bombazine. We have forgotten that Christ wore a crimson cloak and Mary a bright blue mantle. His followers' bravest colors are a sober black and a saucier white; and the followers of these followers go about like jaunty-minded smuts. If those who follow won't, then those who don't will demand more color in life and motion; on the body and in the mind. Color on pillar and post, on door and window; color on cushion in little garden and in little hall. Look at the gaily-colored funnels of life's ship on every sea: the crimson of the United States Lines with its white and blue bands; the Cunard Line with its crimson funnel, too, and its broad and narrow black circles; little Ireland's funnel a rich yellow, with green and white bands, and lesser Iceland, with its richly-white funnel, decorated with a broad circle of blue and a narrow one of black; all carrying about a message that the business of the world is neither afraid nor ashamed to show bright color to those who buy and to those who sell.

The flags are out. Come to the Fair! Life isn't La Danza, neither is she La Dirge. Though the dirge may be heard through the whirl of the dance, the dance is always stronger than the dirge. So let us go gaily about under the flags; not forgetting that a few black ones still fly among the colors, symbolizing the things and diseases that still torment us and sometimes carry us from the Fair before it is time to go.

These flags will, one day, be hauled down, and no one shall depart from the music and the fun before he and she have had their fill.

We are tired of glum and gloom; let voices sound from the wilderness—heed them not. Though a community cannot forever stand on its toes, neither can it lie forever in a slough of despond. Never mind the wailers, lads and lasses —come to the Fair—the dangerous and delightful Fair of Life. Through the desert places and the rose gardens. Come, lasses, with a bow of ribbon in your hair; come, lads, with a bow of ribbon on your shoulder. Come you who can play a Beethoven Symphony, and you who can play on the old banjo. Come to where

The fiddles are playing the tunes that we know,
Where drums are all beating the way they should go:
Hey, ho! Come to the Fair!

Windfalls: Four Short Stories

I Wanna Woman

JACK AVREEN WAS WAITING FOR A GIRL TO COME
and have a light little supper with him in his flat. Between
half-past eight and nine she was to arrive, and it was now a
quarter to nine. Any minute she might be here now, tossing
all his emotions into a hot and exquisite whirl of uncertain
anticipations. The packed bud of anticipation might burst
into a rich-colored realization tonight if he was careful
enough. It wanted a little careful handling, that was all. A
girl didn't come along to a man's flat for nothing. Sit down
calmly together and sing hymns? Not damn well likely. He
would have to move cannily tonight, though. Bring her along
gradually. A hasty movement might frighten her and spoil
everything. It would be maddening if she fought shy of it
again. Like the night a week ago when she was with him
here, and he hurried the pace on too suddenly. Everything
was going grand, and if he only had had the patience to
spread the final fuss over another half-hour or so, he'd have
got her sure—but no, he must try to rush things, and in ten
minutes she had her hat on saying she'd have to go, and
biding him an agitated good-night. Then for a week he had

to bring her to a theater, to meals in public restaurants, and to walk respectfully and respectably with her till he had subdued her timidity into coming again to his flat for a light supper and an hour or so of secluded companionship. She was a Catholic and that made it more difficult, though it shouldn't, for plenty of Catholics were hot stuff too. But Catholic or no Catholic, if he couldn't get her going this time, he'd just shunt her off finally about her business. She went too far altogether without going far enough. It was a bit thick to applaud desire till it was a passion ready to overthrow everything, and then to expect a sudden thought of shyness or fear to trim it down to a cool-centered flame of torturing self-control. Pandering to passion, playing with passion, and then asking passion to behave itself. She wouldn't get him to stop so easily this time. When he saw that passion had filled her with a wild, throbbing, and delicious confusion he would go on determinedly and exact a full and perfect satisfaction out of her. She could even do a faint if she liked; that wouldn't lure him into any frightened, pitiful, or conscientious withdrawal. In fact a faintness would make the job easier. When she weakened with emotion, that was the time to hammer a job on her. So long as she didn't start to yell. That would make everything impossible. He remembered the last time she was with him here how she started to yell when he tried to show her how nice she'd look lying down stretched out on the divan. The roars of her . . . let me up . . . let me up . . . let me up! Pretense, the whole of it. Imagine a girl, even a Catholic, living in London all her life not knowing her way about. The idea was stillborn. He would carry on this time if only she didn't start to yell. Then he'd have to put the brake on, for he couldn't afford to let the people in the other flats hear a girl yelling in his room. He didn't want to have a cloud of witnesses to the thing he wanted to do. But he didn't think there was any real risk of a yell tonight. Even though she did yell the last time there were signs that she was beginning to get into her stride. She came, if she came at all, expecting things to happen, and she had no reason to grumble if she wasn't disappointed. Besides there was the present he had bought for her nestling up on the mantel-shelf in its satin-lined casket: a twenty-guinea gold and jewelled wristlet watch which was worth something more than a kiss. A big expense, he thought, but she was worth it. . . . Oh, she was fairer than the evening air clad in the beauty of a thousand stars. . . . Not quite so wonderful as that, but she was fair, and he was mad for her.

Everything was ready, and everything was waiting for her. The room was aglow with the heat from a blazing fire. Everything whispered encouragement to, and tolerance of, the solace of sex enjoyment. Food, fruit, and flowers; light glowing softly through amber shades; the bottle of wine offering exhilaration; cushions coyly clamoring for the vivid conclusion of passion. And all would contribute to, and form, a happy harmony, hiding in softness and color the savageness and sadness born in the energy and ecstasy of the sex encounter.

After they had taken supper they could sit down courageously and cozily on the divan. He wouldn't force or even press her to take any wine, but if she would take a glass or two, all the better. After a little while he would place the watch around her wrist . . . and listen to her cries of admiration . . . he would kiss and kiss her while he was looking quietly to see how her things were fastened . . . then fondle some of them open here and there . . . so that when the right moment paused in front of him, a little struggle, sweet and rapid, would be a sweet beginning of a sweeter end.

He glanced around the room to see that everything was in

order. To see that there was nothing that would even deli-
cately interfere with the plans or the excited emotions of the
evening. There now; look at it, look at it, look at it! He
had overlooked the print of Lochner's picture of the Crucifixion, hanging on the wall so that when she was lying on
the divan, it would be staring her in the face . . . that grue-
some, beautiful, tranquil, primitive expression of the last
terrible act of the Passion. . . . To the right on the Cross the
stark, wasted figure of Jesus with the look of predestined,
agonizing resignation on His tortured, peaceful face. . . .
Three wondering, funny-looking angels, fluttering like little
birds in the air, each with a tiny chalice in tiny hands; two
of them catching in the tiny cups the blood that trickled from
the nail-wounds in His hands; the third gathering in the cup
the blood that streamed from His wounded side. . . . Mary
Magdalene, dressed in brown and modified purple, kneeling
at the foot of the Cross, the train of her gown sweeping
around a bare skull and a bare bone. . . . To the left of the
picture, the rich purple-mantled St. John supporting the
fainting, black-gowned figure of the Savior's Mother. . . .
Behind, the peaceful features of a valley, with a narrow, curving, swift-flowing brook in its bosom. . . . And high up in the
background, to the left, on a tiny indication of a road, the
little figure of a soldier marching up and down on guard.

That picture would have to come down and be hidden
away for a while. It was bound to be a disturbing element.
Once let it catch her eye, and superstitious fear would make
her briskly button up all her secrets, and fend her back into
a condition of agitated and implacable primness. Besides he
wouldn't feel perfectly comfortable himself, now that his
attention had hovered around it. Something strange and sor-
rowful would be there contesting silently everything they
said, everything they did. It must come down and be set

aside. Perhaps that very picture was the influence that stood in the way on previous occasions when she was here, and was ready apparently to go the whole hog, and then suddenly became hard and denying. . . . Curious that it never occurred to him before. He extended his hand to take it from the wall, and withdrew it again. He wished the picture had never been where it was. . . . He felt a chill thrill at the thought of removing it. Was he getting superstitious too? He laughed softly and deridingly at the thought. . . . It was pitiful that this silly feeling of nervousness should dart through him. . . . He wasn't a Catholic or even a Christian, so down, down you come. He turned his head a little aside, and pressing his lips together, he lifted the picture from the wall, smiling, to rebuke his infirmity of sudden fear, went into another room quietly and deliberately, and placed the picture behind a bookcase there. Returning he sat down, lighted a cigarette, and puffed and puffed, and waited tremulously. She was twenty minutes behind her time now, and that wasn't promising. She really was a provoking little bitch. Between eight-thirty and nine—that was what she had written to him, and have a nice little supper ready for his little darling. Well, the supper was here, but where was the little darling? And at the end of the letter that she wouldn't be later than nine-fifteen, so if she wasn't with him by nine-twenty, he needn't wait, for she wouldn't be coming. . . . Nine-twenty now, and she wasn't here. . . . One thing certain —if she didn't come tonight, she had seen the last of him. He toyed with the flowers in the vase on the table; he read the label on the bottle of wine; he put some more coal on the fire; he crossed to the window, pulled the curtains aside and looked out on to the street; he pulled the curtains back, returned to his seat by the fire and smoked furiously. . . . A quarter to ten, by God, and she hadn't come. If she wasn't

coming, couldn't she phone, and not keep him waiting this
way for her? Or if she was afraid of reproaches if she phoned,
couldn't she at least send a telegram? He took a little book
mechanically, opened it and began to read a few lines. . . .
"Critics have referred to Monet as being of Norman birth,
when as a fact his mother was of a Lyons family, and the
artist was born in Paris. . . ." Happy Paris, happy Monet. . . .
Lucky fellows these artists who could make a high hill of
dainty, fragrant garments stripped from pretty women. . . .
If he were a sculptor or a painter or something of that kind,
this jade wouldn't be keeping him waiting like this, time
nipping into his anticipations of delight with uncertainty and
misgiving. . . . Still she might come yet. . . . Many things in
London might delay her. . . . The traffic . . . a bad jam. . . .
Ticking of the clock getting on his nerves. . . . He'd just
wait patiently a little longer, then if she didn't come he'd
seek a compensation down in Piccadilly. . . . Ten times the
little clock on the mantelpiece struck. . . . He sat like a stone
listening, puffed up with rage and disappointment. The
clock stopped striking and resumed its laughing tick, tick,
tick. He sat there still as a stone. . . . He saw his maid come
in, leave a small tray of things on the table beside him, and
heard her say "Cup of tea" while he was "wyting" . . . "didn't
look as if she'd come tonight . . . wot a shime, and things so
nice and comfy. . . ." He sat there still as a stone, sick and
hot with rage and disappointment. . . . His mind went forth
savagely and sought her out; his hands went round her throat
and he shook her and shook her. Perhaps it was just as well.
. . . What fools men were to lacerate their senses with these
delicious and dangerous emotions. . . . He sipped his tea with
a stiff, set face, and nibbled his toast, while his hands in
imagination circled her throat and shook and shook and
shook her. . . . He would go out and take a long walk, a

swift walk, a furious walk, and sweat all his longing and disappointment out of him. . . . He put on his heavy coat and wrapped a muffler round his neck. . . . His eye fell on the little blue box on the mantelpiece, and snapping it open he fixed the gold and jewelled watch round his wrist. . . . She had missed something, anyhow, by not coming to him. . . . Then he descended the stairs and passed out into the street. She could come now if she liked. . . . Hoped she would. Price of her to come and find him out. . . .

Here was a taxi coming up the street. . . . No, but she might be in it. . . . He'd peep as it passed. Damn fellows allowed to drive too quickly. Couldn't snatch a glimpse of whoever was in it, he flashed past so fast. . . . Dangerous speed altogether. He'd go back a little just to see if it stopped at his place. . . . Wouldn't go back though if she was in it. . . . No demeaning himself that way. Damned taxi had flown past his place. Might have known it couldn't have been she.

He tightened again his loosened emotions, and walked swiftly, never lowering the quickness of his pace till he came into sight of a glow in the near distance that told him he was coming into the color-lighted sprightliness of Piccadilly Circus. Pausing at the corner by Swan and Edgar's, he looked on at the streaming, hurrying, pleasure-seeking, prettily dressed, neatly dressed, snappily dressed hordes that surged along and around, that crossed and passed and crossed again in all the curious, bewildering, merging and rejecting jugglery of human life and movement. The circle of life streamed round and round, moving off the Circle down Shaftesbury Avenue, towards Leicester Square, or up Regent Street. Long, lithe limousines, purring confidently, joining in the orgy of movement, slipped by with a majestic glide, passing superciliously the perky little two-seaters that raced vehemently alongside for a while, then shamedly dropped

behind and followed afar off with a cringe in their perkiness.
Bull-bodied taxis, graceless, assertive, self-absorbed, facing
forward, ignoring all the wheels around them, nosing boldly
up to the front of a traffic jam, standing still or rushing along,
ever determinedly minding their own particular business.
Buses, big and red-faced, abrim with strength, bullying their
rumbling way through the traffic, trumpeted around corners
with engine-whir and horn-hoot. And all this streamed in,
rushed round, and poured out within a blazing halo of lights,
rich blue, light blue, purple, bright red, pale red, rich green,
light green, mauve, yellow, and orange, flashing, dimming,
vanishing, moving slowly, whirling fast, rippling down yellow, rippling up green, gliding across to the left red, gliding
purple across to the right, making an endless flow and ebb of
animated color. Over opposite, a steady, dignified, silvery
yellow glow told that a Cochran Revue had a home there.
The name of an actress that carried a terrible load of loveliness about with her blazed imperiously in golden lights on
the breast of Shaftesbury Avenue. Over to the right, on a
great broad space, a shower of red, yellow, and green stars,
flanked by zigzagging, curving lines of red and green,
merged into a huge, gorgeously flamed announcement of
an unction of beer in flashing yellow, changing in a moment
to half green and half yellow; then all yellow again, with a
crimson strip in the center of each letter; then the upper half
became red and the lower half remained yellow; then it was
entirely red; then all green; then the upper half red and the
lower half green, then it became all yellow again, to vanish
in darkness and give place again in a few moments to the
shower of red, yellow, and green stars that recommenced
its cycle of announcement. On the wall of a restaurant in
brilliant colors were the orange sunbright blue sea and
emerald-green trees of some resort in Southern Europe. The

whole place flamed with the gaudy gusto of advertisement.

But he hadn't come here to look at the lights, he hadn't come here to look at the lights. He came to get a woman. But the woman must be something worth while to compensate him for what he had missed. He hummed softly to himself:

> I wanna woman, oh, bo, I wanna woman,
> With wavy hair and time to spare to banish care,
> I wanna woman, I wanna wanna woman, wanna woman.
> That's always gay, doesn't pray; for last hours o' night, first hours o' day;
> I wanna woman, I wanna woman.
> That'll say, oh gee, my guy, you know the way; now my clothes are astray, you know the way, my guy; oh gee,
> I wanna woman, I wanna wanna woman . . . today!

He watched a man coming towards him with a placard hanging over his breast looped over his shoulders to another hanging down his back. He read the one in front, "The wages of Sin is Death." He looked at the face of the man passing and saw there a sign of severe, sodden, and enviously imagined sanctity. He watched him, moving quietly and obstinately onward, mingling with the crowd, looking to neither the right nor the left, carrying his holy placard glorified with the reflected glow of the vanishing, reappearing, gleaming, twisting, rippling, colored lights of the Circus. Nobody took the slightest notice of this wandering herald of heaven. He wondered—oh that wasn't a bad little bird that passed; face just a little bit too coarse though—at the curious sensations different people sought to bring them pleasure. Churches were old-fashioned. Hanging on still to pulpits and placards. No novelty in them now; what was wanted were Stations of the Cross in colored electric lights.

Ireland's one-up there, for, in Dublin, he remembered seeing a statue of the Blessed Virgin with a ring of colored electric bulbs around her head for a halo. Unbecoming thoughts for a man on a mission like his, so he crossed the Circus and wandered down Piccadilly towards Leicester Square, humming softly to himself:

> *I wanna woman, I wanna woman,*
> *For first hours o' day, last hours o' night,*
> *I wanna, wanna, wanna woman.*

He kept watching out keenly for a suitable bit of skirt. They were streaming past him, many giving him an inquiring and desirous glance as they went by. No, thank you, he wouldn't have any of those. They were all so common, so coarse, and so obvious. He wanted just a little elegance of manner and a saucy reticence that surrendered with a sad, sham charm what it was paid for and had to give. These were rare among birds, for their life muddied their manners as well as their bodies.

He passed into a bright patch of colored light on the pavement flowing from a window display of green, black, crimson, and yellow dresses. Glancing casually at the richer light and color in the window, he saw a woman leaving it and walking off in the opposite direction. Pretty, dressed in a smartly-made tailored suit, covered by a fur coat that reached to the hem of the skirt, short enough to show the full knee when she took a step forward; a delicious helmet hat of modest red made a sweet frame for her face. His indifference flaming into excited interest, he swung round, said "Sorry" to a man he bumped into, and hurriedly walked after her. Was she one? Hard to say. She seemed to have an elegance and taste in dress, and a gracefulness in walk that few tarts had, but there still seemed to be something about her that suggested the possibility of hire. He'd walk on quickly, get in front of her, stop at a shop window, and eye her as she passed. He went by her rapidly, walked on in front for a few moments, stopped at a shop window, watching her sideways as she came along. His heart beat a little faster as he saw first the right, then the left leg from the knee down issuing out of the narrow sweep of her neatly-tailored frock. Trim, and he loved them trim, and with this bird everything else seemed to be in coy conformity with the pretty legs. He wheeled around as she came level with him, and looked longingly and inquiringly at her, but she apparently took no notice and walked on. This was disappointing, and made things doubtful. Was she one, or was she not? She was worth following for a while, and if she only would turn down one of the quieter streets, he'd tighten up to her, and ask her how she felt towards the world. Wouldn't be nice to get a choke-off in a crowd, so he'd wait a quieter chance to find out if her clothes came off easily. He hadn't the courage yet to go up and say "Good evening" and chance it. She might be waiting for some man to do the clicking quietly. Some birds were like that—only out occasionally to add a little week-end tail to their wages; or, those that were a little new at the game, still frightened and shy. If he wasn't quick some johnny was bound to nip in and she'd be snapped up before his eyes just because he hadn't enough of the pure stuff in him to Charleston up to her and whisper, "Say, kid, you'd look nicer with a little less on; oh, you'd look a lot nicer with a lot less on. . . ." Damn this leisurely moving crowd that was hindering his efforts to keep close to her. He could see in the distance the little soft red hat dodging forward, in and out through the people, apparently with ease and certainty, while every man and every woman that came toward him seemed to plonk themselves right in front of his face, and then begin to dodge the wrong way to get by. He hurried and twisted as cleverly as he could. She was a lovely bird, and he'd willingly bury four or even five quid under the world-forgetting trickeries of a night with her. There was the soft little red hat crossing Wardour Street. He'd hurry, reach her, walk side by side and get it over before his halting hesitation lost her. . . .

Now he was caught in a crowd gathered at the edge of the path gaping greedily at something that probably wasn't worth a flickering thought, coming up Wardour Street. . . . Oh, procession of people singing something like a hymn. . . . Church Parade. Leader carrying a cross. . . . Lift the cross higher, brother. . . . Choir in white surplices and black cassocks with heads reverently bent over their hymn-books. Jammed here now for at least three minutes and the soft little red hat getting farther and farther away. . . . Why do the authorities shut their eyes to this sort of wandering, maundering, philandering missionary mania holding up regular and necessary traffic? My God, listen to them:

Lord in this Thy Mercy's day, ere it pass for aye away
On our knees we fall and pray.

No use, gentlemen; no one in Piccadilly has the slightest intention of falling on his knees. . . . She'd be miles away before he'd get himself out of this mess. . . . Hurry up, hurry up; get along, please. . . .

Holy Jesus grant us tears, fill us with heart-searching fears
Ere that awful doom appears.

Soft, sloppy, winding, creeping, crawling, snaily, snobby, snaring bastards dividing him from all the heart-quickening

gifts beneath the red hat, the tailored suit, and the silk stockings. . . . Oh, if he were a savage how he'd like to jump in
and spear a hundred per cent of them. . . . Not a sign of her
now. That procession had crossed the hunt and saved the
quarry. He breathed deeply in disappointment and rancor.
And they did this sort of thing out of their love for men.
Annoying thing to come up against and mingle with his
present mood. Even if he did manage to get into touch with
her again, things wouldn't feel so comfortable, for he knew
the hymn by heart, and here it was maliciously humming in
his mind, blunting the innocence of his eagerness. She might
be anywhere now. . . . Grant us tears . . . fill us with heart-
searching fears. . . . No use of looking any longer. . . . To
go home is best. . . . Nothing in skirts could interest him now
till he'd forgotten a little about the girl in the soft red hat.
A peach. . . . No doubt about it, he'd missed a peach. . . .
Lord in this Thy mercy's day, ere it pass for aye away. . . .
Bakerloo, from Piccadilly to Baker Street, and then a bus to
Swiss Cottage. . . . On our knees we fall and pray. . . . It
was just twelve anyhow, and only the "Pros" that time has
tossed a lot paraded now. . . . Strange, determinedly sliding
movement of the escalators. . . . Wonder how the procession
would look coming up or going down one of them. . . . Keep
time and step off together, please. . . . Trains going west . . .
that was his platform . . . empty carriage . . . drowse to Baker
Street. . . . When eyes are closed curious feeling runs through
body with the gentle, rumbling shake in the movement of a
tube train. . . . Feeling of motion and of rest . . . Oxford
Circus. . . . Two more stations. . . . Somebody coming in . . .
sitting opposite him. . . . Woman . . . see so by shoes. Some
uninteresting looking old cow or young heifer not worth
noticing. . . . Keep his eyes closed. . . . Regent's Park. . . .
Next stop. . . . Nothing exciting in the night after all his

hope. . . . Procession spoilt everything. . . . Procession spoilt sport. . . . Perhaps it was just as well to get a check now and again. Thoughtless compliance with the complaints of sex was bound to overbalance his nervous system, and that wouldn't do at all. He was almost glad now that the procession had poked its way between him and his desire to make a fool of himself. He wouldn't feel that seething sense of remorse that invariably followed a night with a new woman; the dead, revolting dissatisfaction of deliriously misspent energy and passion; the miserable surge of empti-ness that followed the feat of giving too much for a short enjoyment. He could rest and go to sleep without the soul-nagging sense of sex weariness. Perhaps this would be the first step towards a stronger self-directed life, of decided and persistent effort towards self-control. Back to a virtuous bed. . . . Good bed; better bed; best bed.

Baker Street . . . oh hell, don't stir. . . . Fur coat, tailored suit, and soft red hat sitting opposite. Damn fool keep eyes closed. Where's she getting. . . . Passing Marylebone. Oh, that was a cute glance. . . . Measuring up his naughtiness. Opening her fur coat. Too hot in here, dearie. Good sign; wants to show her legs. . . . Passing Warwick Avenue. . . . She's a peach, boys, she's a peach. . . . A sense of uncom-fortable fullness made his heart beat faster. . . . He lighted a cigarette, and his hand shook. . . . His nerves were tingling again. . . . Oh, gee, my guy, you know the way, now my clothes are astray, you know the way, my guy, oh gee, you wanna wanna wanna woman. . . . Getting out at Maida Vale. . . . So was he, you bet. . . . Along the passages to the lift. . . . He feverishly paid his excess fare from Baker Street to Maida Vale to the attendant, watching her from the other end of the lift. Anyhow, she knew that he was interested in her. She had seen him look at her with suggestion in his eyes, and had shown no annoyance. Indeed, she had sent him glances that seemed to venture an invitation. The lift doggedly moved upwards, came to the road-level, the gates crashed open, and they passed out into the street. If she hopped off quickly now, all was over, but if she went on slowly the thing promised fruit. The street was quiet and restful, animated only by an odd taxi cruising past. Up in the sky, in the northwest shone The Plow and in the north-east sparkled The Lyra. . . . She went along slowly. His mouth that had dried twitched a little, and his heart beat unpleasantly as he hurried on and walked by her side. . . . "Good evening," he murmured nervously. She gave a slow, careless glance at him, and continued to walk on slowly. . . . "The air is very clear tonight," he went on, "and the stars are remarkably plain. . . ."

She turned her head to him, smiled and said, "What are you doing with yourself at this time of night?"

He stammered a little as he murmured, "Oh, just taking a stroll round about thoughtlessly."

"You passed me in Piccadilly," she asked, "didn't you?"

"Yes," he said, "I think that I did see you somewhere in Piccadilly."

She's very cool about it all, he thought; she must be a bird after all.

"Well, now that you've seen me again," she said, "do you fancy me as much as ever?"

She was a Pro then, so he'd have to be carefully indifferent, for the more desire he showed, the higher would be the fee. So he kept silent.

"You'd like to come up to my flat and have a drink or a cup of tea, wouldn't you?" she asked.

"Yes, I wouldn't mind," he answered.

"I'm afraid if I let you come you might want to be naughty, would you, my dear?" she asked smilingly.

"I might, you never know," he answered.

"If I let you come, and was very nice to you, you'd give me a little present, darling?"

"Oh, of course," he replied.

"How much?"

"Two pounds," he murmured.

"You're not out to spend much!" she said disdainfully, hastening away from him. "Cheerio, darling!"

He hurried after her and said, "Don't run away, dear; let's talk together for a minute or two. There's no necessity to rush off in a rage."

"I'm not in a rage, dear," she said, "but I don't let myself be man-mauled for two quid. Go back to Piccadilly and you'll get lots of girls ready to accommodate themselves to your idea of generosity."

He was fascinated; she was a rare bird, and he didn't want to lose her, but he wanted to get his pleasure as cheaply as possible.

"How much do you want then, to let me go home and make a fuss of you?" he asked.

"Five pounds, at least," she said.

"That's a lot of money for a few hours. I'll give you four," he bargained.

"Five, dear, or there's nothing doing. If you fancied me so much, and followed me so long, I'm worth a fiver."

He walked beside her pondering, fingering in his pocket one note from another and counting thoughtfully. . . . One . . . two . . . three . . . four . . . five . . . six . . . seven . . . and a ten-bob note.

"Oh, be a sport," she said encouragingly, "and I'll give you a right good time."

"All right," he answered, "I'll give the fiver."

Stopping at a house of flats, she took a key from her bag, opened the hall door, ascended to the first floor, where she rang a bell; the door of the flat was opened by a maid who gave him a quick, furtive look as they entered. She brought him into a sitting-room, quietly and comfortably furnished with easy-chairs and lounges. Some ordinary landscapes were on the walls, and on the mantelpiece were two large photographs of pretty women pictured in a state of saucy and semi-nudity. She pulled brilliantly green curtains that were on the window closer together as she said to him: "Take off your coat, dear, and make yourself at home."

To the right of the fireplace were six shelves filled with books. Spicy, naughty, and nonsensical, the lot of them, he thought.

"Tilly," she called to the maid, "bring me and my gentle-man friend some tea and biscuits."

She took off her fur coat and soft red hat, and sat down in one of the easy-chairs before the fire, crossing one leg over the other. "Nice to be sitting before a fire on a cold night like this," she said as she sipped her tea.

"Nothing better," he said, "with a pretty girl waiting to be nice to you."

"And with a man that wants to be naughty," she added.

"I see," he said, "you're interested in books."

"Just a little," she answered, glancing at the shelves. "They pass in a pleasant way many a dull hour."

"Who's your favorite writer?" he asked.

"I've none," she said. "I like Hardy, France, and Dostoev-sky a lot."

"Dostoevsky's one of the Russian fellows," he said; "don't know how anyone could be interested in such a writer, though I haven't read him myself."

"If you haven't, how do you know?" she asked.

"I know from those that tried to read him," he said, "that he's a terrible writer."

"Yes," she admitted, "he is, sometimes . . . terrible."

"Who's the johnny that wrote all the books you have covered in green?"

"Balzac," she said. "Wonderful writer. Never read his *Poor Relations*? *Madame Marneffe, Baron Hulot,* and *Cousin Pons* —far greater than his better known *Père Goriot*. Powerful realism, and pathetic, remorseless imagination."

"Come over here," he said, "and sit beside me; I don't want to be bothered about Balzac just now."

She got up out of the chair, smiled, lifted her skirt a little, danced over to him, and sat down by his side on the settee. She put an arm round his neck, kissed him quick and cooed into his face, the suggestive look in her eyes hardening a little.

"Now, darling," she whispered, "what about my little present? Not nice to talk about it, but it's best to get all the nasty things over at once."

"Oh, I'll give it to you all right," he said.

"I know, but I might as well have it now."

"You won't trust me?" he asked peevishly.

"I know you're a sport," she said, "but it's just as well to get it over and done with before we begin to amuse ourselves."

He took the notes from his pocket with a serious, half-timid sigh, and handed her five, saying, "Here you are, five of the best and brightest."

She quickly and gently caught hold of his hand, and with

a confident smile said, "The ten-bob note as a little present for the maid, dear."

"Oh, now you've had enough out of me," he protested.

"I always get a present for the maid," she insisted; "she's a dear woman, and I never forget to ask for a little tip for her. . . . Go on, don't spoil things now by a mean refusal of such a small thing; we're getting on so nicely together."

And the ten-shilling note was pulled gently from his hand, added to the five, and all were locked away in a drawer of a cabinet that stood quietly and expectantly close to the window. Then she removed her skirt, coat, and blouse, pulled loose the ribbons threading the shoulders of her cami-nickers, showing her breasts, animatedly sat beside him, put her arm round him, and murmured, "Now, darling, don't you like me a lot better with a little less on?"

He abandoned himself to the surge of desire that swept through him. He caught her in his arms and tried to bend her back on the settee. With a sour laugh she freed herself, crossed the room, and opened a door opposite.

"Come into the bedroom, dear," she said, "where we'll have plenty of room."

*　*　*

What a fool he had been to stop so long with her. It was maddening to have to stay on here in bed beside her, after having got all that he wanted. She had fallen asleep, while he was still awake listening to the ticking of the little clock at the other end of the room, thinking and cursing deeply in his mind about the weariness and waste of affection, energy, and money that made this honeycomb a bitterness and a loathing to him. He sat up in bed and winked his eyes several times to press the heaviness out of them. The first glimpse of a cold dawn was trickling in through the green curtains that covered the window. The room that had looked so full of nimbly dancing promises of pleasure was now filled with a sickly sense of weariness, and seemed to be stuffy with the breath of dead things. He moved as far away as possible from his companion, and looked down at her sleeping there with her bare breasts, tossed hair, and partly open mouth. Attractiveness had ceased to meddle with her now. He felt a wish to beat till he bruised the breasts that he had fiercely fondled only a few hours ago. Tear and rend them for the ruin of tiredness and silent agony of remorse that they had helped to bring upon him. Lying here for three hours he had been trying to deafen himself to his thoughts, and put away the memories that had stormed his mind before he had bargained with this unashamed whore that now lay asleep and naked beside him. . . . The procession that had cut across his path and the hymn they had been singing. . . . "Holy Jesus, grant us tears, fill us with heart-searching fears. . . ." Keep it out, keep it out. . . . I wanna woman, I wanna woman, with wavy hair, to banish care, I wanna woman . . . keep it out, keep it out. . . .

She had felt him moving and was murmuring drowsily, "Lie down, sweetie; cold coming in under clothes, and I've nothing on . . . lie down, sweetie."

He plunged down into the bed again, and roughly pushed away a leg of hers that had wandered over near him. "Not so rough, dear," she murmured.

What vice-armored souls these women had. But perhaps it was better if one wanted to be anything, to be that thing right out. Wallowing grandly in her own shame. Let the light of dawn but mount a little higher up and he'd slide from bed, and dress and leave this place of poisoned satisfaction.

Her eyes opened a little and a peculiar, spiteful smile darkened them, and her hand began to fondle him. "Keep that damned hand quiet," he said, as he jerked it away with a savage and resentful movement.

"Sweetie doesn't want pretty Alice any more," she murmured, giving his cheek a malicious caress.

"I'm going out of this," he said surlily, getting out of bed and beginning to creep shiveringly into his clothes. Glancing in the glass he saw himself hollow-eyed, hair-tossed, with his chin darkened where his beard was beginning to show strongly.

She sat up sleepily, resting on her elbow, took a card from a drawer in a bedside table, held it out to him and said, "Card, dear, double ten double nine Berkeley. You might like to ring me up some evening."

Paying no attention to her, he tugged on his heavy coat, pulled on his hat, wrapped his muffler round his neck, glanced at the cabinet where his five pounds ten were stored, and said, "I'm off now, good-bye."

She snuggled down in the bed, pulled the clothes warmly round her shoulders and under her chin, and murmured, "Don't make a noise, dear, to wake the maid . . . she's such a dear woman, and I'm very fond of her . . . close the street door after you as gently as you can. . . . Cheerio, darling."

It was cold and damp coming into the air of the street. Leaving that whore warmly nested in her bed, too. He was done with women for a long time. He kept his head bent as he slouched sleepily homewards. The exhaustion of the night was letting this dampness into his marrow. Ding, dong, ding, dong, dell. . . . Some damn church bell ringing for some damn service. Waste of time. . . . Never keep people from making fools of themselves. . . . Ding, dong, dell, sinners sent to hell, to clothe their pain in an everlasting yell; so cease to do evil, learn to do well; ding, dong, ding, dong, ding, dong, dell. . . . Palpitating nonsense, these bells.

He opened the door of his flat, and let himself shivering in. He would sleep till about five in the evening, then he would have a warm bath, a brandy and soda, a good dinner, and he would feel a lot better. He stripped to his shirt, and let his clothes slide from him in a heap on the floor. He slipped his pajamas on over his shirt. Must be getting on for eight, now. ... He bent his arm to look at his wrist. ... Jesus, he had left the wristlet watch in the house of the whore! He didn't—he couldn't—have stuck it in one of his pockets. ... He rummaged fiercely in the pockets of his trousers. ... No, and he flung them savagely back on the floor. ... His coat? He rummaged through the pockets of the coat ... no, and flung it down again on the floor. ... He remembered ... he had put it down on the little table beside the bed, and had forgotten it was there in his eagerness to get away from the place. ... Oh, the idiot, the fool, the ape, to forget to take it up and put it on when he was leaving. Oh, what a stinkingly stupid thing to do. ... What did he want to bring it out with him for? And he had no idea of the street or the house, only that they were somewhere in Maida Vale. ... He had hurried away noticing nothing. ... Wouldn't take her card even. ... Hadn't the least idea of her telephone number. ... A big-brained idiot, that's what he was. ... She had been well paid for her favors—five pounds ten and a wristlet watch and bangle worth twenty guineas. ... She was laughing at him now ... and fitting it on. ... Pity it couldn't turn to steel and stop the circulation of her blood. ... He turned down the clothes and stormed into bed. As he lay down his eye caught sight of Lochner's Crucifixion hanging again on the wall over his bed. ... That blasted maid of his couldn't keep from ferreting around. ... Fished it out from behind the bookcase and replaced it on the wall. ... Frantic to meddle with everything. ... Mocking him there with its tale of tragedy. . . . Take him weeks now to recover from the shock of his stupidity. He pressed himself down on the bed in a rush of rage. His head throbbed with the nerve-rack of his loss. Forget it and sleep. . . . That's all he could do . . . sleep and forget it. . . . He lay silent. . . . The telephone bell rang, rang . . . rang. He snapped down the receiver and bellowed, "Hello? yes, this is Mr. Avreen. . . . Yes, it's Jack. . . . No, you can't come tonight. . . . I'll be engaged till long after midnight. . . . If you long to see me, why didn't you come last night? Explain . . . yes it will need some explanation . . . Angry? why of course I'm angry. No, I won't post the watch to you, or see you tonight either. . . . Must go now to keep an appointment." And he firmly and angrily replaced the receiver. . . . Then he gathered the clothes tightly around him, closed his eyes, and quivered in a mad medley of thoughts. This was the crowning of his foolishness. He stiffened with repressed and remorseful rage. . . . The telephone bell rang . . . and rang . . . and rang. . . . Ringing me again, he thought; well, let her ring.

A faint trickling beam of light from a timid rising sun crept in through the window and spread over the picture of the Crucifixion, showing wanly to the right the figure of Christ hanging on the Cross, the three funny little black-robed angels with tiny chalices in tiny hands catching the blood that dripped from hands and side; Mary Magdalene, in her brown and purple robes, kneeling at the foot of the Cross; to the left the crimson-mantled St. John supporting the fainting Mother; the brook swiftly flowing through the peaceful valley, and away in the dim distance, the little figure of a careless soldier marching up and down on guard.

And he tightened his teeth together, cursed deeply and lay still, as the telephone bell rang . . . rang . . . rang.

The Star-Jazzer

THE STARS GLITTERED IN THE SKY AND THE FROST glittered on the ground as she bent her head and watched the water flowing slowly into the bucket. It was a blasted shame that they didn't get a pipe to give a quicker flow for the poor people. It was terrible when the ten families that lived in the house were looking for water at the same time. And when the people that lived in the houses on each side were at their own pipes, this one dwindled down to a tiny, maddening dribble of drops. She often ground her teeth when she came into the yard for a bucketful to find before her one washing a cabbage under a flow of water, another waiting her turn with a basin of spuds, and a third humming a tune, with a kettle to be filled. The best plan was to fill a pail overnight, so as to be certain that nothing would delay her husband from his hasty wash and hurried breakfast before he sallied out to work. That was the bell of St. George's chiming twelve o'clock, pushing another Tuesday up against the pile of Tuesdays that she had put behind her. Tuesday . . . the day she hated, the day she dreaded, the day she felt was always in front of her. The day that, when she thrust it behind her, seemed with a rapid, wheeling circle to stand before her again. The day that, when through the week she had dried the clothes, ironed and aired them, came up, shook her from bed at six o'clock to restart the washing of them and kept her going sullenly, ceaselessly, and silently, with pain and without pity, till twelve o'clock at night, carrying up clean water, washing, wringing, rinsing, washing, wringing, and rinsing and wringing, and carrying down ten flights of stairs the water soiled with the mud of clothes after a week of wearing. For eight years now, every Tuesday, on the stairs coming down, on the stairs going up, or standing in the yard as she was now, except when she was having a kid, she had listened to the bell of St. George's chiming the twelve strokes that divided one day from another.

She shivered, glanced up at the sky, and wondered what they called the star that glittered right over her head. It seemed to stand out in the black breast of the sky in a fuller and more friendly way than the others; you could say the others shone, but this one gleamed. Her mother had often told her when she was a kid that God was hiding behind the stars; that they were resting-places for the angels' feet when they were flying from one part of the heavens to the other; and that at midnight on Christmas Eve all the stars danced. She wondered would it be a schottische or a waltz they danced. She had never yet met anybody that saw them dancing. Like many another yarn, she supposed it was all a fake. Though anything could have happened on the first midnight eve of the first Christmas. She could picture the Infant lying in the manger motionless, or stretching out His arm towards His Mother, with St. Joseph standing stiff behind her, and the shepherds in one corner, and the kings in the other, staring open-mouthed at the now delicate, now delirious dance of the stars in the heavens. . . . Wouldn't it be

funny now if they started to do a jazz dance across the sky?
She'd pick the movement up, and join them with a rush.
"Chase me, Charlie, through the clouds and over the sky-i-i!"
Not tonight though, after a day of washing the clothes of
Jack and herself and the kids that were dirtied through the
week's wear in the streets and in the tenement. An elegant
sight she'd look with her legs all soppy wet from the thighs
down, stiff and tightened up with the work she'd done, doing
a Jazz or a Charleston round a star. Step, step, together, dip;
step, step, together, dip. Dipping, maybe, when she should
be bringing her feet together; and stepping when she should
be doing a dip. She'd have to postpone it to a happier day;
but give her a month's rest from the husband and kids, a
few pounds for a new little frock, and she'd do a Jazz or a
Charleston in the full, flooding light of the biggest star in
the firmament. . . . How do you do do dodoodle loodo do
dooo. . . . Kick them up and kick them high; show a knee and
show a thigh, don't be shy, to the stars shining bright in the
sky . . . in the sky. . . . She felt a surge moving through her
body. A desire to circle around the lonely yard, surrounded
by the surly-featured tenements, now dark and still, sheltering the sleeping, to sing softly, to move and wag her body
to the rhythms of a Charleston or a Jazz; to show the star
that, in spite of seven kids carried in eight years, her figure
was still shapely; that her hair was still long and thick, and
the gold gleams in the brown weren't all gone; that her face,
hiding its lines in the darkness, had all its beauty left. She
bent back her head and stared up at the star. Then she began
to move her body to the tune and motions of a Jazz, circling
round the yard while the water poured lazily from the pipe,
filled the pail, and flowed over the rim, down the sides, and
disappeared into the gully beneath. She stepped forward
with her left foot, then with her right, brought her feet to-

gether and dipped by bending her legs backward from the
knees. She moved forward, twisted, turned and came back
again. Step, step, step, together, dip, with her head bent
back, gazing at the star. As she moved she felt her wet skirt
sopping, sopping against her knees, so as she moved on, step,
step, she unloosened her skirt at the waist, together, dip;
and as she rose to step forward again, the skirt fell from her,
and she danced on in her short black petticoat. With her hair
flowing down, in her untidily buttoned blouse, dingy black
petticoat, patched shoes, and imitation silk stockings, ribbed
and scarred with many a mended ladder, round the tenement-
enclosed yard she turned, bent, circled, advanced, retreated,
across and around the yard, singing with her head bent back,
staring at the star—

Now a woman, and once a kid
That came from God—oh yes, I dih-i-d;
I came from God and I settled down
In this damn'd and dreary one-horse tow-ow-n;
I came from God and I settled down
In this damn'd and dreary one-horse town!

I met a man and lost my head,
Oh yes, I did, I lost my he-he-head;
And him I wed; he gives me bread,
And fits my life into a four-post be-he-ed;
And him I wed; he gives me bread,
And fits my life into a four-post bed!

I'll sing and dance beneath the sky,
Out of my cage, with no one ni-i-igh;
Not caring why—make joy a rage,
The clouds a hall and that bright star a sta-a-age,
Not caring why—make joy a rage,
The clouds a hall, and that bright star a stage!

She was getting excited. She danced down the yard, dipping, rising, and stepping more rapidly than before. Now a woman—and her eyes gleamed grandly—once a kid that came from God . . . oh yes—her breath was coming in quick, impulsive pants—she did. She came from God, and she settled down in this damned town and—she whirled to the right and hurried forward—dreary one-horse town. She met a man and lost her head, oh yes, she did, she met a man and lost her . . . step, step, together, dip, and him she wed; he gives her bread, and fits her life into a four-post bed. . . . She swung her arms wildly as she plunged along, dipping, stepping, and bringing her feet together, dipping again and moving forward, going round and round the yard furiously, heatedly, wagging her behind, swaying her body madly, sweat beading her forehead and trickling down her cheeks. . . . She was tiring, her legs were aching vividly; her heart beat and beat so rapidly that she was almost unable to breathe. . . . She staggered on, bending stiffly and clumsily now, losing her balance frequently so that she almost fell several times. . . . She stiffened her muscles determinedly and, struggling on, danced out the wild, reckless, happy-mad rhythm of the song she sang, with savage, panting breath, with movement of leg, sway of body, and stamp of foot, with her head bent back, and her eyes staring up at the star. . . . Out of my cage, with no one ni-i-igh, not caring why—make joy a rage, the clouds a hall and that bright star a sta-a-age. . . . She began to sag at the knees. A sharp pain was shooting through her legs. . . . The small of her back was a dull, gnawing ache. She lifted her feet in a dull, heavy way from the ground as she swayed along. The star was moving from side to side and up and down as she stared at it. She felt all the vim was going, going out of her; the chant became a murmur, a fading murmur slipping lifelessly from the feverish

breath-pants. Then suddenly in the center of the yard she
sank down on her knees, and leaned heavily and wearily
against the wooden upright that held the pipe from which
the water still lazily flowed, filling the pail, trickling down
the sides, and disappearing down the gully underneath. . . .
There she lay lingering in a glow of weariness, head bent,
shoulder leaning against the wooden upright, and her body
cooped up in a kneeling curl in the center of the paved yard,
the tall, lounging, filth-fostered whores of houses all around
her. . . . She held her right hand out and let the water from
the pipe flow over it, making a tiny cascade as it fell over
into the pail, and she listened curiously to the gentle gurgle of
the overflow as it slid down into the gully beneath. . . . One
of her kids gurgled something like that a moment before it
went west. Where was it now? Up, up, up, somewhere, dodging about in heaven, behind the bloody star, maybe. Blast
the star and damn the star, anyway. I want to look at it no
more, never again. Let it rot, rot, rot in the sky. . . . No, no,
she mustn't curse a star; dangerous thing to do. . . . No one
could tell how close a star could be to God. . . . Badges of
the blessed angels maybe. . . . Silly thing to do, but she was
always doing silly things. . . . Rings on the finger of God,
maybe. . . . Wish she could get hold of one to pawn. . . .
Imagine her going into Lowry's with a star in a basket. Taking it out, planting it down on the counter, and asking
Sammy how much he would give on that. Oh, she must try
to keep these desecrational thoughts from creeping into
her mind.

*　　　*　　　*

She slowly and unwillingly gathered herself together, and
pulled and pulled herself up on to her feet. She turned the
tap and stopped the water flowing from the pipe. She tilted

the pail and spilled some of the water out, bent and lifted up the skirt that had fallen from her in the dance, and flung it over her shoulder, took up the pail in her right hand, walked unsteadily across the yard, lifted the latch of the yard door, and passed into the darkness of the back hall of the house. She groped her way along the darkness, her fingers brushing the wall, her lungs, after the coolness and freshness of the outside air, sensing the hot, human, thicker density of the air in the house that gave breath and took breath from the forty-five breathing bodies that lived there. Her hand touched the foot of the banisters, and gripping the handrail she began to go up the stairs. With the pull of the pail intensifying an ache in the muscles of her right arm, and the pull of the handrail intensifying an ache in the muscles of her left arm, she climbed the first flight, crossed the little landing, climbed the second flight, crossed the lobby and went on. . . . Her foot slipped on something soft and slimy on the stairs; dirty gang of mellowing apes; some kid misbehaved on the stairs, and nobody bothered to clean it away. She climbed on heavily to the fourth floor of the tenement. . . . Here she left her pail on the floor, and paused and panted. . . . She felt very unsteady; her legs were hot and quivering with a curious tremble. What a fool she had been to do that dance. . . . Two more flights of damned stairs to climb before she got to where the bed harbored a hope of sleep. . . . No, there wouldn't be much sleep tonight with those aching muscles and trembling legs. . . . Eight flights done, and two more before her still. Ten altogether. She must have climbed these twenty times today. That was two hundred flights climbed carrying water, and two hundred flights done downwards, without counting the washing, the wringing, and the cooking. Well, God could see her job wasn't a soft one, anyway. All done to keep life pure and wholesome. Well, the majesty of God gilds the homes of the poor. She offered the burden and the pain of the day to Jesus. She forgot the dance; she couldn't offer that. It would be blasphemy or something like that. The dance had taken the good out of the offering of her day's hard labor. She must have gone out of her mind for a few moments. She felt curious. As if there were things near that were about to touch her. . . . A shivering tremble that tingled her skin passed slowly over her whole body. She was frightened. . . . She shouldn't think of speaking about God in this dark landing at this time of night. . . . She always felt shuddery whenever she thought of sacred things in the dark. . . . She looked backwards down the stairs and saw a large bright star shining in through the window of the lobby below. She could sense a cold mockery in its gleam. She never felt the place so quiet before. Everybody must be fast asleep. . . . Yet she felt that there were things very near her, breathing on her, stretching out hands to touch her. Again she felt the tingling shiver, cold and creepy, passing up her legs, through her body, right up and over the skin of her head. She stopped quickly, caught up the pail, and ran swiftly up the other two flights of stairs, pushed the door of her room open, stepped inside and closed it rapidly and fearfully behind her, standing against it trembling and thankful to be hemmed in from fear of the darkness and silence by the satisfying reality of her one-roomed home. There were the strings stretching from wall to wall that carried the washing; the three chairs, side by side, around the fire, hidden by the damper clothes steaming steadily into a drier condition. The kitchen table, pushed back against the wall, with an oil lamp on it that was giving a smoky light to the room: the large rosy-featured wallpaper that did its best to look cheery and contented; the huge bed that gave a grudging rest to them all, with her three eldest asleep at the foot, her husband lying on his back at the head, with the youngest lying on his right side.

Placing the pail in a corner, she went to the fire and, stripping one of the chairs of the steaming clothes, she turned it around and sat down wearily upon it. Lifting her petticoat, she warmed her legs. She was frozen, and she felt a little sick. Near one o'clock now, it must be, and she had to be up at six in the morning. Five hours of sleep was hardly enough for a young woman that had to work so hard. Hoped the kids at the bottom of the bed would sleep tonight without their usual kicking and squirming and plunging about. Hoped to God they would. Six kids in eight years. Her belly must have been working like a steam engine; cranks twisting, piston rods shooting out and shooting in; wheels revolving . . . chih, chih . . . chih chih chih, without a stop, going the whole time . . . like a steam engine. Full steam pressure all the time to increase, multiply, and replenish the earth. Spinning out her destiny in record time. . . . She glanced up at the mantelpiece to see the clock. . . . She should make her mind resolute to burn that photograph. . . . It was merely a sigh for a lost slim figure, pretty face, and a curly mass of brown hair. If she went to a dance there wouldn't be many boys nosing around her now. . . . Eight years of it had skimmed the cream out of her life. . . . It was only alone now and in the dark that she could dance before the stars.

She heard the drowsy and querulous voice of her husband asking her if she was coming to bed or going to sit up all night. "Just arranging the clothes for the night," she said. "For Christ's sake, come to bed, woman, and put out the light; impossible for anyone to sleep with that lamp burning on the table!"

Rising she turned the back of the chair to the fire, and

replaced the damp clothes over it. Then she undressed down to her chemise, went over to the lamp, turned the wick down as low as possible, and with a vigorous puff put out the flame. She pulled the clothes on the bed down a little and thrust her feet in under them.

"Get in quietly now," grumbled her husband, "and don't slap yourself down as if no one occupied the bed but yourself."

She pushed her legs down cautiously, and gradually separated the four pairs of legs at the end of the bed to make room for her own feet, and lay on her side with her arm around her youngest and her back to her husband, stretched crookedly so as to occupy as little as possible of the bed, and to fit in comfortably at the same time. She remained motionless, every muscle aching in a dull way. Her mind was vaguely painful and clogged against free or clear thought by the heavy, dull, jading work of the day that was over. What she wanted now was rest . . . rest . . . and . . . sleep . . . sleep and rest . . . till six o'clock tomorrow morning. Deli . . . cious to be . . . in bed . . . and ge . . . get to sleep, to ge . . . get to slee. . . . Dimly she felt an arm sliding around her waist . . . and a leg lifted across her body. . . . She tried to shake the leg away, and unfasten the arm that was clinging around her waist. . . . But the hold tightened, and she felt herself being turned over and over on her back. . . . "No, no, Jack, not tonight . . . too tired for that sort of business. . . . Give it over, give it over, Jack. . . ." She tried to plunge away from him, and one of the kids at the bottom of the bed yelled in fright and pain as her toes plowed his thigh. "Shut up, there, you!" she heard her husband say viciously to the kid, "or I'll leather hell into your hide!" She struggled sleepily and wearily against him so as to hang on to a little rest, for it wasn't fair for him to bully her into his embraces when she was so tired, tired, tired. . . . He sank his fingers into the flesh of her shoulders and roughly held her from moving. . . . "Keep quiet for a few moments, can't you?" he said.

She yielded to him in weariness and from habit as she lay stretched on her back; her sleepy eyes opened and she saw the star that had seen her dancing gleaming grandly down at her through the window of the skylight.

The Job

SHE WATCHED HIS HEAD BENDING OVER HIS DESK, lifted now and again to glance at her approvingly. She knew she looked enticing in her well-cut tailored suit. Her slim legs were catching his eye. She leaned back in her chair and crossed one over the other. He stretched his hand for some papers at the end of the desk, but she knew that he sought an opportunity to see for a moment a fuller vision of things that stirred him. She suddenly sat straight and uncrossed her legs, for she remembered that her cami-knickers weren't as fresh as she'd like them to be. Idleness had left her no money for laundry, and she had worn one pair after another till she was now wearing the last pair that was in any way presentable. The others had been washed and were waiting to be ironed, but she had been too lazy to finish them off. She should have finished them a week ago, but she had put it off from day to day because she was too tired each day, or too lazy. But, then, look at the time she spent going from audition to agent, and from agent to audition, so that when she got home she was always too tired to do anything. She wanted a job; she must get a job soon or things would be too bad to bear. The rent—there was the rent due. The grocer wouldn't let her go on much longer—he was beginning to threaten already. Her mind was tired out thinking of them. Everywhere she went she carried her anxiety about with her. But it must be kept hidden. She must be free from care and bright when she spoke to managers, or sang and danced at auditions. She hadn't done too badly today. If she could only forget the rent and the grocer. She had danced and she had sung before one tall, thin, tremulous man, and two others, puffy-eyed, balloon-bellied money-cuddlers, and had been selected among fifty from a hundred others. Then she had sung again, and had danced again, and had been selected among twenty from the fifty girls. That was something that held a little hope. The grocer's book was red, a red book with the name in gold letters on the cover. Six pounds fourteen and eightpence, that was all; it really wasn't a great deal to owe. Oh, it was more, though; she hadn't counted in what she had got this week. Three, five and six-pence—seven and ninepence; ten shillings would more than cover the lot. Ten and fourteen—seven pounds four and eightpence; no, it wasn't a big debt. When she got work, she wouldn't be long paying it off—all, the whole lot—rent, grocer, and everything. The milkman's book was blue-royal or navy blue, she couldn't exactly say which. Curious the colors they liked; one blue, the other red. No, she didn't remember seeing a green book. Oh, yes; where she had lived last, the fishmonger had issued green books to his customers. Sixteen were to be engaged from the twenty chosen; sixteen only. Pity they didn't want the twenty, then the job would be sure. After all, twenty wasn't a lot to take on, the few additional pounds wouldn't break them. They were a mean crowd, these theatrical producers; wanted a hell of a lot for their money. Pretty face; well-shaped legs; good figure;

clever dancing; fair voice, all the better if it was good;
agility, stamina, patience, and personality. Oh, yes; personality was very important. Didn't want much; just a little
more than what you'd go to church with. If luck came her
way, she was sure the show would go for at least five weeks.
Four pounds for five weeks would be twenty pounds. Not
much, but enough to scrape her out of debt. It might run for
ten weeks, might be a success and run for a year, right
through for a whole year. Nothing like putting a halo round
a hope. It would mean two hundred pounds for her. That
would bring her liberty to get some things she sorely needed,
if she was to keep up appearances, and appearances counted
a lot when you were looking for a job. She wouldn't want
for a fresh petticoat or dainty cami-knickers for a special
occasion—when she went out to a dance with Jim, for instance.

Pity Jim wasn't one of these managers or producers. Why
wasn't he this one here, sitting at his desk eyeing her legs?
But if that were so, it would be the other way round, and
this manager would be Jim, so that would make a difference
the same thing. What was she thinking of? Her mind was
really getting muddled. She must bring it on to the things
immediately in front of her. She would soon have to fence,
and very shortly she might have to fight. So she must keep
her mind clear. Jim would be calling for her tonight at eight;
they were to have a little snack in her place, and then go
off together to a dance. And all the work she had before
her yet, to make an alteration in her dance frock, and to iron
and arrange her undies.

It was annoying that this fellow should still keep her
waiting. Pretending to be looking through his papers while
he was eyeing her thoughtfully and glancing at her legs.
During the last few years he must have seen hundreds and

hundreds of legs, and ought to be a little tired of them now. It was something else: some funny, peculiar, unusual motion or twist of her body; a look on her face or in her eyes, or even the way she moved her hands, that drew his attention to her.

How he twisted and rustled his hands through his papers. He would soon want to be twisting and rustling them through her—she felt it. Well, not yet, sir, anyhow; she would have to think it out a little first. If he tried, however, she wouldn't make a great fuss. She would put him off, fence him, and wait till she was sure, or nearly sure, that it was worth while. When she saw him whispering to his two companions, she knew he was whispering about her. She fancied faithfully all he said: she had stuff in her; didn't they think so? Graceful. . . . Oh, lively too. Would he mark her down among the twenty? And she was marked down among the twenty, so here she was sitting before him, and he was eyeing her legs . . . and twisting and rustling his hands through the papers on his desk. She wished he would say what he had to say, and let her go. It would take her all her time to be ready when Jim called for her. This old buffer in front of her didn't care, didn't even know. It was a month or more now since she had had a dance, and if the old man didn't soon make a move, she'd have to rush things.

If she went with Jim tonight, she'd have to be careful not to let him go too far. Oh, dear, she had to be careful of everyone. Careful of Jim because he was too poor; and careful of this old buffer because he was too rich. Careful of Jim because she wanted to give herself to him, and careful of the other because she didn't want to give herself to him. It was a curious world. . . . It was easier to put Jim off than this one. Jim was young and poor, and could wait; this one was impatient and rich, and she wanted the job. She knew that this old gilded pig couldn't really enjoy or understand the com-

panionship of girls. He brought them to dinner or supper
just to fill in the time before he asked them to take their
clothes off. Jim could do that too, but clothes on or clothes
off, supper was supper to Jim, and a dance was a jolly exciting passage of time. His love-making was brisk and fresh,
with nothing stealthy in it; there was fear and shyness in it,
but there was no shame. Here there was fear, no shyness, and
a good deal of shame. But she was bound to meet this sort
of thing sooner or later, and she would have to put up with
it and go careful. . . . She heard him speaking to her. . . .
"You didn't do badly, dear . . . you showed promise, distinct
promise. . . . Dancing good, very good indeed, and singing
not bad at all. . . . It's a toss-up between you and Miss
Brierly. . . . Hanley favors her, but it can be wangled . . .
we'll wangle it, never fear. . . . Show's going to be a sure
thing. . . . Keep at it, and you never know. . . . Understudy for
a little and then, perhaps . . . leading lady. You're as good as
there, my dear. . . . First rehearsal next Friday, ten o'clock
sharp. . . ." How like a tumbling jelly he looked when he
stood up. . . . She didn't want him to tell her that the
brooch in her breast was a pretty one. A lot she cared
whether he thought the brooch pretty or not. . . . He could
see right well that the little rubies were real without fingering them. . . . A lot he cared whether they were real or
not. . . . Jabbing his fingers into her bosom, and talking about
the shape of the brooch, as if she didn't know what he was
up to. And look at his picture, do, dear, do. . . . Painted by
someone that wanted work badly. His smug, smiling, smutty
face looking like a first-fruit of God's creation. . . . If she
had a face like that she might get it photoed, but she'd think
twice before she got it painted. Beside a table piled with
papers and his hand on an open book. . . . Good idea, the
bust of Shakespeare at one end of the table. . . . With his

knee pressing against her thigh while he was telling her about it, and showing her where the picture was particularly good. . . . The look of deity-tinged irritation that came to his face when she inched away from him. . . . "Good-bye, and thanks" . . . the way he held her hand. . . . Take supper with him tonight. . . . Indeed. Wanted to start off at once. . . . Come along, please, you mustn't keep me waiting. . . . Cheek of these men. . . . Open their arms and expect you to jump into them. . . . Bring his car round for her. . . . No thanks. . . . Wait till she got her job first. . . . Tuesday. . . . Sorry, engaged. . . . Oh, Wednesday night, then. . . . All right, Wednesday. . . . Good-bye. . . . It was something to be breathing the air even of Piccadilly again after that somber, stuffy, sinister-looking torture-chamber of an office. . . . Wanted a lot for four pounds a week. . . . Little enough for work that sweated her for hours every night without having to let herself be mauled about into the bargain. She wished she was a little better at that kind of game. She could make quite a lot out of it if she wasn't so damned shy. Somehow or other she couldn't make use of it as other girls did. No good at a business deal. She'd try this time, anyhow; everyone had to learn, and after a little practice she'd get going all right. How to start, that was the difficulty. . . . She might hint that she owed some rent. No, that would be too common. She'd have to find a fairer way than that. . . . The look that fellow gave her when she was passing; thought she was another kind of woman. . . . Wonderful the number of men that do nothing but prowl, prowl, prowl for women. . . . One thing, she'd have to hold him off for a time, job or no job. A woman shrinks in the mind of a man when he swings her easily into his arms. She was sorry now she'd accepted his offer to supper on Wednesday. Should she put him off a little longer? Wednesday? Oh, no, couldn't; sorry; full up the

whole week. Something on every night. Every night? Every
night, my dear man; sorry. Next week, maybe; ring me up
some evening and we'll see. Instead of that she hesitated,
stammered, and gave him Wednesday. How is it she couldn't
do these things properly, like other girls? Some kink in her
somewhere. . . . A quiet little restaurant that he occasionally
goes to. Fancy that now. A quiet place, to have an unquiet
time of it. She'd go to an unquiet place to have a quiet time,
or she'd go nowhere. She wouldn't let him handle as much joy
out of her as he thought for a job that she had not got yet.
If he really wanted to get going, it would cost him a lot
more than four pounds a week. She must decide upon a
definite line of action between this and Wednesday night.
Wednesday's a good way off, however, and tonight will be
full of hours of dance and joy with Jim.

Curious that there was hardly a part of London in which
you could slide out of view of a tree. It was nice to see
London plumed here and there with a tree, though Leicester
Square hadn't the cool, rich look of the other London
squares. Looked rather like a roof-garden that had been
taken down and planted carefully in the streets. Wonder
what the trees are that grow there. Wouldn't know them
even if she knew. She'd know a holly tree anywhere, and
could guess at an oak because of its funny leaves, and because she had read when she was a kid so much about it
hiding a Harry, or an Edward, or a Charlie in its branches at
Boscobel. Mahogany must be a lovely-looking tree, but it
couldn't grow here. But she had other things to think about
besides trees. . . . As soon as she was a little flush the first next
thing she'd buy would be a brassiere. The one she had was
going west, creased and uncomfortable; no use to her figure
for it had lost all its resiliency, as the motorists say. Pity she
couldn't ask Jim to buy her a brassiere instead of a few hand-

kerchiefs. Or the manager—God, imagine her asking the manager to buy her a brassiere! He'd rush one to her and want to try it on to see if it would fit. Jim would want to do that too. A man needs to give very little to get big ideas rushing into his head. To be or not to be a brassiere, that's the question. Strange if she met a bee buzzing along round Piccadilly Circus. . . . A bee buzzing along to buy a brassiere. . . . What she wanted wasn't a bee, but a bus buzzing along to bring her home. There was her bus just starting. Just like her to buzz in on top of a rush-hour crowd. . . . She'd have to push, shove, and fight if she didn't want to be kept for half an hour. . . . Here was one coming again, now. . . . Push . . . pull . . . and sho-o-ve! Here she was on the top with a nice fresh breeze blowing. The look on the fat one's face when she skidded out of the way. Don't knock her down, please. It was a mercy from God that most people one met were strangers to each other.

Tonight she would leave anxiety and fear and troubling thoughts alone and apart for a while in Jim's arms, responding in every nerve of her body and every motion of her mind to the blood-inflaming rhythms of the drum, fiddle, and saxophone. She could see the gaily colored lights gleaming already. And feel the arms of Jim clasping her. And the boys and the girls swaying softly, turning gently, wriggling closer together, moving, moving, moving along. . . . How these buses crawl along. . . . Brrrum tumtumtumtumbrrrum- tum brrrumtumtum tootle tootle lootootleloo tootleloo brrrum looloo tootle loo. . . . Glorious, Jim, isn't it? . . . tootle loo loo tootle loo. . . . Clasp me closer, clasp me closer, clasp, clasp closer. . . . Brrrum loo loo tootle loo. . . .

At her door she was at last. Slipped into the bottom of her bag again, her key. . . . Irritate a saint. Not a great measure of time left now to get everything ready. Get the iron, get the iron. . . . Mauve or green or cream-colored undies, which would she put on? The green would look sweet under the tulle of her black skirt. . . . They would blend harmoniously in the swing of the dance, and do delightfully. . . . Now we're well away. . . . Tootle, tootle brrrum loo loo tootle loo. . . . She'd dance tonight; miss only what would pass in the time of taking a sandwich and a glass of wine. . . . She'd just about be able to get everything ready before Jim would come to hurry her, happy-faced, off to the labor and joy of the dance. . . . She'd see the tensing look on Jim's face when he felt the motion of her legs in the movements of the dance. . . . Tootle loo loo loo tootle loo. There's the postman . . . a telegram. . . . No answer, boy. . . . She went in and read it again, slowly and tensely. . . . "Mother and Dad up in town for a few days. Everything off tonight. Arranged another dance for Wednesday night. Love, Jim." . . . She sent the iron flying into a far corner with a vicious swing, and clenched and crushed the green cami-knickers in her hands, and her lips quivered as she sat silent.

A Fall in a Gentle Wind

MOLLSER SAT MOTIONLESS ON A DEAL CHAIR
placed on the five-step landing fronting the widely open
door of a tenement house. It was a lovely day in late spring—
glory be to God! The sun was shining gorgeously, streaming
through the dismal avenue of glowering houses; its rays
were ignorantly gilding the sordid street and degenerate
pathways with a radiant, caressing, golden glow; softly
burnishing into a vivid gleam each of the age-worn grimy
windows, and touching with a shimmering newness the
tattered remnants of cotton lace that curtained them, and
sought to veil from the timid passer-by the haggard, mournful life that crawled or scratched or tossed itself into mechanical motion within the secretive chambers of the slum.

A tremulous shiver passed through Mollser's couched body,
as she mistily seemed to see a sinister vitality gleaming from
the eyelike windows, leering down on the fibrous life that
tottered into or plodded out of the various cavelike hallways.
They seemed to glance in a sidelong, jeering manner at the
horde of uncared-for youngsters playing feverishly in the
street, as if conscious that each slum was a secondary parent

to them, each child subdued by one faith and one baptism, having had to pass through the womb of the slum when they had been safely delivered from the womb of the mother. Having been born first in the image of God, they were afterwards to be molded in the image of the Devil.

Mollser shivered again, for the tenement opposite, a foul, wrinkled, dishevelled, palsied-looking building, like a worn-out harlot, seemed to be muttering across to her.

"Well, Mollser, how are you today; going along well, ay? You're a credit to number fifteen. . . . All the little body's a mass of tubercular rot. . . . Feeling as if you'd like to be laid out? Time enough, time enough, little one. . . . We'll give you a long spell on the broad of your back before we pack you away in the coffin. . . . You're the little masterpiece of number fifteen. . . . Each of us has its own. . . . Mine went a week ago. . . . But I've years of fertility left in me still, and there's many more to come. . . . My own little one above with spinal disease, in a few months, 'll be able to hold her own with the best of you. . . . We've a rich and lush heritage for all our children, and it will go hard with us to disinherit any."

"Christ help us!" murmured Mollser, closing her brown eyes, to shut out the vision of the leering threat that glowered in front of her, and turning her head to deflect from her dim soul the murmur she heard but could not understand.

Dreamily she heard the muffled shout of the playing children, punctuated by the vehement blasts from the horns of the passing motors, the drivers worming their way with sullen faces through the forms darting about in a frenzy of animal unconsciousness.

"Harps, sixpence," bawled a voice to her right, followed by "Heads, thruppence; harps, a wing." "For Christ's sake, keep back there, an' give a fella a chance to toss th' coins."

"The toss school is on again," thought Mollser; "that's

Jimmy Byrne's voice: he must ha' got th' dole today, an' he'll be bringin' Mary Timmins to th' pictures tonight, if he doesn't get too dhrunk. . . . He must be motting her now, for six months. Curious, a sturdy fella like him to be gone on a bloodless one like Mary Timmins. . . ." Mollser instinctively looked at her own hands, pallid with the mournful delicacy of disease. . . . "The summer may work wonders," thought Mollser, "and then——"

Interrupted in her thoughts by shuffling steps coming from the hall behind her, Mollser moodily watched Granny Hennessy climbing stiffly down the five steps as if they were a precipitous cliff, her skinny hands holding fearfully to the railings, her tiny bluey lips aquiver, muttering resentfully as she shambled along: "Holy Virgin, it's nearly time we had a bit of sun. The draughts in that bloody house 'ud skin you. . . . I'm goin' for me oul' age pension; nine shillin's now, only nine shillin's now. Takin' a lousy shillin' off a poor oul' woman. . . . A lousy shillin'. . . . A lousy oul' shillin'."

A rollicking twittering, having in it the lilt of joyous intoxication, roused up Mollser to raise her head, and, shaking back with a feminine swing her shock of dark hair, dimmed with the dirt of street and tenement, she saw a pair of sparrows abandoning themselves to the joy of tumultuous motion in the bosom of one of the little trees that stood at regular distances apart, surrounded by crudely cut wooden palings, along the pathway's edge of the slum street. A vague sense of kinship moved her to sympathy as she looked at the frail, thin trunk, like her own shrinking body; the fragile branches stretching towards the sky as if appealing for deliverance; the leaves murmuring a gentle protest, and the whole nature of the little captive from the wood, pregnant with bewilderment at the loss of its heritage of solitude, and the intimate caresses of sun and shower that had lost their purity and power.

A half-hidden gleam of subconscious envy faintly glimmered from the brown, wistful eyes of Mollser as she watched the animated excitement of the little leaves sharing in the motions of the sparrows springing with an exultant celerity from spray to spray; she gently thrilled as she noticed the rapid pulsing movement of their little throats, chirruping with the recklessness of elemental vigor, their tiny, diamond-like eyes, luminous with the confident hilarity of a natural discipline that gave them the fullness of life.

And Mollser shivered as she vaguely thought that life was more abundant in a common sparrow than it was in her: song and rhythm and motion, against weakness, disease, and death, a fragile feathered morsel of life, that even her little, wasted hand could clutch and banish from the universe, vibrant with the vigor that her body, passive because of tubercular weakness, would never know, and gone, too, for ever from the life that lingered in the coiled-up frame of little Alice Tait opposite, gripped in the Laocoön vice of creeping paralysis.

Like a warning gong the voice of her mother sounded in her ear from the area below: "Keep th' shawl well wrapped round you, Mollser. . . . If you get another chill in your chest, you'll be havin' me stoppin' up all night with you, an' turnin' your father into a divil with th' coughin' keepin' him awake at night."

Mollser tightened her shawl round her, and, like the mechanical swing of a weathercock yielding to a swooning wind, she turned her head and looked down with a dull interest on her mother below, gathering from a frayed and frequently joined line, stretching precariously from one end of the area to the other, the week's washing that had been hung out to dry, and was now to be ironed and made ready to wear on the Sabbath that was made for men.

She saw, one by one, the pitiable articles carefully collected into the gnarled hands of her mother: her own little shift, of flannelette, its once brightly pink stripes faded into dim, unhealthy-looking lines; her mother's, tawny-colored with constant wear, encouraged to live a little longer by the company of a multitude of patches; her artificial *crêpe de chine* blouse, with its saucy glad neck, that long long ago had prompted Jimmy Byrne to dance and dance with her, now bereft of all its glory; one of the two sheets that protected them grudgingly from the shaggy coverings of old coats and sugar sacks; a few pairs of socks living their last days, and her father's cotton shirt, with the hole under the arm growing larger and larger week by week. Her mother gathered carefully lest a thoughtless pull might rip the last remnant of life out of them, and, pressing them maternally against her bosom, looked up at Mollser, a faint smile trying to alleviate her misery-mangled face, and muttered monotonously: "Kippers tonight, Mollser; full week of th' dole he got, an' we have kippers tonight—one for him and one between me and you."

The clang of the bell shook a start out of Mollser: one, two, three, then a pause; twice three again, and a pause, then nine slow strokes—it was the Angelus. She noticed the men sitting on the steps taking off their hats and whipping the pipes out of their mouths as they bent their heads. Mollser inclined her head and murmured an Ave Maria.

Lithe-limbed spring had ripened into a pompous, full-bodied summer. The dingy street sparkled in the golden robe of the sun. The tenements, panting, leaned against each other for mutual support; their open windows and gaping doors seemed to be gasping for breath. Everything seemed to be struggling in a sea of warmth. The passing traffic glided indolently by; children lounged lazily on the paths, or dreamily nursed wornout toys on their laps as they sat on the stone steps of the houses. The groups of men and women had sought the shade of the doorway and the hall. The foliage of the exiled trees drooped languidly in the heated stillness.

Up in the one-room tenancy of the Conways, Mollser, rapidly breathing, lay in the bed that had given a harassed rest to her mother, father, and herself for many years. She could see the ceiling, cracked and tremulous with the pounding of the family overhead breaking sticks or smashing coal. How vividly the picture of the Sacred Heart glowed on the ghastly whiteness of the whitewashed wall! On the hob was the poor little kettle that had to do so much work. And the dresser, the biggest thing in the room, standing proudly with its back to the wall, consciously displaying its array of rugged delph, garnered through many years by the systematic barter of piles of rags and innumerable bottles. She could hear the little clock on the mantelpiece ticking the minutes away with a hoarse impatience. The little table, always covered with a page of newspaper when they were taking a meal. . . . Mollser looked at her father, divested of his coat, looked fixedly from the open window into the street. She heard the swish of the brush her mother was using to wash down the lobby outside, and the soft splashing of her hands into the bucket that held the day's supply of water for drinking and cooking purposes, and in which her father every morning washed his face with a fantasia of blowing, and his feet on the first Sunday of every month.

There had been a strange quietness in the room for the past few hours or days—she could not tell which. Some way or another she didn't like the silent kisses her mother occa-

sionally gave her. Her father, talkative enough, had stilled
his tongue, and rapped his pipe, when it needed refilling,
against the hob or on the window sill with a fierceness that
seemed to drum a rally to some idea that had found a
lodging in his mind.

The nuns had been with her yesterday: she still saw their
fading image in the mirror of preconsciousness. The black-
robed figures standing beside her bed. The heavy, brass
crucifixes, decorations of the Church Militant, glittering on
their bosoms. Their faces sheathed safely within the deep
shelter of their spathe-like bonnets. They had talked of the
goodness of God, of the mercy of Christ, and of the Faith of
the Little Flower. . . . She had heard an authoritative murmur outside the door, divided by her mother: "Yes, Sister"
. . . "No, Sister" . . . "Yes, Sister . . ." faintly audible as they
descended the first flight of stairs. . . . She didn't like the nuns
to come: somehow they seemed to leave dark shadows behind them that continually hovered over her head. If she
had the power in her to get up and go for a walk it would
do her good. She felt better . . . maybe, tomorrow . . .

The door of the room opened, and her mother came in,
hurriedly and agitated, followed by two big men wearing
vivid red shirts, carrying something between them. Her
father rose to his feet, clapped his pipe into his pocket, and
rigidly stood staring at them. Her mother came to the bed,
and bending over her whispered: "Here's the men, Mollser,
with th' stretcher to bring you to the Hospice. . . . You'll be
well looked afther be th' nuns, an' if it is God's will, you'll
get all right again."

The Hospice . . . the Hospice for the Dying! That's where
they wanted to bring her . . . she wouldn't go. She wouldn't
go! She felt better—she knew she was better—and even if

she wasn't, a week longer where she was—even one more day to linger longingly by the side of hope.

The nuns! What did the nuns know? They were always dying to be sending souls safely to Paradise or Purgatory!

"Mother, I can't go, I can't go there; I won't go." She painfully struggled to the far side of the bed, her bloodless hands twitching at the bedclothes, her shift, open at the breast, showing the wan weakness of her chest, revealing one breast that had subsided to a crinkled blob, the nipple, against the ghastly pallor of the skin, gleaming like the red of a cherry.

"It's th' only place for you," muttered her father. "You can get nothin' you want here; th' pair of us is worn out watchin' an' attendin' you. . . . It's nearly time you had a little thought of your mother. . . ."

Gently, the huge, red-shirted men lifted her, motionless and lost, on to the stretcher. She felt herself carried slowly, slowly down the gloomy, dirty stairs, out into the strength-quivering sun, through a group of staring, silent women and children, into the ambulance standing at the side of the street, the throbbing engine giving it the vibration of a living thing excitedly eager to carry her away to the dreadful place of shrinking shadows.

Shawled and wordless, her mother climbed in and sat beside the stretcher. Mollser sidled her hand over till it touched her mother's; she felt a gentle, agonizing pressure that set her body quivering. As if from an infinite distance, she heard the murmur of voices: "Harps a tanner" . . . "Heads a bob" . . . "For Christ's sake, keep back there, and give a fella a chance to toss th' coins."

With a gliding spring, the motor moved away.